The Matter of Critiq

Readings in Kant's Philoso

The Matter of Critique

Readings in Kant's Philosophy

Editors
Andrea Rehberg and Rachel Jones

CLINAMEN PRESS

First edition published Manchester 2000

Clinamen Press Limited
Enterprise House
Whitworth Street West
Manchester M1 5WG
www.clinamen.net

A catalogue record for this book is available from the British Library

ISBN 1 903083 11 7

1 3 5 7 9 8 6 4 2

Typeset in Simoncini Garamond by
Northern Phototypesetting Co. Ltd, Bolton
Printed and bound in the UK by
Biddles Ltd, Guildford & King's Lynn
Printed on acid free paper

Contents

Abbreviations

References to Kant's works are given using the standard English title acronyms, except where a work is only mentioned once. All references to the *Critique of Pure Reason* (*CPR*) are in A/B numbers only, in keeping with standard practice. In the case of all other works the volume numbers (in Roman numerals) and page numbers (in Arabic numerals) of the *Akademieausgabe* are also given. Where the author's have modified translations this is denoted by t.m. (translation modified) and where authors have provided their own translation, this is denoted by m.t. (my translation).

Ak   *Kants gesammelte Schriften*, herausgegeben von der Deutschen [formerly Königlich Preussischen] Akademie der Wissenschaften, 29 Bände (Berlin: Walter de Gruyter 1902-).

Anth   *Anthropology from a Pragmatic Point of View*, trans. M. J. Gregor (The Hague: Martinus Nijhoff, 1974). (*Ak*.VII)

AS   *Aus Sömmering, Über das Organ der Seele* (Königsberg, 1796). (*Ak*.XII)

CAJ   *Critique of Aesthetic Judgement*, in *CJ*.

CF   *Conflict of the Faculties*, trans. M. J. Gregor (Lincoln: Nebraska University Press, 1992). (*Ak*.VII)

CJ   *Critique of Judgment*, trans. Werner S. Pluhar (Indianapolis: Hackett, 1987). (*Ak*.V)

CoJ   *Critique of Judgement*, trans. J. H. Bernard (New York: Hafner Press, 1951). (*Ak*.V)

CPR   *Critique of Pure Reason*, trans. N. Kemp Smith (London: Macmillan Press, 1989). (*Ak*.III (B) and IV (A))

CPrR   *Critique of Practical Reason*, trans. Lewis White Beck (Indianapolis: Bobbs-Merrill, 1956). (*Ak*.V)

CPRR   *Critique of Practical Reason*, trans. Lewis White Beck, 3rd edn
       (London: Macmillan Press, 1993). (*Ak*.V)
CTJ   *Critique of Teleological Judgement,* in *CJ.*
EG   *The One Possible Basis for a Demonstration of the Existence of
       God*, trans. Gordon Treash (Lincoln: University of Nebraska
       Press, 1994). (*Ak*.II)
JL   *Jäsche Logic*, in *LL.*
KH   *Kant on History*, ed. and trans. Lewis White Beck et al
       (London: Macmillan Press, 1963). (*Ak*.VII-VIII)
LL   *Lectures on Logic*, ed. and trans. J. Michael Young (Cambridge:
       Cambridge University Press, 1992). (*Ak*.IX)
LM   *Lectures on Metaphysics*, ed. and trans. Karl Ameriks and Steve
       Naragon (Cambridge: Cambridge University Press, 1977).
       (*Ak*.XXVIII and XXIX)
MNS   *Metaphysical Foundations of Natural Science*, trans. J. Ellington
       (Indianapolis: Bobbs-Merrill, 1970). (*Ak*.IV)
Op.p. *Opus postumum*, ed. and trans. Eckart Förster and Michael
       Rosen (Cambridge: Cambridge University Press, 1993).
       (*Ak*.XXI and XXII)
P   *Prolegomena To Any Future Metaphysics That Will Be Able To
       Come Forward As A Science*, trans. J. W. Ellington (Indianapo-
       lis: Hackett, 1985). (*Ak*.IV)
PW   *Political Writings*, ed. Hans Reiss (Cambridge: Cambridge
       University Press, 1991). (*Ak*.IV, VI, VII, VIII)
RLR   *Religion within the Limits of Reason Alone*, trans. T. M. Greene
       and H. H. Hudson (New York: Harper Torchbooks, 1960).
       (*Ak*.VI)
RT   *Raising the Tone of Philosophy*, ed. and trans. Peter Fenves (Bal-
       timore: Johns Hopkins University Press, 1993). (*Ak*.VIII)
TP   *Theoretical Philosophy 1755-1770*, ed. and trans. David Walford
       (Cambridge: Cambridge University Press, 1992). (*Ak*.I
       (1747–56) and II (1757–77))
UNH   *Universal Natural History and Theory of the Heavens*, ed. and
       trans. Stanley L. Jaki (Edinburgh: Scottish Academic Press,
       1981). (*Ak*.I)

Notes on Contributors

Martin Bell is Professor of Philosophy at Manchester Metropolitan University. He has published on the philosophy of David Hume in a number of journals and edited collections, and has edited a new edition of Hume's *Dialogues Concerning Natural Religion* for Penguin Classics. He has a special interest in the relations between philosophy and its writing. J.M.Bell@mmu.ac.uk.

M.J. Bowles has taught Philosophy at the University of Greenwich since 1990. His main areas of interest are Kant, Nietzsche and Deleuze. M.J.Bowles@greenwich.ac.uk.

Howard Caygill is Professor of Cultural History at Goldsmiths' College, University of London, and author of *Art of Judgement* (1989), *A Kant Dictionary* (1995) and *Walter Benjamin: The Colour of Experience* (1998). hcaygill@hotmail.com

Paul Davies teaches Philosophy at the University of Sussex. He has published widely on phenomenology, aesthetics and the philosophy of Kant. He is currently completing a monograph entitled *Poems, Works, Contexts* and working on a longer term book-length project entitled *Kant and the Continuation of Philosophy*. P.Davies@sussex.ac.uk

Iain Hamilton Grant is Senior Lecturer in Cultural Studies at the University of the West of England. He has published essays on modern and contemporary philosophy, including Deleuze, Lyotard, Baudrillard, Kant and Schelling, and has translated major works by Lyotard and Baudrillard. He has also published on the philosophy and culture of science and technology. He is currently writing a book entitled *On an Artificial Earth: Schelling,* Naturphilosophie *and Absolute Empiricism* (Athlone, forthcoming). Iain.Grant@uwe.ac.uk

Joanna Hodge is Reader in Philosophy at Manchester Metropolitan University . Her study of Heidegger, *Heidegger and Ethics*, was published by Routledge in 1995 and she is currently working on Derrida and Benjamin. J.Hodge@mmu.ac.uk

Kath Renark Jones is lecturer in Philosophy and Combined Studies at the University of Greenwich. She has published a number of papers on Kant, Foucault and Irigaray and is the editor of *Mapping Woman*, a collection of papers on feminist philosophy. She is currently working on a book entitled *The Subject and Community* and jointly organises the Community 2000 conference series, now in its third year. Her research interests are Kant, Foucault, Lyotard, feminist theory and philosophy of the body. K.Jones@greenwich.ac.uk

Rachel Jones is a temporary Research Fellow in Philosophy at Manchester Metropolitan University; from September 2000, she will be a lecturer in Philosophy at the University of Dundee. She has research interests in Kant and post-Kantian European philosophy, aesthetics, Nietzsche, and feminist philosophy, and was co-editor of a Special Issue of *Hypatia*, *Going Australian: Reconfiguring Feminism and Philosophy* (Spring 2000). She is currently working on a book on Jean-François Lyotard. R.E.Jones@mmu.ac.uk

Simon Malpas is Lecturer in English at Manchester Metropolitan University. His main research interests are in philosophy and literature, particularly the relationships between Romanticism and German Idealism. His publications include *William Cowper: the Centenary Letters* and *Postmodern Debates*, as well as a number of articles on the relationships between Romanticism and contemporary critical theory. S.Malpas@mmu.ac.uk

Andrea Rehberg is Postdoctoral Research Fellow in Philosophy at Manchester Metropolitan University. Her main research interests are Kant, Nietzsche, Heidegger, and Deleuze and she has published a number of papers on them. She is currently working on a book on Nietzsche and Deleuze. A.Rehberg@mmu.ac.uk

Jim Urpeth is senior lecturer in Philosophy at the University of Greenwich. He has written on Kant, Nietzsche, Heidegger, Foucault, Bataille and Deleuze. He is a co-editor of *Nietzsche and the Divine* (Clinamen Press, 2000) and is writing a book on themes in aesthetics from Kant to Deleuze. J.R.Urpeth@greenwich.ac.uk

Alistair Welchman works as a consultant to a biotechnology company, applying artificial biological techniques to irrational molecular synthesis. He studied variously philosophy, politics, economics and evolutionary systems at the universities of Oxford, Warwick, Wisconsin and Sussex, and has published several articles.

Editors' Introduction

I

The pivotal position which the Kantian *oeuvre* holds for all subsequent philosophy is undisputed and cannot be overstated. That Kant's influence also reaches outside philosophy, to those working in other areas of the humanities, in the arts, and in the social and natural sciences, is a further mark of his centrality. Kant's reinvigoration of philosophical conceptuality and of the philosophical lexicon has inspired philosophers since his own time and continues to do so.

Kant's Copernican revolution in philosophy – the conformity of objects to our modes of knowing them, rather than vice versa – made possible many of the most important intellectual developments of the nineteenth and twentieth centuries and will no doubt continue to exert its influence in the future. Beyond the technicalities of the Copernican turn, beyond its specific context in the project of the *Critique of Pure Reason*, what it opens up is the possibility of disrupting our commonsensical or realist assumptions about the world we encounter. In Kantian thought what is empirically real or given must at the same time be transcendentally ideal, i.e., constituted, constructed or produced, and cannot be considered merely as given. And so the question of how experience comes to be what it is, what its modes of production are, enters the philosophical scene explicitly for the first time. Hence, in the nineteenth century, such diverse projects as those of Nietzsche's thought of will to power, Freud's theory of the unconscious and Marx's understanding of Capital are on one level made possible by this Kantian reversal, as are, in the twentieth century, those of Deleuze, Heidegger, and Irigaray, to name but a few. The fact that many of these thinkers are in turn mobilised for rethinking Kant in several of the pieces in this collection points to the central issue of this volume, reflected in its title, namely that of critique.

Kant initially 'invented' critique to counter the conflicting claims of dogmatic rationalism and empiricism in the field of metaphysics, or what would now be called the theory of knowledge. But as a consequence of the problematisation of representational thinking – a movement which is itself traceable to elements in Kant's thought – the term 'critique' has taken on a much wider sense, beyond any merely epistemological concerns, to mark a further profound reversal. What is decisive about Kant's conception of critique is that it always takes the form of a self-examination, it is always the critique *of* x *by* x. Hence, after Kant, critique must always follow the course of an immanent, rather than an oppositional approach. This clearly points the way to a different kind of philosophical hermeneutics, one which is precisely non-oppositional, in which texts can be read against themselves, can be 'destructed', deconstructed or immanently radicalised at the edges of, and beyond, their metaphysical construction. Although there is a considerable variety in the hermeneutic approaches employed by the essays presented here, they share this fundamental understanding of critique as immanent radicalisation. What this means concretely is that, in a variety of ways, Kant's texts are here read against themselves and hence are radicalised from within. Throughout, this is based on the implicit assumption that a genuinely critical reading requires a re-thinking which opens up an apparently fixed text anew and thus leads to a re-animation both of this text and of the thinking which proceeds in this way.

Kantian philosophy has often been characterised as unhistorical, overly formalist and, of course, as merely idealist. Whilst such charges cannot be simply dismissed as completely unfounded, the task for a critical philosophy is to show that in the interstices of texts which display such characteristics, richer veins of thought can also be discovered. The case in point here is that of matter. By privileging the transcendental constitution of experience, rather than the materiality which it presupposes as given, Kant appears to write matter out of his account of how experience, cognition and finally science, become possible. In contrast to such a traditional reception, and in contrast to any essentially hylomorphic understanding of it, matter here becomes itself the object of a critical rethinking. After the Kantian reversals have taken effect (even if Kant himself did not fully realise them), matter can no longer be conceived in dualistic Aristotelian terms, nor can its mere opposite – an equally metaphysical materialism – make good this deficiency. Instead, the texts in this collection set out how matter can be understood in the

Kantian context, including the matter of art, of politics, of the divine, in short, the matter of critique.

II

Kant's texts, and above all the three great *Critiques*, have inspired a vast number of readings, commentaries and reconsiderations in the form of monographs, collections and articles. To single out any number of them for discussion here would do a disservice to the wealth of existing texts. Collections of contemporary writings on Kant in the continental tradition have primarily consisted of work by European, and particularly French, scholars.[1] These important volumes have clearly contributed to the wealth of debates in the English-speaking world. What is all the more surprising, then, given this obvious abundance, is that no collection such as the present one, of original essays by English-speaking authors working on Kant in the continental tradition, has been produced up to now. Where the last years have seen reconsiderations of, among others, Hume and Nietzsche, no such overview of new writing on Kant has been attempted.[2]

This volume does not of course claim to give an exhaustive account of writings on Kant from a continental perspective – the field is too large and varied for that. Its more modest ambition is to indicate some of the transformations of which Kant's texts are capable when read in this way. It is hoped that this will in turn inspire further explorations of the Kantian *oeuvre*, and thus further developments in an area which understands Kant not just as a central figure in the history of philosophy but as a thinker who is also capable of becoming our contemporary.

The readers of these essays will discover the wide variety of approaches, of texts under consideration, and of philosophical orientations present here. They will also notice that no sustained interpretation of any of Kant's works on ethics is carried out by any of the contributors. Whilst many of the authors featured here go beyond the critical texts – to the pre-critical works, to the *Opus postumum*, and to many of the shorter texts in between – they eschew engagement with Kant's ethical writings. On one level, this is undoubtedly due to the emphasis placed on this part of Kant's work by many analytic commentators. More positively, it underscores the fact that this collection aims to provide exemplars of contemporary continental work on Kant, and that this tends to focus on the issues discussed here. This is not to say that these authors have not in the past written on Kant's ethics, nor that they (and others) will not do so in the future. It merely indicates that the contributions to *The Matter of Critique* found their impetus elsewhere in the diversity of Kant's works.

III

Throughout this volume, it is matter itself which provides the impetus to thought: matter as thematised in the critical project, but also in its wider relation to force, to thought, to life itself. The complexities of Kant's thinking on matter are immediately apparent in Mick Bowles' paper, 'Kant and the Provocation of Matter', the first of three papers in Section One that bring the issue of matter to the fore. These papers seek to allow matter to emerge from within the critical project in ways that offer an immanent critique of some of Kant's attempts to contain materiality within more hylomorphic or anthropocentric modes of thinking. In so doing, they aim to mobilise Kant so as to extend critical thinking from within. In Bowles' paper, an oppositional, Aristotelian conceptualisation of the form/matter relation is displaced in favour of a more unsettling dynamic where matter is the threat of annihilation that brings thought to life. The concern with subverting an oppositional model of matter also underpins the second paper in Section One. But whereas Bowles links the complex dynamic traced in the first *Critique* across to a reading of the sublime in the third, thereby opening these texts up to new readings both individually and in conjunction, Rachel Jones interrogates two key paragraphs of the third *Critique* – on crystallisation and on the productive imagination of genius – so as to produce disruption from within. By contrast, the paper by Iain Hamilton Grant questions the relation of thought to the earth by moving across Kant's writings, from the *Universal Natural History*, through the first and third *Critiques*, to the *Opus postumum*, as well as by drawing in a range of post-critical texts. Both Jones and Grant seek to disrupt the analogical method Kant employs in the third *Critique* from within, Jones by rigorously extending the analogy between art and nature to the question of their production, Grant by examining the material basis of thought in ways that begin to unravel the delimitation of analogy as merely reflective. In ways that point back to the opening paper, Grant positions the sublime as provoking the transition to a re-making of nature, and, ultimately to a metaphysics of nature as a science of transition.

Grant identifies the stakes of his reading as the production of new species, thereby pointing up the intersection of matter with life which is also central to Bowles' paper. The place of life within the critical project is an issue which cuts across the first two sections of the volume, as it is developed in Section Two by way of the following genealogical questions: What type of life is implicitly invested with value in Kant's philosophy? What kinds of pleasures and pains, what forces of desire underlie the investments of critique in its particular structures and strategies? What is the affective and evaluative economy, the internal dynamic driving the critical delineation of aesthetic and teleological judgement? Such questions, addressed primarily in the papers by Jim Urpeth and Andrea Rehberg, are complemented and extended by those addressed by Howard Caygill and Paul Davies, respectively: What is the genealogy of the concept of life within Kant's writings? How legitimate is the genealogical thought that thought must make a difference, must directly affect – and be affected by – a mode of living?

In Urpeth's reading of the sublime, the Kantian mode of immanent critique becomes a genealogical critique which does not stand outside the text it evaluates but traces the libidinal investments running through it. Such tracing does not lead to an oppositional reading but to a more complex reversal and revaluation. As Foucault reminds us, and as Urpeth's analysis of an asceticism driven by libidinal forces shows, genealogy is a search neither for 'the inviolable identity of ... origin', nor for 'unbroken continuity', but for the disparity and differing at the beginning of things.[3] This theme of the self-differing implicit within production, including the on-going productivity of texts, is echoed in Rehberg's examination of the tensions and instabilities that are generative of and generated by the *Critique of Teleological Judgement*. Rehberg, like Urpeth, locates the ground of the transcendental principle of purposiveness in a transcendental affectivity.

However, whereas Urpeth positions his analysis in direct contrast to readings of the sublime sited in a Heideggerian and deconstructive tradition, Rehberg mobilises a Heideggerian reading in order to take Kant's text beyond its own apparent limits. And whereas Urpeth argues that Kant's notions of self-preservation and of the 'feeling of life' conceal an uncritical anthropomorphism, Caygill, in 'Life and Aesthetic Pleasure', extends our understanding of Kant's concept of life by linking the ways in which life exceeds the language of representation in the third *Critique* to the incompatible models of life to be found throughout Kant's *Lectures on Metaphysics*. The shift from life thought in relation to representation, to life as a dynamic principle, casts light back onto both Grant's comments on vitalism, and Bowles' exploration of matter as integral to a dynamic of life and death. However, the relation of life to matter within Kant's texts is further complicated as Caygill delineates another model wherein life is opposed to lifeless matter. This last model is itself modified by Kant in ways that raise the spectre of hylozoism, a possibility that might provide a route out of the anthropocentrism that is critiqued elsewhere in this volume.

Given the manner in which genealogy is understood and indeed practised by Urpeth, Rehberg and, to a degree, by Caygill, namely, as an extension of Kantian critique that can interrogate the pre-critical elements within the Kantian project, the final paper of this section poses a challenge that cannot be straightforwardly foreclosed. By contrast with the foregrounding of the third *Critique* that has characterised the papers thus far, Paul Davies examines Nietzsche's criticisms of Kant's critique of the ontological argument, where Kant stands accused of offering a critique that makes no difference. However, Davies' paper raises the suspicion that genealogy would itself succumb to the significantly different and more modest form of Kantian critique which it seeks to radicalise and displace. Davies' paper employs a method of reading Kant by placing him in conjunction with other key figures, not in order to supersede Kant but, on the contrary, to open up the implications of the Kantian project in unforeseen directions, and in ways that suggest that Kant's texts often contain at least as much – and sometimes more – radical potential as those of some of his successors. Such a method is one of the common features of this volume, and can be found at work in papers which are otherwise diverse in the themes and arguments they address. However, in the third section of the volume, productive conjunctions are doubly manifested, as both method and theme.

In Kath Jones' paper it is the thematics of conjunction/disjunction which come to the fore, in a mode of thinking community that is made possible by Kant and yet goes beyond restrictive models grounded in identity or unity. One of Jones' strategies is to juxtapose Kant and Lyotard *contra* Hegelian models of community. In the next paper, by contrast, it is Lyotard's reading of the sublime which is itself called into question and, instead, Simon Malpas conjoins Kant's sublime with Hegel's critique of spurious infinity. Rather than seeking to oppose or reconcile these two thinkers, Malpas deploys Derrida to delimit a space between Kant and Hegel such that they meet at a limit that is also a passage.

This matching of a method which conjoins to an argument about spaces and modes of conjunction is most fully exemplified in the third paper in this section. Here Joanna Hodge approaches Kant through Irigaray, arguing that the latter's productive disjunctive reading allows her to hold together both Heideggerian and Lacanian reworkings of Kant. In ways that point back to previous papers in the volume, the theme of radicalising critique from within is once again linked here to a mode of reading for differences that exist both between texts and their readers, and within texts and readings of texts. Whereas Hodge argues that disjunctive reading can sustain a multiple critique, Kath Jones argues that both the epistemological community based on exclusive disjunction, and the *sensus communis* that underpins judgements of the beautiful, are dependent on a model of community based on unity and identity. The latter obscures a more primordial affective being-in-common thought as an undetermined polyvocity. Jones' characterisation of this ontologically prior community as a voice that is a chorus – as a non-self-identical *Einstimmung* rather than the voice of consensus – extends Rehberg's emphasis on the importance of the register of a non-determined *Stimmung* in Kant's third *Critique*. However, one of the most original aspects of Jones' paper lies in her argument that *sensus communis* as an affective being-in-common is to be found in the sublime, rather than the beautiful.

This privileging of the sublime as a site through which the subversive potentiality of Kantian critique can be maximised is visible across the volume. In different contexts and registers, the sublime is seen as opening up thought to that which thought cannot determine. It is via their differing recastings of the sublime that the papers by Kath Jones and Malpas are linked. Malpas carefully distinguishes between Derrida's characterisation of the sublime as an inadequation within presentation, and the Lyotardian topos of 'presenting the unpresentable'. Elsewhere in the volume, and in more or less explicit ways, the readings offered by Urpeth, Bowles and Grant are sharply differentiated from those in the Heideggerian-deconstructive vein. Instead, they read the sublime as a libidinal economy of negative pleasures: as joy in cruelty and sacrifice; as the desolate failing of the understanding that provokes synthesis back into life; and as the violence which impels the powers to the invention of another nature. Indeed, Kath Jones' interpretation of the sublime as affective being-in-common belongs with these papers insofar as it can be read as folding Lyotard's later work on Kantian aesthetics back into his earlier explorations of libidinal economy.

This process of folding one reading back into another to generate an original interpretation of Kant is continued in the final section, on transcendental empiricism. Whereas Kant is usually characterised as responding to Hume, Martin Bell provocatively reads Hume's thought – via Deleuze – as a critique of Kant. Deleuze is also key to the final paper of the volume, in which Alistair Welchman draws on a new kind of Kantian psychologism to go beyond the orthodox opposition of 'continental' and 'analytic' readings and to point to a 'deepened' Deleuzian understanding of the transcendental. Thus both papers envisage new modes of negotiating the analytic/continental divide such that productive 'cross-fertilisations' are engendered, whilst Bell's paper also complicates any simplistic understanding of the history of philosophy as linear. This methodological emphasis on divergence and discontinuity as productive is in keeping with the aim of both papers and, indeed, with the aim of many of the papers in this volume, namely, to open up Kant's transcendental philosophy to the movement of differing by extending critical thought to any uncritical privileging of unity and identity.

In particular, Bell and Welchman call into question Kant's uncritical privileging of the *a priori* nature of the mind understood as a formal unity of self-consciousness. Bell seeks to fold a Deleuzian understanding of empiricism, where the latter is characterised by the externality of relations, back into Kant's account of the faculties such that it is the differences rather than the harmony between them that become critical. Welchman argues that the synthetic activity of the subject of the first *Critique* is dependent on a mode of synthesis prior to any such unity governed by laws. Both thereby aim to release Kant's thought into a 'properly critical' thinking that would of necessity take the form of a transcendental empiricism.

The transcendental empiricism yielded explicitly in these last two papers is a thought that can also be traced across the previous sections of the volume. The *a priori* constitution of the subject in a transcendental unity of apperception is continually shown to be in turn reliant on a non-unifiable play of multiplicities and differences, identified by Urpeth, Rehberg and Kath Jones as a play of transcendental affectivity. Indeed, in their search to reconnect the empirical and material to the transcendental, so as to think the latter fully transcendentally, the papers by Bell and Welchman take us back to the beginning: through Grant's reworking of a physicalist sublime and a non-anthropocentric metaphysics of nature, to Bowles' location of a constitutive dynamic of life and death at the very heart of synthesis. In this way, the themes and methodologies which hold each section of the volume together productively intersect with the concerns and questions that are inflected across the volume as a whole. Hence 'The Matter of Critique' itself explores its interwoven themes multiply and differentially, such that we can only conclude, with Irigaray, that '[t]he Copernican revolution has yet to have its final effects'.[4] Nonetheless, some of the aftershocks of the explosive force of critique can be felt to resonate across all the essays in this volume.

Notes

The editors would like to express their gratitude to Martin Bell and Joanna Hodge for their invaluable support and encouragement in the preparation of this volume.

1   For instance, Eduardo Cadava, Peter Connor, and Jean-Luc Nancy, eds., *Who Comes After the Subject?* (London: Routledge, 1991) and Courtine et al, *Of the Sublime: Presence in Question*, trans. J. S. Librett (Albany, NY: SUNY Press, 1993).

2   For instance, David B. Allison, ed., *The New Nietzsche* (Cambridge, MA: MIT Press, 1986), David Farrell Krell and David Wood, eds., *Exceedingly Nietzsche – Aspects of Contemporary Nietzsche Interpretation* (London and New York: Routledge, 1988), Warren Montag and Ted Stolze, eds., *The New Spinoza* (Minneapolis: University of Minnesota Press, 1998), R. Read and K. Richman, eds., *The New Hume Debate* (London and New York: Routledge, 2000), to name but a few.

3   Foucault, 'Nietzsche, Genealogy, History', trans. Donald F. Bouchard and Sherry Simon, in *The Foucault Reader*, ed. Paul Rabinow (Harmondsworth: Penguin, 1984), pp. 79, 81.

4   Luce Irigaray, *Speculum of the Other Woman*, trans. Gillian G. Gill (Ithaca, NY: Cornell University Press, 1985), p. 133.

1

Kant and the Provocation of Matter

M. J. Bowles

Matter at the impasse

Without a doubt Kant's thinking on the subject of matter owes a debt to Aristotle. Both thinkers maintain that matter is what is left when we remove all form: that matter marks the negation of form. Kant applies this negative definition of matter in the analysis of experience which he undertakes in the first *Critique*. There he tells us that we must not suppose that experience is simply the given: rather conscious experience only arises because the given is made to conform to the *a priori* patterns which the mind imposes. Hence it is not the object of experience, but whatever it is which occurs prior to experience, which Kant calls matter. Matter, it seems, is the unformed, the absence of order; but this is only something for us to the extent that we impose structure.[1]

We must not, however, pretend that the notion of the unformed is easily grasped. In particular we must be careful not to misread the opening move which Kant makes in his analysis of experience.[2] For whilst the Transcendental Aesthetic asks us to consider sensation in independence from conceptuality, Kant is not thereby claiming access to matter. Indeed the goal of the Transcendental Aesthetic is to show us that it is not a *conceptual* necessity that objects of experience are always within space and time. Hence form cannot, as Leibniz had maintained, be entirely reduced to logic. Kant famously declares that even the necessity employed in the inferences of mathematics involves something more than the law of non-contradiction. Accordingly, the pure form of experience must be comprehended by a transcendental logic; that is to say, a logic which maintains that the form imposed on the given is *already* a relation between the conceptual necessity of traditional logic and a necessity which does not stem from the law of non-contradiction.

Indeed, Kant's critique of rationalism is reducible to the claim that traditional logic is an abstraction from the more primary relation studied by transcendental logic, and, as such, is insufficient to comprehend the world of experience. For Kant the principal failing of traditional logic is its inability to comprehend change, for it can only register change as contradiction ('for instance, the being and the not-being of one and the same thing in one and the same place'),[3] whereas Kant insists that change becomes comprehensible only if we add to comprehension a non-conceptual factor: 'only in time can two contradictorily opposed predicates meet in one and the same object, namely, *one after the other*'.[4] We should not pretend for a moment that the latter remark in any way makes clear what time, as the non-conceptual aspect of all experience, might be. But it does make clear that for Kant it is only if we include this non-conceptual necessity that the everyday experiences we actually have become comprehensible.

Thus the Transcendental Aesthetic does not offer an insight into the nature of matter prior to the imposition of form, as though matter itself were spatial and temporal. Rather, it attempts to show that the nature of form is richer and wider than traditional logic has allowed for. If we should wish to apprehend matter in complete independence of form then we must not only attempt to remove logic (the conceptual), but space and time as well. Accordingly, we should be very careful not to equate the Kantian notion of matter with the notion of sense data beloved of empiricism. For whilst 'sense data' clearly indicates the pre-conceptual, it is not at all clear that empiricism also invites us to think sensation independently of space and time.[5] The momentary sense datum, whilst non-conceptual and perhaps non-spatial, is nevertheless an event in time. And yet the implication of the Transcendental Aesthetic, which argues that space and time are part of the formal contribution to experience, is that the rawness of the given, stripped of all form, indicates that which must not be grasped in terms of time. It is this finding which leads Kant to challenge all attempts to comprehend that which occurs prior to formation: 'The true correlate of sensibility, the thing in itself, is not known, and cannot be known'.[6] For how can we remove time? Kantianism maintains that a rigorous ontology, that is, the attempt to purge our own contribution from what we comprehend and let things be as they really are, will only ever lead to blindness. If the formal structures of experience are removed, then the ability to grasp something also vanishes. This is why for Kant to try to think matter is to confront the impasse: that the content of form, pure nakedness, is always beyond our reach.

Hence Kant persists in maintaining the distinction between the appearances of experience and the blindness which overwhelms us when we try and remove all formal structure. Of course, Kant's persistence on this point has been questioned. If we can never know the 'in itself' why do we continue to maintain it? And indeed, if the distinction is dropped, ontology becomes possible again: now ontology becomes the study of phenomena – there is nothing else.[7] If we cease to maintain the distinction between phenomena and the 'in itself' then we no longer face the Kantian impasse of trying to remove time from the equation. In this way it becomes possible to maintain the decidedly non-Kantian position that time is at one with how things are in themselves. Ontology and the study of temporality become one. However, we should not fail to note that to proceed in this way is not without its casualties. What we lose is the insistence on matter. Kant maintains the impasse – that the analytic of phenomena can never stretch as far as the 'in itself' – precisely because it is at such moments of incomprehension that matter is encountered.[8]

Zero degree intensity

We must be most careful not to identify the Kantian location of matter with the bright intensities of sensation. Kant offers his argument for this position in the Anticipations of Perception.[9] We cannot regard a sensation as the matter which fills out form because a sensation itself only occurs to the extent that it too takes place within a certain structure. When we feel a sensation it is always with a certain degree; and of course we do indeed speak of strong and weak feelings. If a sensation has a degree it is because it involves measurement. It involves a relation whereby the specific degree is fixed in relation to a common reference point. Kant is quick to point out, however, that the way of grading the 'size' of a sensation must be distinguished from how we measure the size of a spatial object. A large table and a terrible pain both involve an act of measuring, but the size of the table and the size of the pain take place in terms of different registers. Thus for Kant it is a category mistake to maintain that tables and pains are measured in the same way: we fail to distinguish quantity from quality.[10] Instead of extensive we must speak of intensive magnitudes. It is not a question of counting parts but of noting the distance between what we feel and the complete absence of feeling: 'a magnitude … in which multiplicity can be represented only through approximation to negation = 0, I entitle an *intensive* magnitude'.[11] It is only because a feeling involves a comparison between itself and the cessation of feeling that we hold feelings to be diverse, so that some are stronger than others. A weak feeling is closer to zero degree intensity, a strong one has greater distance. It is precisely because this comparison is involved that Kant locates a sensation as a representation and not the immediacy of raw matter: 'sensation is not the transcendental matter of all objects as things in themselves'.[12]

If Kant uses the Anticipations of Perception to correct a naive assumption found in empiricism – that sensation is raw[13] – he nevertheless does not disagree with the empiricists' claim that sensation is the criterion of reality: 'what corresponds in empirical intuition to sensation is reality'.[14] For Kant it is indeed the case that we regard something as real only if we feel it, but it is not the case that the feeling precedes the judgement of reality, as though the feeling were pre-conceptual. In that a feeling always occurs with a certain degree of intensity it must involve structure: the degree is set in relation to the complete absence of feeling (= 0 degree). It is this act of measuring, which must be distinguished from how we count extensive magnitudes, which marks the formal component of a sensation. Thus for Kant, contra empiricism, reality is not the judgement we make after experiencing a feeling, it is that element of a feeling which makes it possible that it has a certain degree. Consequently, the term 'reality', in part, marks the procedure which generates intensive magnitudes. Such a procedure, Kant famously tells us, is an act of synthesis. It is the movement of locating a degree of feeling in relation to the complete absence of feeling, for only by way of such a comparison can a certain degree be generated. Moreover, Kant is quick to point out that we must not take it that the measuring of feeling is a process which generates a product and then shuts down. Sensations are clearly not static: their degree of intensity rises and falls. Even boredom has its peaks and troughs. Accordingly, Kant insists that the synthesis which generates intensive magnitudes is continuous: the determination of one intensive magnitude is but the starting point for the generation of a further one. Hence when we claim that all sensations take place in time we are merely noting the fact that the synthesis which produces intensive magnitudes never shuts down. Accordingly, sensations always have the characteristic of flowing: 'Such magnitudes may also be called flowing [*fließende*], since the synthesis of productive imagination involved in their production is a progression in time'.[15]

Thus it is vital to realise that whilst Kant agrees with the empiricists' claim that sensation is the criterion of reality, he does so because the intensity encountered in a sensation is not something that simply comes from without but is the working of the synthesis. It is on this basis that Kant attempts to explain the troublesome notion of 'being'. We maintain the existence of something when we take it to be real; and we ascribe reality when we feel the act of synthesis taking place. It cannot be emphasised too strongly that for critical philosophy the term reality and the related notion of being, when properly understood, refer first and foremost to the act of synthesis:

> [T]he real, which corresponds to sensations in general, as opposed to negation = 0, represents only that something the very concept of which includes being, and signifies nothing but the synthesis in an empirical consciousness in general.[16]

Kant famously applies this theory of being in his critique of the Ontological Argument for the existence of God. The problem with this argument is that it treats 'being' as a concept, whereas Kant maintains that the criterion for speaking of existence is not conceptual – 'we could not confound the existence of the thing with the mere concept of it'[17] – but is the feeling that occurs through the act of synthesis. Thus a purely formal argument, which the Ontological Argument purports to be, can never convince us to speak of being. The argument fails not because of formal considerations but quite simply because it fails to move us. What is missing from the Ontological Argument's presentation of God is the production of an intensive magnitude: it fails not through conceptual error but because of a lack of feeling. For Kant, by contrast, if we are to speak of God existing, it is only because an act of synthesis occurs commensurate to this concept. And indeed the most extraordinary claim in the whole of critical philosophy is that we are capable of such a synthesis.[18]

If, however, critical philosophy maintains that the terms 'reality', 'being' and 'existence' first and foremost mark the act of synthesis which produces the degree of intensity felt in a sensation,[19] we should not thereby infer that Kant has abandoned matter. That is to say that if Kant calls the act of synthesis 'reality', it is not because he wishes to maintain that such an act takes place in the void; as if when we act we are not thereby relating to something other than the act. Kant maintains throughout the first *Critique* that a synthesis is always a response: it is a reactive faculty. It is this claim which lies at the heart of Kant's refutation of idealism. Synthesis only occurs because it meets something. Indeed, Kant maintains that the entire edifice constructed out of acts of

synthesis, the domain of theoretical cognition, comes about because we
meet with that which resists us: 'we are dealing with an object about
which nothing can be done [*unternehmen*] by us, and in regard to which
our judgment is therefore purely theoretical'.[20] Kant argues for this claim
in the following way: experience is not composed simply of passing time
(the rhythm of repeating, flowing synthesis) but determinations of time.
We always meet a measurement of time and never pure flux. But a determinate measure presupposes a fixed point from which it takes its bearings. For Kant this fixed point, which gives determinate experience its
basic orientation, is not something with which we provide ourselves. If
Kant is correct to maintain that the work of the mind is the act of a continually repeating synthesis, then how could this flux of time, of itself,
give rise to the notion of a fixed point; that is, something permanent, in
terms of which a determinate measurement could take place? Moreover,
we cannot take it that such a fixed point is provided by the spatial
objects of the empirical world. Such a suggestion merely avoids the
question, *viz.*, how does determinate experience arise in the first place?
Kant rejects *both* the suggestion that the mind itself provides the fixed
point from which determination starts and the muddled view that spatial objects are the ground. Instead he claims that the basic orientation
in terms of which we measure our empirical world comes from that
which bears down on us as a power 'about which nothing can be done.'
It is this fixed point which makes it possible that a *determinate* (measured) cognition arises. And it is this which Kant calls matter:

> we have nothing permanent on which, as intuition, we can base the concept
> of a substance, save only *matter*; and even this permanence is not obtained
> from outer experience [i.e., objects in space], but is presupposed *a priori* as
> a necessary condition of determination of time.[21]

What Kant locates here as the necessary condition for the production
of a determinate experience is the meeting with a power 'about which
nothing can be done'. Hence from the fact that we are creatures who
always insist on comprehending facts, on determining what we meet, we
can infer that we have met with a power greater than ourselves. For it is
this meeting which is the stimulus that brings synthesis to life. There-
after this foreign power is employed as a fixed point in relation to which
the capacity to produce a determinate synthesis becomes possible. Theoretical cognition does not take its bearings from truth, or from what, in
our more naive moments, we might be tempted to regard as simply the
given waiting to be moulded. Certainly cognition always takes account

of matter, but precisely because matter is that which intrudes, that which threatens to annihilate our capacity to respond. With matter the issue is not letting be what is given but whether comprehension can survive. Indeed, it is most important to realise how close Kant's notion of matter is to the threat of death.

We saw that in the Anticipations of Perception Kant locates the production of sensation as the result of a synthesis. In that every sensation always has a degree of intensity we can infer that a sensation involves an act of measurement. Further, we also saw that Kant argues that the term 'reality', when correctly used, refers not simply to a sensation but to the act of synthesis which every sensation presupposes. If then 'reality' marks the act of synthesis, 'negation' indicates the cessation of synthesis. Consequently, the generation of a sensation with a degree of intensity requires the relation between the act of synthesis and the cessation of synthesis. It seems then that an intensive magnitude, whilst the most common event in the world (after all, we generate sensations all the time we are alive), is something which borders on the incomprehensible, for how can we possibly grasp that which is located as the cessation of synthesis? If Kant is correct to maintain that we comprehend by way of the activity of synthesis then that which is located as the cessation of synthesis will always be beyond our reach. And yet Kant maintains that the very activity of productive synthesis involves a relation to such a black hole. Thus we can see that the zero degree of intensity implied in the generation of a sensation would be death. If synthesis is annihilated, time ceases and life is no more.[22]

Zero intensity does not simply mark an inert and featureless domain, but rather the threat of annihilation. It is that threat, however, which brings us to life. For Kant, synthesis does not simply happen, it is provoked. Zero intensity is always involved in synthesis because synthesis is a reaction to the threat of extinction. Thus in the Anticipations of Perception we have advanced from the situation of the Transcendental Aesthetic, where the content of thought is encountered as the impasse we reach should we try to strip away all form, to the suggestion that what such an 'operation' would encounter is extinction (zero intensity). Extinction is not simply a blind spot, it is a threat. It is at the moment of zero degree intensity that life bursts forth in the face of the threat and the act of synthesis is engendered once more.

Accordingly, we can see that when Kant speaks of the content of thought it is to the strange, problematic notion of zero degree intensity which he refers. Now we are no longer dealing with an interesting dilemma but with extreme provocation. Zero degree intensity is a threat to life. If we approach it we will be repelled. But for Kant this is precisely the way in which synthesis works. The activity of synthesis is galvanised by zero degree intensity and that is why synthesis always involves a relation to its own cessation. Kant maintains that content is a necessity of thought ('without matter [*Stoff*] nothing whatsoever can be thought')[23] precisely because the dynamic of synthesis, that a synthesis occurs, requires this 'relationship' to annihilation.

A non-determinative synthesis

There can be no denying that the association of synthesis with death does not sit comfortably in the Analytic of the first *Critique*. For, initially, Kant maintains that the act of synthesis is not simply that of movement but that it marks the specific procedure whereby dispersion is gathered and made into a whole.[24] However, if synthesis is defined as the movement from difference to identity we will ask what provides the patterns in terms of which such arrangement takes place. One never simply gathers but rather arranges according to a pattern one already has in mind. It is on the basis of this reflection that Kant declares that the activity of synthesis is forever tied to and governed by the understanding. If synthesis can gather the manifold it is only because another faculty provides the templates which direct the operation. Consequently Kant declares that 'Pure synthesis, *represented in its most general aspect*, gives us the pure concept of the understanding'.[25] We should not underestimate the significance and the status of this claim. For, firstly, we cannot, with any ease, maintain that this crucial claim is incorrect. We cannot comprehend the suggestion that a synthesis takes place *without* the guidance of a pre-given code. To grasp the activity of synthesis we locate it as the act which imposes a pre-given order upon what it meets. Secondly, it is this claim which provides the principal consideration that underpins the deduction of the categories. If we agree that experience is always the result of synthesis and that a synthesis always needs a pattern in terms of which to work, then we will indeed accept that there must be *a priori* patterns which make coherent experience possible in the first place. Accordingly, we must note the extent to which the Analytic of the first *Critique* presents the act of synthesis as that which *can* be comprehended, i.e., as that which is only possible because it is governed by the understanding.

However, the difficulty with such a comprehensible account of synthesis is that it forgets that the energy of synthesis comes about by way of incomprehension. For what the Anticipations of Perception show us is that synthesis needs to fail; it needs to come to the point where it can no longer gather, where the activity of moving from the manifold to unity ceases and synthesis plummets to zero degree intensity. We saw that for Kant 'matter' comes to mark the moment where synthesis bursts back to life. This energy is provoked by the threat of annihilation, by the cessation of synthesis. This is why Kant maintains that synthesis is impossible without matter, why thought always has content. The threat of death, it seems, is part of the very pulse of life. Such collapse is not without consequence for the understanding. For it must be the case that this failure of synthesis is also the failure by the imagination to generate the pattern demanded of it by the understanding. Zero degree intensity threatens when we can no longer comprehend in terms of the categories. But, as we saw, it is this paralysis which fires the synthesis, which ensures that thought has content. It seems then that, according to the Analytic of the first *Critique*, the term synthesis is at once comprehensible and incomprehensible. Comprehensibility demands that synthesis has a pattern given to it and so synthesis is simply the creature of the understanding; but the energy of synthesis requires the failure of the understanding.

Thus it is difficult not to see inconsistencies in the presentation of synthesis found in the Analytic of the first *Critique*. Kant at once maintains that synthesis is measured by the understanding and yet requires the failure of the understanding. It is this tension that has led some commentators to speculate that synthesis must be grasped in independence of logic. The inconsistency is cited as evidence that Kant fled from the radicality of his discovery, or, more specifically, that the inconsistency occurs because Kant presents the forces of production in terms of their product. The only reason to insist that synthesis occurs in relation to logic is because we are refusing to give up the orientation of the ontic world, the world of conscious order. Hence, after Kant, philosophers have given themselves the task of overcoming these inconsistencies and providing an account of synthesis which dispenses with the demand that synthesis enacts the patterns of logic.

However, before leaving Kant and embracing thought without categories, we should note that Kant also felt the need to explore the notion of a synthesis not controlled by pre-given patterns. The first part of the *Critique of Aesthetic Judgement* distinguishes between determinative and reflective judgement. The latter contains the suggestion that the act of synthesis can attain autonomy and is not obliged forever to serve the understanding. However, we should not simply assume that Kant is, at last, getting round to resolving the problems which the Analytic of the first *Critique* had left hanging. Rather, it is the case that Kant's account of autonomous synthesis is consistent with the inconsistencies of the first *Critique*. Indeed, in the account of autonomous synthesis which Kant provides in the Analytic of the Sublime, we can see that all the claims of the first *Critique* still hold. Synthesis, even in its autonomy, continues to both meet and reject the understanding. And this will be the case because, at least for Kant, the event of the sublime is never simply an ascetic act, an event only concerning the internal balance of the mind. Rather, a synthesis always has content, it only ever occurs by way of a relation to matter. It is because of the insistence on matter that the inconsistent relation of synthesis with the understanding is repeated by Kant in his discussion of the sublime.

That the sublime involves a relation to matter is seen most clearly from Kant's contention that the sublime is born of failure: 'it is produced by the feeling of a momentary inhibition of the vital forces'.[26] The non-determinative synthesis of the sublime is not decided upon, it is provoked. It is forced out of us through the collapse of the understanding. Kant tells us, 'that it is … in its chaos that nature most arouses our ideas of the sublime',[27] but we should not take it from this that chaos is ever something we can simply decide to accept. The core argument of the Analytic of the first *Critique* was that consciousness is a function of the mind's ability to grasp the manifold of sensations as a determinate object. If, in the third *Critique*, Kant does suggest that the order of the empirical world can break down, it is not because he is now contending that consciousness stretches further than the categories. The failure which provokes the sublime is a crisis for consciousness. We meet with that which we cannot understand. But that which we cannot understand must not be presented as an object which we do not quite recognise, as though we only have to wait for the development of science for the crisis to pass. That which can be grasped as an object, even if it remains unrecognised, is purposive for the understanding: it *is* something which the understanding can handle. However, when Kant tells us that 'a pure judgment about the sublime … must have no purpose whatsoever of the object as the basis determining it',[28] he is indicating that with the sublime the understanding does not simply meet a pause in its deployment, it encounters that which is completely non-purposive for it. We cannot understand what it is going on. Even the simple logical connectives, which provide the shell for all empirical objects, fail. We must not make the mistake of thinking that non-purposiveness, chaos, is an object of the understanding.

Moreover, it is precisely because we *necessarily* reach the sublime by way of the failure of the understanding, that pain, or, as Kant calls it, 'negative pleasure', is always a feature of the sublime.[29] The understanding, consciousness, is part of us. If this should collapse it is we who suffer the failure. When consciousness approaches the sublime it cannot help but tremble[30] – it suffers vertigo at the prospect of its own annihilation: '[the sublime] is, as it were, an abyss in which the imagination is afraid to lose itself'.[31] In such encounters the understanding loses confidence in its ability to comprehend in terms of the categories; we fear that with the failure of cognitive synthesis, the very act of synthesis will also collapse. In other words, the sublime always begins when the prospect of death intrudes into the order of the understanding.

For Kant, as indeed for many philosophers before and after him, such intrusions are not without a certain benefit. However, we should note that it is not a benefit which the understanding will ever appreciate or indeed be able to register. Kant claims that if we suffer the collapse of the understanding it might occur that a different kind of synthesis, a synthesis no longer regulated by the categories, appears: 'the subject's own inability uncovers in him the consciousness of an unlimited ability which is also his'.[32] It is by way of the collapse of the understanding that we become aware that what we can *do* is not limited to what we can know, that the power of synthesis can function otherwise than as a creature of the understanding. Of course such an expansion is invigorating. A feeling of delight always surges through us when a block is removed, when a code ceases to hold a force to its patterns. Such is the pleasure that we feel in the sublime. But we should note carefully that this pleasure is only available at a price: it is necessary to suffer the increasing desolation which overwhelms the understanding as it approaches its collapse. To feel the power of unrestrained synthesis it is necessary that the understanding should go under: 'the imagination thereby acquires an expansion and a might [*Macht*] that surpasses the one it sacrifices'.[33] The sublime does not occur without a death – the death of the understanding.

It is vital that we do not convert the autonomous synthesis which Kant calls the sublime into an ascetic act, as though the understanding suffers its defeat simply because of an internal manoeuvre within the mind. To interpret the sublime in this way would be to lose the Kantian insistence on matter, and yet certain remarks by Kant seem to suggest precisely this view of the proceedings. For example, Kant locates the mathematical sublime as arising when we realise that cognition is unable to measure the infinite;[34] he then notes the following: 'But – and this is most important – to be able even to think the infinite as *a whole* indicates a mental power that surpasses any standard of sense'.[35] It is well known that for Kant the notion of infinity is not learnt but stems from a power of the mind which he calls reason. Is it then the case that the crisis of the understanding comes about simply because the mind brings two faculties together: the understanding is shown the idea of sufficiency ('the infinite as *a whole*') and for the first time realises that its determinations never achieve such completeness? We have decided, as it were, to subject the products of the understanding to the absolute criteria of reason, and found them wanting. However, the event of the sublime cannot be the result of such an ascetic measuring of the faculties precisely because it is only by way of the collapse of the understanding that we *first* come to feel that we are more than creatures who produce cognitions. Indeed, if we are ever to come close to what Kant might be attempting to speak of when he refers to the faculty of reason, we must start by noting that the gateway to this power is the death of the understanding.[36] We must not forget that the constant theme of all Kant's critical writings is that pure reason is something that we can never understand.[37]

We will never meet the sublime if we regard it as a purely internal affair which can be accounted for by way of a relation between the structures of the mind. It is certainly the case that this autonomous synthesis marks a relation between the powers of particularity and universality (understanding and reason), such that we cannot ground the relation in either faculty: the understanding, in its failure, shows itself to be incomplete, but the power of reason only comes about by way of this failure. However, we are still too formal if we locate autonomous synthesis as merely concerned with a relation between these faculties of the mind. We must notice that something has happened between the hegemony of understanding and the non-determinative synthesis which is no longer held to the categories. It is precisely because synthesis has, as it were, shut down that we are able to waken to a new day in which we and the world are more open. The systole and diastole of synthesis do not mark an auto-affection: as though synthesis were sufficient unto itself and the breakdown comes from within. For Kant, the heart beat would not fire without the provocation of matter. Matter intrudes when form fails, when the capacity to comprehend the world deserts us, when we are no longer able to find within ourselves the power to respond. Such a break-down is not a self-managed affair, it is the refutation of idealism. For now we meet what we are no longer able to resist; now we cannot even comprehend what is happening to us. It is at such moments of zero degree intensity that we are closest to matter. What is so extraordinary about Kantian philosophy is that it is at such moments of collapse that it discovers the very fount of life. Somehow or other, zero degree intensity can serve to 'raise the soul's fortitude above its usual middle range and allow us to discover in ourselves an ability to resist which is of a quite different kind'.[38] What Kant clearly shows in the Analytic of the Sublime is that without the intrusion of matter a non-determinative synthesis would not occur.

It is because Kant contends that the autonomous activity of synthesis only comes about by way of the encounter with zero degree intensity that we find that the Analytic of the Sublime assembles the same problematic relation between the energy of synthesis and the categories of the understanding which is evident in the first *Critique*. If free synthesis is provoked by matter then it requires the failure of the understanding. It is not a question of simply giving up the categories and returning to the primordial ground of free synthesis, for we do not meet matter by stripping away the non-essential structures of logic; matter only ever intrudes through the failure of logic. If Kant is right and a free, non-determinative synthesis is only ever provoked, then such freedom will always take place in an atmosphere of desperation and trauma. We hold on to the order of consciousness to the very last and as its failure grows, so does the fear and anxiety aroused by the coming collapse. It is this build-up of crisis and darkness which suddenly becomes the energy of a non-determinative synthesis. This is why Kant tells us that the feeling of the sublime is at once pain and pleasure. And this is also why a non-determinative synthesis must involve at once a relation to the categories of the understanding and the failure of that relation. Energy only ever flows when form breaks down. If we ignore the movement whereby a free synthesis bursts forth in desperation out of the unbearable failure of synthesis determined by the categories, we will indeed simply note an inconsistency in Kant's analysis – an inconsistency which, it seems, is found in both the Analytic of the first *Critique* and the Analytic of the Sublime in the *Critique of Judgement*. However, Kant's consistency in repeating the inconsistency occurs because, in each case, he is trying to show us that the energy of synthesis fires by way of the collapse of the understanding, by way of the provocation of zero degree intensity.

Synthesis requires a relation to the understanding because it is provoked by the failure of the understanding.

Kantian materialism

We can see that the dark thoughts of the Anticipations of Perception are attempted again in the Analytic of the Sublime. Synthesis does not simply happen, it is provoked, provoked by way of crisis and failure, where the systems of comprehension and order fail to grasp what is happening. It is at such moments, where the exhilaration of the act of synthesis has almost disappeared, when life hardly stirs and we are left in the desolation of depression, that we come closest to matter. We reach matter at the moment when form collapses, when we no longer possess the power to meet and comprehend whatever it is that is pressing in upon us: zero degree intensity. And yet Kant insists that such paralysis is necessary for synthesis. If a synthesis has content, if the imposition of form is not empty, it is because from out of the depths of collapse a response has been forged. Matter makes us create anew: nothing works, we must think again. Synthesis fires in response to its own collapse: it collapses when the imposition of form fails and matter draws near. It is on the basis of such reflections that Kant gains the premise which is so fundamental for his Refutation of Idealism.

Of course, the question we cannot help but ask is how synthesis returns after the devastation of zero degree intensity. If the light goes out completely, how is it possible that it can flare up once more? Such considerations lead us to insist that there must be a meta-narrative which can guide us through the death of zero degree intensity. We insist that synthesis must be determinate, that there has to be a code which grounds the mechanism of synthesis. However, for Kantian philosophy the extent to which we are able to respond to what we meet by way of a pre-given code (form) is also the extent to which matter has not yet fully intruded into our life. In the face of matter all determinate synthesis collapses, indeed synthesis itself apparently freezes as it drops to zero degree. If synthesis fires again it is not because there is a code which determines what will happen on the other side of death. In contradistinction to all philosophies that try to give the last word to formal patterns which tell us what to do, Kantianism insists that synthesis requires, as a necessary condition, that we do not know what to do. The encounter with matter, which we reach when form collapses, is the provocation which stings synthesis back to life. This, presumably, helps us to understand why so much of life is drawn towards death.

Notes

1 '[E]xperience contains two very dissimilar elements, namely, the *matter* of knowledge obtained from the senses, and a certain *form* for the ordering of this matter.' Kant, *CPR* A86/B118.

2 'In the transcendental aesthetic we shall, therefore, first isolate sensibility, by taking away from it everything which the understanding thinks through its concepts.' (Kant, *CPR*, A22/B36).

3 Kant, *CPR*, A32/B48.

4 Kant, *CPR*, A32/B48–9.

5 Certainly there have been attempts to remove the dimensions of space from raw sensation. Berkeley made precisely this suggestion in *An Essay Toward a New Theory of Vision* (London: Dent, 1954); and indeed Russell, by implication, removes spatiality from the reality of sensation when he tells us that reality is ephemeral: 'The things that are really real last a very short time.' ('The Philosophy of Logical Positivism', in *Logic and Knowledge*, ed. R. C. Marsh (London: Allen and Unwin, 1956)). Yet neither empiricist considers the Kantian claim that to reach the rawness of the given we would also have to strip away time.

6 Kant, *CPR*, A30/B45.

7 For example, 'Behind the phenomena of phenomenology there is essentiall nothing else.' (Martin Heidegger, *Being and Time*, trans. J. Macquarrie and E. Robinson (Oxford: Blackwell, 1980), p. 60).

8 In *CPR* Kant marks the impasse of matter with the term 'noumenon'. This term is used first and foremost to indicate Kant's recurrent theme that the content of cognition is something other to the forms of cognition. Consequently 'noumenon' is both a 'limiting concept' and 'problematic' (Kant, *CPR*, A255/B310–11). It marks the limit of the impasse: that without form we cannot approach matter, but with form, matter as such is never encountered. Moreover, the impasse is not to be solved by simply dropping the suggestion that form has content. The problematic status of 'noumenon' is irremovable precisely because critical philosophy insists on content, insists on matter.

9 This section occurs in the part of the Analytic of *CPR* which Kant calls the Principles of the Understanding. Here it is no longer a question of examining the faculties of cognition individually but considering the product which occurs when they work together. This product Kant entitles a principle and claims that it is principles which lie at the bottom of all explanations of experience. For one of the few modern readings of Kant to register the importance of the Anticipations of Perception see Deleuze's 1970s Kant

lectures: 'So there are twelve extraordinary pages entitled "Anticipations of Perception".'(Gilles Deleuze, *Second Lesson on Kant, 21st March 1978*, trans. Melissa McMahon (http://www.imaginet.fr/deleuze/TXT/ENG/210378.html), p. 4).

10 Precisely this category mistake appears to be present in Bentham's famous attempt to measure sensations. In *Introduction to the Principles of Morals and Legislation* (London: Hafner, 1948) he seeks a calculus for determining policy: that which promotes the greatest quantity of pleasure should be chosen. Accordingly in chapter four, 'Value of a Lot of Pleasure or Pain. How to be Measured', Bentham does indeed present suggestions for quantifying sensation. After such a translation it then becomes possible to mathematically demonstrate that one course of action is superior to another because it will lead to more units of pleasure and fewer of pain. The category mistake is to suppose that the intensity of a sensation can be measured as if it were a quantity and not a quality. Indeed the sometimes heard reservation concerning Utilitarianism, that it is fair but insipid, can be traced to this attempt to treat the quality of an intensity as nothing but a number.

11 Kant, *CPR*, A168/B210.

12 Kant, *CPR*, A143/B182.

13 We should not fail to note that Kant's critique of empiricism on this point owes an enormous debt to Leibniz. Indeed, the principal motif of Leibniz's response to Locke was that Locke's starting point, sensation, is always already a product of activity: 'sensation is something more than a simple perception' ('Monadology' in *Philosophical Essays*, trans. R. Ariew and D. Garber (Indianapolis and Cambridge: Hackett, 1989), § 19).

14 Kant, *CPR*, A168/B209.

15 Kant, *CPR*, A170/B211. This is perhaps the appropriate point to note that for Kantian philosophy time is merely the collective term for the different types of synthesis which compose experience. Hence time is a necessary condition of experience because experience is produced by way of transcendental syntheses.

16 Kant, *CPR*, A175–6/B217.

17 Kant, *CPR*, A600/B628.

18 We touch here on the most controversial stratum of Kant's later writings. Whilst Kant is adamant that we cannot *theoretically* speak of the existence of God, we can encounter this existence *morally*: 'it is morally necessary to assume the existence of God.'(*Critique of Practical Reason*, p. 130; *Ak*.V: 125). We should not, however, assume that Kant is simply being inconsistent: that he did not have the courage to maintain the findings of the first *Critique*. If Kant does go on to speak of the *existence* of God it is because he believes he has discovered an act of synthesis which theoretical reason can never comprehend.

19 I have used these terms almost as equivalents. This, I would contend,

reflects Kant's own usage.
20 Kant, *CPR*, A825/B853.
21 Kant, *CPR*, B277–78.
22 This suggestion is certainly not unique to Kant. For example, Leibniz, using
    a slightly different vocabulary, maintains that when no synthesis occurs,
    when no combination is made in the face of what we meet, then 'we ha[ve]
    nothing distinct or, so to speak, in relief and stronger in flavour, we would
    always be in a stupor. And this is the state of bare monads' (Leibniz, 'Mon-
    adology', § 24). And earlier Leibniz tells us 'Death can impart this state to
    animals for a time.' ('Monadology', § 21). However, whilst Leibniz does
    appear to locate death as the cessation of synthesis, we should not fail to
    notice a radical difference between the two thinkers. For Leibniz, death is
    merely an event in time (he suggests it is merely temporary), whereas for
    Kant the extinction of synthesis is the death of time.
23 Kant, *CPR*, A232/B284.
24 '[I]f this manifold is to be known, the spontaneity of our thought requires
    that it be gone through in a certain way, taken up, and connected. This act
    I name *synthesis*.' (Kant, *CPR*, A77/B102).
25 Kant, *CPR*, A78/B104.
26 Kant, *CJ*, p. 98; *Ak*.V: 245.
27 Kant, *CJ*, p 99; *Ak*.V: 246.
28 Kant, *CJ*, p. 109; *Ak*.V: 253.
29 For example, 'the sublime contains not so much a positive pleasure as
    rather admiration and respect, and so should be called a negative plea-
    sure'(Kant, *CJ*, p. 98; *Ak*.V: 245). Kant calls the pain which always occurs
    at the beginning of the sublime a negative pleasure because he knows well
    that pain and pleasure are not mutually exclusive: that the most intense
    pleasures go by way of pain.
30 Indeed, Kant tells us that the sublime 'can be compared with a vibration'
    (Kant, *CJ*, p. 115; *Ak*.V: 258).
31 Kant, *CJ*, p. 115; *Ak*.V: 258. The imagination to which Kant refers here is
    the power of synthesis as ruled by the understanding. This arrangement is
    so much part of us that we cannot help but feel fear at the prospect of its
    collapse.
32 Kant, *CJ*, p. 116; *Ak*.V: 259.
33 Kant, *CJ*, p. 129 ; *Ak*.V: 269.
34 We should note that, according to Kant, the sublime can have two differ-
    ent kinds of beginning. He distinguishes between the crisis which is pro-
    voked when we are no longer able to measure what we meet (the
    mathematical sublime); and the catastrophe which follows from meeting a
    power (*Macht*) which overwhelms us (the dynamical sublime).
35 Kant, *CJ*, p. 111; *Ak*.V: 254.
36 'Yet this inadequacy itself is the arousal in us of the feeling that we have

within us a supersensible power'(Kant, *CJ*, p. 106; *Ak*.V: 250).

37   For example, when speaking of our power to act when the ability to know
      has failed, Kant states that 'the basis of this might [*Macht*] is concealed
      from it'(Kant, *CJ*, p. 129; *Ak*.V: 269).

38   Kant, *CJ*, p. 120; *Ak*.V: 261.

2

Crystallisation: Artful Matter and the Productive Imagination in Kant's Account of Genius

Rachel Jones

At the salt mines of Salzburg, they throw a leafless wintry bough into one of the abandoned workings. Two or three months later they haul it out covered with a shining deposit of crystals ... a galaxy of scintillating diamonds. The original branch is no longer recognizable.
What I have called *crystallization* is a mental process which draws from everything that happens.[1]

Under the described circumstances, formation then takes place, not by a gradual transition from the fluid to the solid state, but as it were by a leap: a sudden solidification called *shooting*; this transition is also called *crystallization*.[2]

Throughout the *Critique of Judgement,* Kant's examination of reflective judgement is itself structured by a series of reflections between art and nature, reflections which sometimes seem to trap the reader in a captivating hall of mirrors. Thus, we read not only that nature is to be judged as if it were art, and that nature's technic proceeds artistically, but that art in turn is to be judged 'fine art' only when it appears to be like nature. This complex mirroring is structured by analogy, which Kant himself describes as a 'double function' of judgement.[3] This paper will begin by tracing the complex movements of Kant's analogy between art and nature. However, I will go on to argue that in addition to the differences and similarities on which Kant's text explicitly draws, there is a further vital relation between art and nature concealed within the terms of his analogies, a relation which needs to be mapped out in terms of *production* rather than *judgement*.

Exploring this relation will involve examining the passages on crystallisation which occur in one of the final paragraphs of the *Critique of Aesthetic Judgement*. Although this paragraph points ahead to Kant's

examination of teleological judgement, here I will primarily be concerned to map the notion of crystallisation back on to Kant's account of
aesthetics, by reading it in relation to his account of art and genius. In
what follows, I will suggest that rigorously extending Kant's own analogical comparison of art and nature to the case of art and crystallisation
has a transformative effect on the models of production Kant employs
to account for both art and nature. Pursuing Kant's analogical method
in this way thus introduces a productive disruption into the Kantian
frame.[4]

Nature as art and art as nature

One of the most pressing concerns of scientists in the late eighteenth
century was the relation between classificatory systems and empirical
nature. As James Larson notes, it was at this time that naturalists began
to think that their artificial hierarchical method of categorising 'was
potentially an accurate representation of natural order.'[5] Kant's analogy
between art and nature reflects this concern with the relation between
the artificial and the natural, between human capacities to structure and
order on the one hand, and nature's empirical complexity and diversity
on the other. The *Critique of Judgement* is itself necessitated because
although the *Critique of Pure Reason* guarantees that nature forms a
system under the transcendental laws conditioning all objective experience, nature's manifold empirical forms, together with the empirical
laws they instantiate, might still be 'infinitely diverse and heterogeneous
… a raw chaotic aggregate without the slightest trace of a system.'[6]

Hence Kant argues that to be able to order nature's material diversity
in terms of systematic empirical laws, we must first *presuppose* that
nature forms a coherent system, even in its empirical multiplicity. Only
on the basis of this presupposition can judgement connect the particularity of singular experiences to more general and universal laws through
which we form an understanding of nature as an ordered whole. This
presupposition is the guiding principle for judgement's reflective use
and makes the meaningful investigation of nature possible: it is the subjectively necessary principle prescribed by judgement to itself.

This necessary principle of reflective judgement is explored throughout the *Critique of Judgement* and entails a perspectival shift in the way
we see nature. If nature in all its empirical variety is to be seen as lending itself to the power of systematic judgement as such, it is no longer
enough just to see nature as blind mechanism. Even though nature's

empirical diversity is merely contingent, we must see it *as if* intentionally designed, *as if* its arrangement were the result of a deliberate ordering which corresponds to our capacity to find coherence and systematic unity. Hence this perspectival shift entails seeing nature as if it were art:

> [T]he concept that arises originally from judgment, as its own concept, is the concept of nature as *art*; in other words, it is the concept of the *technic of nature* regarding its *particular* ... laws. This concept ... gives us only a principle by which we [can] proceed in terms of empirical laws, which makes it possible for us to investigate nature.[7]

We can introduce coherence into our reflections on empirical laws by attributing to nature a capacity to construct its objects in an artful and deliberate way, such that they lend themselves to judgement's search for organising principles. Strictly speaking, it is judgement itself that is technical, rather than nature. It is only judgement which presents nature as specifying itself according to its 'technic' or design. We do not know objectively that nature is designed, and thus Kant writes that when we regard 'nature as *art*', judgement itself is functioning '*artistically*', in terms of a principle that is universal but also indeterminate'.[8]

For Kant, this human ability to judge nature not just as a random aggregate but as if it had an inherently lawful order is most directly reflected in aesthetic judgements of taste. Judgements of taste are grounded in a pre-conceptual free play of the imagination over a manifold of intuition presented to it. This 'play' generates a heightened sense of the way we see nature as lending itself to the ordering potential of the faculties. As determinate concepts would restrict this free play, judgements of taste refer to this heightened mental state through feeling alone. Yet as all human subjects must be able to see the world as harmonising with the potential of their own ordering faculties, this singular feeling of pleasure reflects a universal *a priori* principle, which is nothing other than the indeterminate principle of judgement itself. Judgements of taste are thus grounded in our necessary ability to see nature '[by] analogy with art'.[9]

Yet it is worth noting that when Kant turns to the interest reason has in our ability to make judgements of taste, he extends his analogy to draw on the difference rather than the similarity between art and nature. For if we were to find out that something aesthetically pleasing was artificial, if the nightingale's song was in fact being played on a reed, we would lose all intellectual interest in our aesthetic appreciation of it. It is only through natural beauty, where the world seems to freely accord with the lawfulness of the understanding, that we are given a 'trace' or 'hint' that nature might also accord with the lawfulness of reason, allowing us to hope that our moral ideas might one day be objectively realised.[10]

Ultimately, judgements of taste lead us to inquire as to whether we can in fact form any judgement about the determinate purposes underlying nature's production. These 'profound investigations' are pursued in the *Critique of Teleological Judgement*.[11] Kant's analogy between art and nature is extended to teleological judgement by drawing on exactly that aspect of the artificial which had to be excluded from aesthetic judgement, namely, its production in terms of rules. We know from our own experience, Kant argues, that something artificially constructed depends upon an underlying idea of what it is meant to be, of its organisation as a whole. Teleological judgement involves ascribing such causality to nature: we judge nature's products as natural purposes by thinking of them as objects which are only possible because they too are united and organised according to an underlying design or concept, determining what they are 'meant to be'. In this way, he concludes, we judge natural objects not just insofar as they appear like art, but as products of art.[12]

The final way in which the analogy between nature and art is deployed is when Kant is discussing fine art (*schöne Kunst*) itself. If we were to judge works of art only as deliberately produced objects, our judgement would be constrained by the rules in terms of which we judged the work to have been intentionally organised. Thus if we are to find an art work beautiful, then even though we know it to have been deliberately produced, its form must seem free from all rule-governed production such that, like beauty in nature, it appears to accord freely with the faculties. Only in this way can a work of art encourage that pleasurable free play of the imagination on which universally communicable judgements of taste are grounded. Hence, 'fine art must have the *look* of nature even though we are conscious of it as art.'[13]

Kant's analogy is to work in both directions: nature is to be judged as art, and art as nature. This interdependency is both highlighted and to some extent problematised in the last section of the First Introduction of *CJ*. Having used the analogy of judging nature as if it were art throughout this Introduction, Kant abruptly declares that in fact it is 'the technic in nature' which is properly called art, and that it is thus art which is to be judged in the same way as nature: 'Our judging of artistic beauty will have to be considered … as a mere consequence of the same principles that underlie judgements about natural beauty.'[14] In this way,

Kant seems to fold his analogy back on itself and to create the dubious situation where nature is to be judged by analogy with art, whilst we can only legitimately judge art on the basis of a nature that turns out to have been art all along.

The threatened collapse of Kant's analogical structure is perhaps averted if we allow that nature is to be seen by analogy with art taken in the broad sense, that is, it is to be regarded as artfully constructed, whilst the artistic beauty which is then to be judged by analogy with nature is art in the narrower sense: that is, it is fine art which must seem 'as if it were a product of mere nature.'[15] His final comments on artistic beauty in the First Introduction can then be read as referring to a special and more limited case. However, it is precisely the 'special case' of fine art which entails that Kant's play of analogies is not completed by mapping the judgement of art back on to the way we judge nature: what is missing from the Introduction's attempt to systematically delineate the matters to be examined by the *Critique of Judgement* is the question of the production, as opposed to the judging, of works of art.

The imaginative art of genius

Kant himself makes a rigorous distinction between the production and judging of works of art. It is this distinction, I will suggest, which complicates his analogy of art and nature in unpredictable ways. Producing art requires genius. Genius is an imaginative capacity to generate and present ideas aesthetically, by restructuring the materials given through experience so as to present more than experience itself could ever give. Whereas rational ideas 'go beyond' nature because they are concepts to which no exhibition is ever adequate,[16] genius surpasses nature by expressing through an imaginative arrangement of its materials more than any given determinate concept could ever describe. Genius allows the artist to imaginatively bind together 'a multitude of kindred presentations' in the art work, reschematising nature so as to generate a wealth of ideas which discursive, conceptual thought could never have arrived at or expressed.[17] Hence genius cannot proceed by following a predetermined concept or rule, but imaginatively generates an original object which 'reveals a new rule that could not have been inferred from any earlier principles or examples'.[18] It is because fine art is produced without following rules that its aesthetic value is not merely objectively determined by concepts. Where artistic creation proceeds by imagination, the work produced allows for an undetermined imaginative play in the minds of those who contemplate it, and hence for non-conceptual, subjectively universal judgements of taste.

The fact that the art work is in the end a determinate object seems to introduce a radical possibility into Kant's framework: here we have an object which is not generated on the basis of a pre-given concept, like the product of a mechanical craft but, rather, produced by a freely creating imagination such that it instantiates an original rule or concept. However, the notion that works of fine art exemplify an 'original rule' can be understood in several different ways, which reveal that the imagination is not simply to be accorded an unregulated freedom. Firstly, the production of any work of art requires not just originality but particular skills and training. Thus it is possible to abstract from any art work the learnt mechanical processes that were necessary to produce it. This alone, however, cannot account for the object as something which could not have been deduced from existing rules or practices.

Hence, secondly, genius is an imaginative capacity to rewrite the rules. Although – as Kant insists – a knowledge of existing artistic practices and traditions is required, these are imaginatively recombined or reconfigured to produce new rules underlying new practices. Kant describes these rules as 'abstracted' or 'extracted' from works of fine art.[19] They would always be historically situated but would involve a revolutionary transformation of tradition, which could not be achieved merely by extending the existing rules. Furthermore, as the rules exemplified in the originality of an artist's work cannot be adequately encompassed in a conceptual formula, they are abstracted not by being summarised in a linguistic precept, but by being acted upon, imaginatively taken up and actualised in the work of other artists. Crucially, these successors will not simply copy the new standards set, but engage with them so as to transform them in turn with originality. On this model, then, aesthetic traditions are shaped by unpredictable moments of creative discontinuity expressed imaginatively through the materiality of the art work.

This historical discontinuity itself seems to be encompassed by the third way in which works of genius can be understood to exemplify a rule. On this model, the originality of all works of genius is produced in the same way, namely, as the expression and result of a particular attunement of the subject's faculties. In this special, animated state, the productive play of the imagination harmonises with the understanding such that the creative presentations generated by the former 'aesthetically expand the concept [of the object presented]' and thereby 'prompt much thought' and 'quicken ... the mind'.[20] In this way, nature in the subject gives the rule to art, whose originality reflects a particular proportion of the mental powers. In the Dialectic of Aesthetic Judgement, Kant goes so far as to ground taste not merely in the transcendental attunement of the faculties, but in the supersensible substrate where 'all our a priori powers are reconciled'.[21] He thus claims that the standard for works of fine art is itself supplied by reference to this supersensible substrate.

Its legitimacy aside, this move is indicative of the problem with this third explanation, which might otherwise seem to provide the final ground for all genius's productions. On this model, the imaginative creativity of genius is measured via judgements of taste against a timeless transcendental ground: the apparent discontinuity of genius's productions is overcome as each original work manifests anew this same productive attunement of the faculties. However, precisely because this timeless ground is purely transcendental – or even transcendent and supersensible – it cannot legislate for the particular material configurations produced by genius, for the specific embodiments of art's originality, or for the discontinuities generated by artistic production considered at an empirical and material level.

In this way, the very problem of the *Critique of Judgement* re-emerges in Kant's account of genius. For as we have seen, in this text Kant seeks to account for the fact that although nature forms a system considered in terms of the transcendental laws established in the *First Critique*, nonetheless, its manifold *empirical* forms and laws might still be thoroughly unsystematic in their heterogeneity, linked together in a purely haphazard manner as a 'raw chaotic aggregate'.[22] In other words, although the empirical world must necessarily be experienced through a spatio-temporal frame, what appears within this frame may still be infinitely chaotic and diverse. In a similar way, regarding works of genius as the exemplars of a transcendental ground in no way contains the productive power of genius as an imaginative capacity to re-schematise matter – and indeed, it is the very indeterminacy of this ground which preserves the unpredictable originality of works of genius in terms of the specific innovations and disruptions, novelties and dislocations which it is capable of producing.

In terms of making it possible to order *nature's* material diversity, as has already been noted, Kant argues that we must necessarily presuppose that nature forms a coherent system even in its empirical variety, and that this presupposition forms the guiding principle of reflective judgement. In terms of containing the material diversity of *genius's* productions, Kant (somewhat notoriously) falls back on judgement again, though in rather less convincing fashion. Having insisted on the essential difference between judgement and production, and having just argued in §49 that genius is itself a capacity not merely for producing a richness of ideas but for communicating those ideas in a way that generates an 'original' concept or a 'new rule',[23] Kant goes on to claim in §50 that genius is 'lawless' without judgement, and that taste must therefore 'severely clip [the] wings' of genius.[24]

Rather than exploring the complex tensions generated by the fact that genius is thereby defined as an imaginative capacity to produce a new rule which is in turn to be ruled by taste, I want to return to the point made earlier, namely, that Kant does not in fact carry through his analogical comparison of nature and art with regard to art's mode of production. In the light of the above, this foreclosure can now be seen as symptomatic of the need to privilege judgement over production so as to restrain the creative capacities of genius. In what follows, I will suggest that the *Critique of Judgement* does in fact sustain the possibility of comparing art's production with nature's productive power. I will suggest that extending Kant's analogical thought in this way shifts the focus away from the legislative role of judgement and on to the potentially subversive power of the productive imagination of genius, whilst at the same time opening a site within the Kantian system whereby the model of matter as essentially inert substance is disturbed.

However, it is first worth noting to what extent Kant's account of the productions of genius complicates the analogy between art and nature. Despite the fact that art must seem as if free from constraint, Kant also stresses that insofar as we think of art as intentionally produced and not a product of mere chance, it is not like the free beauty we find in nature and cannot be judged by taste alone. At the same time, the production of a work of fine art also refuses to be neatly mapped on to the teleological judgement which accounts for the production of natural forms.

In teleological judgement, we cannot make any legitimate claim as to whether nature actually proceeds according to real intentions, for this would involve going beyond the limits of experience. Instead, as was noted above, Kant argues that as we know from our own experience that something artificially constructed depends upon an underlying idea of what it is meant to be, we can proceed by ascribing such causality to nature, that is, by thinking of nature's products as possible only because they too are organised according to an underlying design or concept. In other words, just as judgement's own *a priori* principle allows us to judge nature *as if* designed, it also allows us to judge nature *as if* produced according to rules or concepts instantiated in its products. By combining this guiding principle of judgement with our determinate knowledge of particular objects, we are able to judge these objects in terms of the specific ideas or concepts which would provide the rule for their organisation, ideas and concepts which we think of as the underlying causes of these objects. Thus, although we cannot legitimately claim to know that nature does produce its objects intentionally, nonetheless we can identify particular organising principles and concepts which enable us to make sense of the organisation of the natural world.

In the case of the production of works of genius, the situation is exactly reversed: here, according to Kant, we can indeed know that the object is *intentionally* produced by analogy with our own experience of constructing objects deliberately in accordance with reason. However, we can never think of a work of art in terms of any particular underlying concept which makes its material organisation possible, for the key feature of fine art is that it is created without following any rule for its production. A crucial difference thus emerges between products of nature and those of fine art: nature, Kant affirms, never proceeds by a leap, even in its material diversity, which – thanks to the principle of reflective judgement – can always be ordered as a system of rules and concepts; works of genius, on the other hand, seem to progress by imaginative leaps and bounds.

Analogies with artful matter

What would happen if, despite this difference, we pursued Kant's analogical procedure with the systematic rigour he usually demands of us? For there is, after all, one kind of natural production which is analogous, even within Kant's framework, to this artistic production which proceeds by discontinuous leaps. In §58 of the *Critique of Aesthetic Judgement*, Kant concludes that we cannot legitimately think of nature as deliberately organising itself to provide man with aesthetic pleasure. Were this to be so, aesthetic judgement would become a merely empirical matter of determining whether or not particular objects were in fact intentionally designed by nature to please us. The kind of natural formations particularly conducive to this illegitimate way of thinking are the excessive beauty and apparent artistry of crystalline forms, which seem almost designed for our pleasure – all the more so because Kant tells us that the glitter of crystals is formed merely through nature's

mechanism, and thus we need not contaminate our aesthetic appreciation of them with conceptual teleological judgements about nature's
organic purposes.[25]

Kant's description makes it clear why crystallisation does not conform
to the model of organic production: crystals form by a sudden solidification or '*shooting*', in a transition that proceeds 'as it were by a leap',
exemplified by the formation of ice crystals, where water does not
become gradually more viscous but suddenly solidifies into slivers of
ice.[26] In this way, crystallisation or shooting transforms a fluid matter,
forcing some particles to leave it and emerge into 'definite external
shapes'.[27] Kant suggests that the inside of rocks and mineral crystals is
also formed by the sudden 'leap' of solidification, as mineral elements
dissolved within water react and crystallise. Organic form depends upon
an underlying idea determining the relations between an object's parts
in terms of their unity in a whole; hence Kant emphasises that organic
unities can only grow from within, strengthening the original proportion
of their parts. Crystallisation, however, transforms matter unpredictably,
forming and reforming the whole shape of objects both inside and out,
their external figure as well as their internal fabric. Yet although crystallisation is clearly not organic, purely mechanical explanations also
seem deficient. Even allowing that crystals result from causal processes,
Kant's model of crystallisation as formation by a leap suggests that
mechanistic rules alone would be insufficient either to predict or to
account for the necessity of the moment where specific configurations
of matter suddenly emerge. This sudden solidification creates a curious
gap within nature's supposedly systematic productivity, unsettling
Kant's Newtonian assertion that '*Nature makes no leap in the diversity of
its forms*'.[28]

This account of crystallisation reflects the tensions within the history
of chemistry in the late eighteenth century, as delineated in Isabelle
Stengers' essay 'Ambiguous Affinity'.[29] Stengers explores the complex
transformation of the model of chemical affinity brought about by the
impact of Newtonian physics on accounts of chemical reaction.
Whereas the more traditional, basically Aristotelian, model saw chemical bonds and reactions as the result of particular substances expressing
intrinsic and characteristic properties, newer Newtonian models, like
Kant, positioned substance itself as basically inert, and understood
chemical reactions as a system or ensemble of bodies in reciprocal interaction. Yet Newtonian chemists could find no universal law akin to
Newton's law of attraction for chemical reactions which would allow

specific reactions to be deduced and predicted in the same way as planetary movements. Somewhat paradoxically, on the Newtonian model, chemical affinities could only be empirically learnt, and chemistry remained an empirical discipline, reliant on extensive tabulation, awaiting the formal basis which would make it a 'proper', deductive science.[30] In a similar way, Kant's account of the 'leap' of crystallisation means that at this point in the *Critique of Judgement*, our understanding of such processes is also positioned as empirical and at best as waiting for the proper scientific principle which would allow for their prediction.

Stengers uses Goethe's novel *Elective Affinities* to explore a potentially radical re-modelling of the relation of the empirical and the *a priori* in chemistry. She quotes one of the novel's chief protagonists, Charlotte, to suggest that when two substances are combined with a third, prediction and deduction must be renounced. As in Kant's leaping crystallisation, in Goethe's novel we are told that chemical elements 'attract, seize, destroy, devour and absorb each other and then emerge out of that violent combination in renewed and unexpected form.'[31] Stengers draws on the way in which Goethe's text uses chemical affinities as an analogy for the human passions – 'No more than chemical combination and separation are human passions amenable to rational prediction'[32] – whilst implicitly reversing and thereby extending this analogical structure so as to take the unpredictability of human passions as a model for chemical production. For Stengers, then, Goethe's model of elective affinity suggests not that chemistry is awaiting its proper formal principle, but raises the possibility that 'another kind of science ought to be recognised', one in which 'it will have to be accepted that knowledge through learning, on the basis of real experience, is not inferior to deductive knowledge based on laws'.[33]

In a somewhat parallel way, it is possible to continue and extend the Kantian process of linking art and nature by analogy, and, in particular, to map the productions of artful matter back on to the Kantian model of production as given for fine art. In so doing, we find that there is, after all, a model of production already present in the *Critique of Judgement* which can allow us to make sense of the processes of crystallisation as neither organic nor simply mechanically explicable, a model which raises the possibility at least that another kind of – non-Newtonian, non-organic, self-organising – matter ought to be recognised. For if the imagination is understood in a non-psychologistic sense, as a productive power capable of generating objects through the organisation of its materials, then the 'leap' of crystallisation can be read as analogous to the leap of the imagination in genius, where matter is restructured without following pre-given rules. By mapping crystallisation on to the leaping creativity of the imagination, we find a model of production which accounts for the temporality of crystallisation, for the way in which the specificity of emerging crystalline forms is not deducible in advance from mechanical rules.[34] Read by analogy, the 'shooting' of crystallisation becomes a process allowing unforeseen constellations to emerge through original combinations and restructurings of the manifold of sensible matter. Crystallisation thereby instantiates the creativity of an active and fluid materiality, generating glittering figures and fabrics which are themselves the expression of rules of production whose specific form can only be abstracted in retrospect from the emergent patterns of condensation.

As we have seen, the creative leaps of crystallising matter are neither regulated by reason's idea of organically unified wholes, nor deducible or predictable in terms of mechanical laws. Nonetheless, if crystallisation is read by analogy with the productive power of the imagination, its activity does not degenerate into the lawless chaos of raw material plurality whose possibility so troubles Kant. Rather, as Kant himself says, this leaping process allows matter to 'take on a definite shape or fabric (figure or texture)', temporarily unifying matter in crystalline forms which are always open to further transformation.[35] Again, this process is akin to the imagination of genius: crystallisation continually generates 'another nature' out of nature's sensible manifold, producing original objects which can be thought of as the discontinuous unfolding of a genealogy of active matter.

Such a reading, then, introduces an anomaly into the Kantian system. For Kant, matter thought as inert substance requires processing via the organising activity of the faculties for form and order to be constructed out of its manifold appearances. Pursuing Kant's analogy between art and nature generates another kind of model for thinking about matter, one which disrupts this hylomorphism. By using as a model the account of production given in the paragraphs on genius, crystallisation can be read as the activity of a materiality capable of producing complex shapes, textures and figures without following rules, yet in ways which allow form to emerge – though not necessarily in predictable ways. In Kant's model, matter as substance only takes on the coherent form of objects if reworked by a human mind in terms of mechanical laws or ideas of organicism. This account involves denying the possibility that emerges by tracing his analogical thought to the limit, namely, that the leaping productivity of an excessively artistic matter exemplified by crystallisation might itself be enough to generate both the figure and fabric of its products. On this reading, if snowflakes and stalactites are 'such shapes as art might invent', this is because they are generated by a productivity neither organic nor mechanical, but via crystallisation as a materially embedded power of production akin to that of the imagination.[36]

Re-reading crystallisation in this way, namely, by analogy with the production of fine art, in turn has implications for the Kantian model of the productive imagination itself. If we continue Kant's analogical procedure of not only seeing nature as if it were art, but art as like nature, we can return to the imagination and re-read its leaping productivity on the model provided by crystallisation. The latter does more than serve as a powerful metaphor for the processes of aesthetic production, although the Kantian imagination can readily be understood via Stendhal's image of crystallisation as 'a mental process which draws from everything that happens', producing a rich fluidity of ideas from which something unforeseen eventually coalesces and solidifies.[37] However, if the analogy between art and nature's crystallising productions is fully elaborated, it has more than metaphorical implications, for it also suggests a potential reworking of the relation between the imagination and reason.

As a capacity for aesthetic ideas, the animated imagination of genius is positioned in a necessary interrelation with reason. This relation takes two key forms, both of which are reconfigured if we read the imagination by analogy with crystallisation. Firstly, genius's imaginative capacity allows it to give rational ideas – God or eternity, for example – which cannot be directly exhibited what Kant calls 'a semblance of objective reality' through their aesthetic expression.[38] Yet this does not entail that the productive imagination is restricted by the attempt to reflect reason's unexhibitable concepts. For the aesthetic expression of ideas always goes beyond what reason alone can give, and involves an imaginative expansion generating 'more thought than can be expressed in a concept determined by words.'[39]

This imaginative capacity to generate thought through the material re-figuring of ideas – a material expression that would include the figurative uses of language – is radicalised if the imagination is in turn read via its affinity with crystallisation. For crystallisation is a *non-organic* mode of production, generating its figures and fabrics without reference to limits set by pre-conceived ideas of organic wholes. Read by analogy, the imagination would not merely allow our thoughts surrounding a particular idea to grow, whilst having to remain within the limits of what reason considers to belong to that idea. Rather, an imagination which functioned non-organically would generate a richness of thought surpassing the limits and transforming the internal organisation of ideas, reworking the very fabric of our thought, and so allowing unforeseen ideas to emerge. This non-organic, crystallising imagination would not simply be cut loose from reason, but instead of merely exploring and extending pre-existing notions, thoughts and ideas themselves would only crystallise when provoked by the originality of material figures and forms. Reason itself would first be made to think by unpredictable imaginative leaps. Kant suggests that the fluid matter which takes shape through the shooting of crystallisation might be the most ancient kind of matter.[40] In a parallel way, it could be suggested that the last and newest offspring of this generative materiality are the linguistic ideas and concepts that emerge as the final gloss on the imagination's crystallisations. Reason's ideas glitter like the polished surface of a crystal, but they are also the most hardened of forms, at the furthest remove from the fluid dynamics through which they are generated.

Hence the final way in which the imagination's relation to reason is transformed: for Kant, when the imagination attempts to go beyond what experience or determinate concepts can give us by exploring ideas aesthetically, it is to be seen as following reason's principle of striving for totality or completeness in our thought. Yet if the imagination's work proceeds non-organically, allowing ideas to leap in unexpected directions, if thought itself only takes shape through productive discontinuities, it can no longer coalesce in the ideal wholeness of a single complete system. If the imagination is a power to transform thought by folding it back through material figures and forms, then thought itself unfolds through genealogies of stratification and condensation whose order emerges in the breaks and shifts in direction generated by an unpredictable imaginative impetus.[41] This is not the *progress* of Kant's 'ever advancing culture', which strives towards reason's eternal ideal of unity and totality, but the *movement* of a materially embodied thought whose very fabric is shaped and reshaped by productive discontinuities that originate in imaginative leaps.[42] If crystallisation is a mode of production akin to the imagination of genius, and the imagination functions as crystallisation, then neither nature nor reason can be unified into a single ideal system, for both develop through a leaping crystalline movement rather than a seamless organic growth. Thus the unconditioned Nature towards which, according to Kant, reason strives can no longer be thought of as a horizon of supersensible totality, but becomes the as-yet-undetermined, an infinite potential for the emergence of future crystalline forms.[43]

At the end of the *Critique of Aesthetic Judgement*, Kant suggests that the future will need fine art more than ever, because art will offer a standard for combining culture and nature, moral ideas and material existence, to peoples who will be 'ever more remote from nature'.[44] In fact, although at the beginning of the twenty-first century the West can indeed be seen to be preoccupied with a distancing from nature, this estrangement is often seen as the legacy of oppositional models of culture and nature, subject and object – such as those which mark Kant's philosophy. This paper has pursued Kant's analogical comparison of art and nature so as to map crystallisation on to the reschematising imagination of genius in ways that place the focus on a leaping mode of production which can be seen as functioning at different levels to produce unforeseen rules, figures, or thoughts. On this model, the transcendental production of form and the activities of thought would no longer be opposed to a lifeless material substance, but the shaping of matter and thought would each become an aspect of the manifold and immanent expression of a power – or even a faculty? – of crystallisation. Thus it could be suggested that in the complex folds of the *Critique of Judgement* there lies a hidden genealogy which opens on to a future different from that foregrounded by Kant. The capacity of a crystalline matter to generate form leaps forward towards Irigaray's insistence on the need for a science of fluids,[45] whilst the model of crystallising imagination outlined above points both towards Nietzsche's critique of concepts as hardened, dead metaphors that belie the creativity that produced them,[46] and to the model of emergent identity explored in *Ecce Homo*. A Kantian philosophy of crystallisation could be augmented via an exploration of the implications of Nietzsche's remark that the greatest danger would have been to catch sight of himself before the day when 'my abilities ... *leapt forth* suddenly ripe.'[47] Thus, by extending Kant's analogical method to investigate the relation between imagination and crystallisation, Kant's text itself can be made to leap and move in unpredictable ways, allowing new possibilities to emerge, and unexpected thoughts to crystallise.

Notes

1   Stendhal, *Love*, trans. G. and S. Sale (Harmondsworth: Penguin, 1975), p.

45. I am grateful to Martin Crowley for drawing my attention to Stendhal's use of images of crystallisation.

2   Kant, *CJ*, p. 222; *Ak*.V: 348 .

3   Kant, *CJ*, p. 227; *Ak*.V: 352.

4   This is not to suggest that Kant's text itself draws the analogy between crystallisation and the imagination of genius in any explicit way. Rather, in exploring this analogy later in this paper, I am suggesting only that a faithful extension of Kant's own analogical methodology as regards art and nature in general – albeit applied 'unfaithfully' to a case which Kant's text does not explicitly consider – generates an interesting possibility from within the structures and tropes of Kant's own text, a possibility with philosophical potential. Furthermore, although the reasons for pursuing this particular analogy are in part strategic, and relate to the possibility of opening up Kant's system from within to non-hylomorphic modes of thinking, as will become clear, this does not entail that the grounds for drawing such an analogy are simply arbitrary. As I will show, the model of production which proceeds by a leap provides a textual basis for relating the processes of crystallisation to the non rule-governed productions of genius.

5   James Larson, *Interpreting Nature: The Science of Living Form from Linnaeus to Kant* (Baltimore: Johns Hopkins University Press, 1994), p. 31.

6   Kant, *CJ*, First Introduction, sec. IV, p. 398, t.m.; *Ak*.XX: 209.

7   Kant, *CJ*, First Introduction, sec. II, p. 393; *Ak*.XX: 204–5.

8   Kant, *CJ*, First Introduction, sec. V, p. 402; *Ak*.XX: 214.

9   Kant, *CJ*, p. 99; *Ak*.V: 246.

10 Kant, *CJ*, p. 167; *Ak*.V: 300.

11 Kant, *CJ*, p. 99; *Ak*.V: 246.

12 See Kant, *CJ*, First Introduction, sec. IX, p. 423; *Ak*.XX: 234. See also *CJ*, p. 179; *Ak*.V: 311–12.

13 Kant, *CJ*, p. 174; *Ak*.V: 307.

14 Kant, *CJ*, First Introduction, sec. XII, p. 440–1; *Ak*.XX: 251.

15 Kant, *CJ*, p. 173; *Ak*.V: 306.

16 Kant, *CJ*, p. 182; *Ak*.V: 314.

17 Kant, *CJ*, p. 183; *Ak*.V: 315.

18 Kant, *CJ*, p. 186; *Ak*.V: 317.

19 See Kant, *CJ*, p. 177; *Ak*.V: 309; and *CJ*, p. 187; *Ak*.V: 318.

20 Kant, *CJ*, p. 183, p. 182, p. 183, t.m.; *Ak*.V: 314–15.

21 Kant, *CJ*, p. 214; *Ak*.V: 341; see also *CJ*, p. 217; *Ak*.V: 344.

22 Kant, *CJ*, First Introduction, sec. IV, p. 398, t.m.; *Ak*.XX: 209.

23 Kant, *CJ*, p. 186; *Ak*.V: 317.

24 Kant, *CJ*, p. 188, t.m.; *Ak*.V: 319.

25 See Kant, *CJ*, pp. 222–4; *Ak*.V: 348–50.

26 Kant, *CJ*, p. 222; *Ak*.V: 348.

27 Kant, *CJ*, p. 223; *Ak*.V: 349.

28 Kant, *CJ*, First Introduction, sec. IV, p. 399; *Ak*.XX: 210.

29 Isabelle Stengers, 'Ambiguous Affinity. The Newtonian Dream of Chem istry in the Eighteenth Century', in *A History of Scientific Thought*, ed. Michel Serres (Oxford: Blackwell, 1995).

30 See Stengers, 'Ambiguous Affinity', especially pp. 379–83.

31 Goethe, *Elective Affinities*, quoted in Stengers, 'Ambiguous Affinity', p. 384.

32 Stengers, 'Ambiguous Affinity', p. 385.

33 Stengers, 'Ambiguous Affinity', p. 385.

34 In exploring this analogical comparison, I am concerned primarily with Kant's account of crystallisation in §58 of *CJ*, and with the images and tropes he employs there, rather than with the way(s) in which crystallisation might be explained scientifically – despite the ways in which Kant's account resonates with the problems eighteenth-century scientists encountered in dealing with chemical reactions, and indeed, the ways in which the analogical comparison I go on to draw could be analysed in relation to contemporary twentieth-century models of matter as generated by some variants of chaos theory (such as that explored by Stengers herself elsewhere). However, such an analysis would require careful plotting and a more detailed account of the history of chemistry as well as of contemporary models of chaos theory than there is room for here.

35 Kant, *CJ*, p. 222; *Ak*.V: 348.

36 Kant, *CJ*, p. 223; *Ak*.V: 349.

37 Stendhal, *Love*, p. 45. Although it is Stendhal's explicit use of crystallisation as an analogy for the processes of the imagination which interests me here, there are significant differences between Stendhal's use of this image and Kant's account of crystalline forms, differences which would provide an interesting direction for further research (in Stendhal's text, for example, crystallisation is linked to a lover's imaginative embellishment of his beloved and thus invokes a process of covering over and distortion).

38 Kant, *CJ*, p. 182; *Ak*.V: 314.

39 Kant, *CJ*, p. 183; *Ak*.V: 315.

40 Kant, *CJ*, p. 223; *Ak*.V: 349.

41 The notion of a discontinuous generation of thought whose patternings can nonetheless be traced via genealogical enquiry could be further developed via Michel Foucault's *Archaeology of Knowledge*, trans. A. M. Sheridan Smith (London: Tavistock, 1995).

42 Kant, *CJ*, p. 188; *Ak*.V: 319.

43 Such a shift involves (re-)thinking the supersensible not primarily in terms of a transcendent undetermined ground underlying all determination, but as a determinable element which reflective judgement's extrapolations from the unpredictable leaps of a crystallising materiality would determine as non-totalisable. A re-examination of the role of judgement, and in par-

ticular of reflective judgement, would thus be necessary at this point, in ways that lie beyond the scope of the current paper. However, to the extent that this re-thinking entails privileging the question of an immanent relation between determination and the determinable, it could be seen as in keeping with the transcendental nature of Kant's thought. Such a re-thinking of the supersensible would involve taking up – albeit at another juncture within the critical system – the force of Deleuze's contrast between Descartes and Kant, when he comments that: 'Blanchot to a certain extent remains a Cartesian: the relation (or "non-relation") he establishes is between determination and the pure undetermined element. Foucault, on the other hand, is more Kantian: his relation or non-relation is between two forms, determination and the determinable element.' Gilles Deleuze, *Foucault*, ed. and trans. Sean Hand (London: Athlone, 1988), p. 140 n19.

44   Kant, *CJ*, p. 232; *Ak*.V: 356.
45   See Luce Irigaray, 'The "Mechanics" of Fluids', in *This Sex Which Is Not One*, trans. Catherine Porter (Ithaca, NY: Cornell University Press, 1985).
46   See Friedrich Nietzsche, 'On Truth and Lies in a Nonmoral Sense', in *Philosophy and Truth – Selections from Nietzsche's Notebooks*, ed. D. Breazeale (Atlantic Highlands, NJ: Humanities Press, 1979).
47   Friedrich Nietzsche, *Ecce Homo*, trans. R. J. Hollingdale (Harmondsworth: Penguin, 1979), p. 35.

3

Kant After Geophilosophy: The Physics of Analogy and the Metaphysics of Nature

Iain Hamilton Grant

I hope to found on incontrovertible grounds a firm conviction, that the world recognizes for the origin of its constitution a mechanical development unfolding from the general laws of nature; and second, that the kind of mechanical genesis which we have presented is the true one.[1]

[I]s it not necessary to represent the very essence of creation ... to be a witness of that power which can be measured by no yardstick?[2]

Kant's ... idea of a Copernican revolution puts thought into a direct relation with the earth.[3]

What is the *nature* of the relation in which Deleuze and Guattari bond Kant's critical revolution to the earth? Neither a manifesto for the necessity of philosophy's transcendent self-grounding, nor an historical or historicising search for origins or emergent structures, geophilosophy takes to the earth as the plane on which philosophical territories (Ancient Greece, Modern Germany, Nietzsche's planet of health resorts, and so on) emerge and dissipate, forming 'diagrammatic movements of a Nature-thought on the plane'.[4]

Yet why bond Kant to this project? Certainly, the well-known political geography of metaphysics that runs through Preface A of the first *Critique* constructs a plane where battles and courtrooms coexist without succession, where nomadic raids are a recurrent threat to successive governments.[5] Yet good sense dictates that this 'geophilosophy' be understood simply as *analogical*, and far from calling forth a new people, let alone a new earth, merely 'inventories' our rational possessions.[6] On what bond, then, are Deleuze and Guattari calling: geological, or merely analogical?

It is widely assumed that Kant's precritical mechanistic cosmogonies and 'universal natural histories' are ended by the insoluble antinomies

consequent upon the critical revolution. The critical philosophy desub-
stantiates 'universe' into mere logical 'universality', by which metaphysics is exiled from physics. Yet, even at its inception, critique is
declared preparatory to a 'metaphysics of nature',[7] a metaphysics that
Kant did not live to complete, the tortured reiterations of the *Opus postumum* notwithstanding. However, echoing the search for something to
span the 'great gulf fixed' between practical and speculative reason in
the third *Critique*,[8] the problem repeatedly posed by the last works is an
elusive 'science of transition' between metaphysics and physics[9] – *the
problem of the relation of thought to the earth*.

   And what is the *nature* of the revolution in question? As Deleuze and
Guattari interpret Kant, revolutions do indeed call forth a new people,
and a new earth. It is the Copernican revolution that Deleuzoguattarian
geophilosophy claims as its precursor, a revolution Kant claims as solely
epistemo-judicial. However, the revolutions which, according to Kant,
do bring forth new earths and new peoples are not epistemological, but
geological. At crucial points in the third *Critique* and the *Opus postumum*,
returning to the cosmological sublime of the *Universal Natural History*,[10]
Kant makes reference to a chaos of 'natural revolutions', in which the
earth itself threatens to lay waste to its present, thinking inhabitants.
Geophilosophy, itself perhaps the precursor of the 'philosophy of
nature' on which Deleuze and Guattari were working before their
deaths,[11] does not therefore go by way of this physical, first natural transition from metaphysics to physics, but by way of practical, 'second natural' revolutions alone. As we shall see, however, the production of a
second *nature* demands material, not merely ideational-moral alter-
ations. However, from the *Universal Natural History* to the *Opus postumum*, and from the first inception of the critical project to the
announcement of its conclusion in the third *Critique*,[12] the metaphysics
of nature, comprising mechanism, dynamics, geology, biology and physiology, remains a component of, rather than an obstacle to, the metaphysics of freedom. If therefore, metaphysics and physics are separated
by a 'great gulf' such as divides nature and freedom, the faces of this
sundered rock meet deep in the earth, and are not merely conjoined by
the technological fix of analogical bridges.

   Deleuze and Guattari begin to reassemble the 'objects' of a Kantian
metaphysics of nature: geophysics, revolution, philosophy and new
species. It is, however, the construction of the material-synthetic chiasmus passing between physics and metaphysics, which Deleuzoguattarian geophilosophy neglects, to which the present essay is devoted. The

metaphysics of nature for which critique was only ever preparatory holds as its guiding thread to the indissociability of physics and metaphysics, a moebian chiasmus most explicit in the third *Critique*. In the broadest terms, it is the fullest stakes of the practical revolution – the *causal efficacy of philosophy upon nature* – that defines the Kantian programme of the metaphysics of nature.

Physiophilosophy: 'how does matter produce a body?'[13]

> Whatever the infinite distance between the ability to think and the motion of matter, between the rational mind and the body, it is still certain that man … is wholly dependent on the properties of that matter to which the Creator joined him.[14]

Although in the first *Critique* Kant makes much of disintricating the empirical from the transcendental in the constitution of the subject, and of reversing the influences of the former on the latter, questions of that subject's empirical, i.e., physiological production insistently accompany those of its conceptual or transcendental constitution, from the *Universal Natural History*, through the second *Critique*, to the *Opus postumum*. As we shall see, the work being pursued in this context, later continued by others,[15] attempts to maintain an asymptotic relation between rational-practical activity and natural production without jettisoning some kind of chiasmatic ideational-neurophysical contact. It is precisely at this moment of conjuncture, however, that the mechanical impetus to physiological critique emerges, before the Copernican revolution, in the *Universal Natural History*:

> If one looks for the cause of impediments, that keep human nature in such a deep debasement, it will be found in the crudeness of the matter into which his intelligent [*geistlich*] part is sunk, in the unbending of the fibers, and in the sluggishness and immobility of fluids which should obey its stirrings. The nerves and fluids of his brain deliver to him only gross and unclear concepts, and because he cannot counterbalance in the interior of his power of thought the impact of sensory impressions with sufficiently powerful ideas, he will be carried away by his passions, confused and overwhelmed by the turmoil of the elements that maintain his [bodily] machine.[16]

Here, what Kant will later call the 'occasioning causes' (*Gelegenheitsursachen*) rather than the 'principle of possibility' of concepts,[17] are criticised if not critiqued: they obstruct and hinder the power of thought.

But this is not an infantile materialism to be dropped at the first hint of mature criticism; rather, even at the 'ending' of the critical project in the third *Critique*,[18] the persistence of mechanistic physiology is manifest, and the problem of how ideas are to become more powerful, is solved. For Kant admonishes that 'to explain all products and events of nature', 'the mechanical must be given its fullest possible extension' in accordance with the essential condition of our powers.[19] On the one hand, this means that as far as the powers may reach, so must mechanics follow; on the other, if mechanical explanation is *not* pursued, there can be 'no insight into the nature of things'.[20] Therefore, the powers themselves must be subject to mechanical explanation, just as the third *Conflict of the Faculties*, between the medical and philosophical faculties, suggests that the 'free play of the imagination [is] a mechanical activity'.[21] What is important here is not whether such explanations – or their teleological counterparts – are *correct*, but rather the establishment of the principle that 'the sum total of all things' is materially instantiated.

The *Universal Natural History*'s physiology of fluids and fibers, however, is not confined to Kant's primitive, dogmatic mechanicism; it is echoed even after the third *Critique*, as for example in Kant's critical afterword to Samuel Thomas Sömmering's *Über das Organ der Seele*:

> As the immediate organ of the soul, this fluid … separates the terminating nerve-fibers from one another so that the sensations from them do not get confused.[22]

Although Kant has qualified this physiological description as 'not confounding a physiological with a metaphysical problem', he adds immediately after the above passage that 'we are dealing only with that matter, which makes the unity of all presentations of sense possible in the mind', and, in a footnote, that matter here denotes 'powers [*Vermögen*], not at all substance'.[23] Although therefore something has changed between 1755 and 1796, it is not Kant's attention to the physicality of the mind, but rather the particular physical theory within which this attention is framed. Instead of a 'mechanical organization', the later work proposes 'a dynamical one, based on chemical principles'.[24]

Kant's 'chemical revolution' reveals a twofold continuity: firstly, as regards the material envelope that provides the historical and philosophical basis for the metaphysics of nature and freedom; secondly, as regards the continuous attempt not only to locate the natural causality – whether mechanical or chemical – productive of the human brain and its powers, but also to produce a reciprocal effectivity on the part of that brain upon those natural causes. In other words, Kant seeks not only to discover 'the physical causes of human philosophy', but also its 'physical effects';[25] not only, that is, 'what nature makes of man', but also 'what man makes of nature'.[26] There is a continuum, a physical substrate, on which nature and freedom depend. Importantly, just because such a continuum is physical – and even physiological – does not entail that it is therefore sensible, and thus epistemologically treatable, but only practically manipulable. It is this non-alignment of the physical and the sensible in Kant that creates the conditions for a practical philosophy that is not reducible to subjective reasoning about actions. Nor does this physical continuum entail that the causal order of philosophy – its retrofitting effects upon material nature – be reducible to that of the mechanical production of the bodily machine. It does entail, however, the *physicalisation of philosophy* and the production of another causal order. It is to this demand that the third *Critique* accedes in the consideration of teleology: the maintenance of mechanical causality, while essential in order to 'gain insight into the nature of things',[27] must equally be susceptible to the production of a parallel and irreducible causal order. Hence, despite the reflective form of the problem in Kant, there is the following anomalously materialistic conclusion: 'matter can receive more and other forms than it can get through mechanism'.[28] Reflective judgement cedes the task of determination only to rid itself of the legislative prohibitions of the first *Critique*, realising its freedom in the production of analogical *but nonetheless material* causalities.

That nature and freedom, intelligible, sensible and practical powers, are physically conjunct in the organ of the brain, and that paralogisms and antinomies, while manifest in ideation, are also neurophysiological pathologies, had already dawned on the earliest readers of the first *Critique*. Indeed, there are hints of precisely such a project throughout that *Critique*, as when, for example, Kant writes that sensibility and the understanding 'perhaps spring from a common, but to us unknown, root',[29] from a *Grundkraft* or 'fundamental power'.[30] The research programme to which this principle gave rise in the passage from Enlightenment science to *Naturphilosophie*, accordingly maintained a parallel series of transcendental and mechanical explanation. The resultant 'vital materialist' programme, as it has been called,[31] drawing on the physiological researches into the 'vital force' or *Lebenskraft* undertaken by the physiologist Albrecht von Haller and the comparative anatomist Johann Friedrich Blumenbach, was explicitly based on an 'attempt to apply Kant's epistemological limits on human reason to concrete physiology'.[32]

How, accordingly, are the powers (*Vermögen*) to be conceived? In accordance with their functioning in rational activity, and thus reducible to ideational structures, or as expressions of physical activity, and thus complex outcomes of a single *Grund-* or *Lebenskraft*? Thus, in his *Versuch über den Schwindel* (*Experiment on Vertigo*),[33] the Berlin physician Marcus Herz, Kant's former student and philosophical correspondent, and a promoter of Kantian philosophy in physiologico-medical researches, proposed that the mental forces were 'like an electrical stream',[34] thus offering a solution to the problem of the physical constitution of the Kantian powers in a single *Grundkraft*. Having a fixed quantity of energy at its disposal, this force modified itself into all the other powers, but all the while attempted to maintain an equilibrium between them, after the Brunonian model.[35]

Again, in 'Von der Lebenskraft' ('On the vital force'), Johann Christian Reil attempted to provide a reducibly physical explanation of the powers of reason and representation from the 'mixtures and forms' of the 'basic elements of matter' (*Grundstoffe*).[36] Against Kant's arguments for the teleological basis of organised bodies, and thus against Kant's perceived retreat from physical causality in explaining thinking nature, Reil writes:

> [T]he basis of the ordered formation of animal bodies lies originally in the nature of animal matter: formation and organization are already the appearance and effect of matter.[37]

All organic powers, including the mental ones, are therefore a function of the complexity of the matter from which they are composed. Both Herz and Reil therefore attempt to answer the question as to the origins and the effects of the powers on the basis of matter.

However, the more immediate problem in the current context is the extent to which such a psychophysical parallelism may be pursued through the third *Critique*. As we shall see, the 'parallel' is misleadingly accommodating; rather, these causal orders, conjoint as the two faces of a moebian band, are brought to the greatest tensions at key points in that work. The rational (insofar as it is constructed by the understanding) and actual nature (as the undeducible domain of the power of reflective judgement) violently diverge under pressure from the latter, buckling the rational envelope through which the physical is determined. The prospect of a physiology of the transcendental subject that was subsequently taken up by Herz, Reil and others is a problem for Kant not insofar as such a 'physiological derivation' might be false or incorrect,[38] but rather to the extent that it poses a merely epistemological, and therefore reductivist, threat to the determination of matter: it would collapse the distance between the powers of reflective and determinant judgement, and render material nature as given through deduction alone.

However, before the third *Critique*'s inclusive disjunctive synthesis of mechanics and teleology; before even the chemical revolution that spawned, in 'Aus Sömmering', the 'dynamical chemistry' and 'fluid becomings' of the 'power of the nerves' (*Vermögen der Nerven*) in the brain;[39] before the extramechanical definition of chemical activity in the *Metaphysical Foundations of Natural Science*,[40] chemistry furnishes Kant with the prospect of a causal agency irreducible to mechanical determination. Prefacing the 'single and sudden' advent of the Copernican revolution, Kant claims as an avatar the productivist lessons taught by the influential eighteenth-century chemist Georg Ernst Stahl,[41] whose experiments Kant cites in the B edition Preface of the first *Critique*, regarding the reversible transformation of

> metals into calxes and the latter back into metal, in that he extracted something from them and then restored it. ... [Thus] students of nature ... learned that reason has insight only into what it produces after a plan of its own.[42]

From the Stahlian inspiration for this manifesto for constructivist chemical philosophy, Kant draws two related lessons. As a natural historian, Stahl was renowned as founding modern vitalism and therefore, like Kant, sought a treatment of matter that was materially and ontologically irreducible to mechanism. Accordingly, Stahlian chemistry distinguishes two types of chemical combinations: whereas the first, 'mechanical aggregation', could be investigated by breaking it down into its constitutive elements, the second, 'mixtive union' or 'mixt', could only be investigated by changing its properties.[43] Such 'reduction' experiments on any chemical body had always to be carried out by the use of an 'instrument', i.e., another mechanical-chemical body such as fire, water or air as a mere vehicle of chemical change.[44] Neutral in aggregates but an agent of alteration in mixts, it is exactly after Stahl's instrumentalism that Kant models the operations of synthesis, which, he notes, 'in chemistry is sometimes entitled the experiment of reduction'.[45] Synthesis, therefore, is a new mixt formed as a consequence of reduction experiments.

Synthesis, then, an instrument in the Stahlian sense, is not something merely brought to intervene in an operation from outside, but an irreducible component of the experimentally resultant mixtive union itself.

Accordingly, it cannot be examined as a merely logical or epistemogenic device, nor as a function to be consciously deployed in the production of representations; rather, it is inescapably the possibilising material dynamic, the mixtive chemistry of human ideation that Kant will explore more thoroughly in 'Aus Sömmering'. This has enormous consequences. How was it ever possible not to read the *Critique of Pure Reason* as an atlas of high-level neurophysiology? In accordance with such readings, the Transcendental Aesthetic would be at least in part a *quaesto facti*, a 'physiological derivation' of the means whereby knowledge is possible for beings of a particular physiological type.[46] At this point, however, the physiological derivation is thus twice relativised: first, as regards the sort of knowledge a particular physiology enables – the *kind* of knowledge human beings can have is dependent upon the physiological constitution they possess; and second, as regards the *instantiation* of that constitution. At the 'blind but indispensable' synthetic core of the subject's critical power of intellection,[47] intellection cannot, by physiological means alone, be determined as the possession of a single kind of organic product. This is why, despite praise for the physiological researches into the derivation of human knowledge by 'the illustrious Locke',[48] such 'material' accounts of possession require supplementary justification, and why that justification must be formal only, a *quaesto juris*. Without such an account, physiological derivations alone furnish the basis for an inclusivist account of 'thinking natures', from which arise Kant's speculations on species and knowledge types: from the wise Saturnians,[49] intellectually empowered by their distance from the sun, to species lost through revolutions of the earth, and those, due to the same causes, yet to come. At this point, we must emphasise that there is, for Kant, nothing wrong in itself in the production of new species; what is wrong is that this should come about by physiological accident rather than by physio-philosophical purpose. To appreciate the *practical necessity* of the production of new species, it is necessary to turn to the third *Critique*. Under physio-philosophical scrutiny, the stakes of that work will be revealed as precisely the practical means open for the preservation or reinvention of the species, given the natural necessity of their coming to be and passing away.

The geophilosophical sublime: on the revolutions of the earth

[Geological] views of the immensity of past time, like those unfolded by the Newtonian philosophy with regard to space, were too vast to awaken

ideas of sublimity unmixed with a painful sense of our incapacity to conceive a plan of such infinite extent.[50]

Species must die out because Time fights against them.[51]

The definition of the naturally purposive organised body in the third *Critique* has prompted some commentators to reduce that work to a philosophy of biology, rather than a component of Kant's long-sought after
metaphysics of nature.[52] Not only the metaphysics of nature, but also the
history of the sciences, however, casts serious doubt over such reducibility. Firstly, the third *Critique* contains more of the *physical* than can be
reduced to biology; and secondly, since biology did not exist as a science
until 1802,[53] it is at best anachronistic to suggest Kant pursued such a
project, although, as we have seen, certain of his successors did. From
the perspective of the metaphysics of nature, the principal problem of
such accounts is that they fail to *philosophise* physiological phenomena.
Such a physiophilosophy will discover that the *only* properly philosophical treatment of physiological phenomena – of 'what nature makes of
man'[54] – is *sublime*. In the sublime, through which the mind first realises
its 'superiority over nature',[55] the 'physical causes of human philosophy'
are pitted against the latter's 'physical effects',[56] in order to demonstrate
the technical-practical purchase of the metaphysics of freedom on
nature, the 'material … totality of all things'.[57] The problem of how far
this reciprocal causality extends is, in effect, the grounding problem of
the third *Critique*, that of *judging* the relation between mechanism and
teleology. As we shall see, the *selection* involved in such judging turns out
to have more than merely epistemic or methodological significance.

If, accordingly, we are to demonstrate a physio-philosophical substrate of judgement as a prelude to a physicalist sublime in the third *Critique*, we must seek the material efficacy of reflection, a *physics of
analogy*. When Kant writes that 'the concept of the sublime in nature is
not nearly as important and rich in implications as the beautiful in
nature',[58] this seems to reject absolutely the prospect of a *reciprocal selec-
tivity* of teleological judgement and nature such as is found in a judgement of the beautiful in nature. If not beautiful, however, nature's
fearful might impels *aesthetic* judgement to realise the powers' superiority *over*, and independence of, nature.[59] Thus, although judgements of
natural beauty reveal 'nature's harmony with the free play of our cognitive powers as we apprehend and judge its appearance',[60] and, through
this consonance with our cognitive powers, reveals a purposiveness that
demonstrates nature's 'favour' for humanity, the reciprocity of this

selection from the 'order of the accidental',[61] is bound together by *analogy* only.[62] And yet, this 'favour' is possible only on the basis of the relation between the sort of constitution human beings contingently possess and, in turn, that of the earth. The possible material basis for such a judgement as a power of selection raises the prospect of a physics of analogy that threatens to undo the merely *reflective* limits within which analogy ought to be confined, ringfencing how far a reciprocal selection of nature and teleological causation might extend.

When, therefore, nature in its *formless chaos* prompts the dynamical sublime – when 'threatening rocks ..., lightning and thunderclaps, volcanoes ..., mighty oceans [and] waterfalls' induce fear in the judging subject and dissonance amongst the powers[63] – analogy is confined to reflection alone. Reflection on the dynamical sublime nevertheless thus reveals a purposiveness other than that given in mechanical nature, whose profligate productivity threatens humanity, epistemologically and physically.[64] That purpose is the subject's capacity to elevate itself above nature's mechanical forces and to operate in accordance with another, 'sublime' causality, that of 'freedom ... [as] itself an *original cause*'.[65] Moreover, Kant adds that the ability to judge ourselves thus independent of and superior to nature provides 'the basis for a self-preservation quite different in kind from the one that can be assailed and endangered by nature outside us'.[66] But this purpose is itself the product of 'an object (*of nature*) *the presentation of which determines the mind to think of nature's inability to attain to an exhibition of ideas*'.[67] That this 'original' causal order is materially grounded in the mechanical causality that produces physical creatures capable of such causative actions, reiterates the inextricability of the material and the teleological, and returns the problem of the sublime to a substrate of freedom and nature that is not solely intelligible, but *also* physical. Thus, the problem of the substrate is precisely what is fleshed out in the consideration of mechanics and teleology, as in the sublime. In neither case, however, is the problem of their physical proximity solved by the restrictions of reflective judgement, but merely displaced to another level.

For the moment, however, we shall follow the twisted paths by which the sublime leads the powers from determination by nature to production, from receptivity to natural forms to spontaneous causation. Turning from an investigation of purposiveness in nature, at the level of the given, to the *production* of purposiveness, the sublime induces the mind to abandon sensibility and the merely reproductive imagination through which natural forms are given. In turn, the imagination becomes 'productive ... when it creates ... another nature [*eine andere Natur*] out of the material [*Stoffe*] that actual [*wirkliche*] nature gives it'.[68] On the one hand, the imagination's transformation in the sublime follows the abandonment of sensibility with a productivity that is intelligible only, thus revealing the nonsensible substrate of nature and freedom. On the other hand, this substrate anchors the heterogeneous causal mesh of mechanism (the physically realised forms that prompt the sublime through the mechanico-psychological reproductive imagination), teleology (the purposiveness it reveals as only contingently embodied in natural forms, but actually only a potentiality of the powers) and freedom (the free production of a *second* nature), which, while it becomes *intelligible* through the sublime, remains materially tied to 'actual nature'.

There is, therefore, a systematic plane of conjunction between matter and practical causation, so that Kant's metaphysics of nature consists of an equally systematic hierarchy of causes that places free productivity at its apex. In the sublime, this hierarchy of causes translates the metaphysics of freedom into that of nature, so that, although desire is defined, in the second and third *Critiques*, as the 'power of causing, through ... ideas, the actuality [*Wirklichkeit*] of the objects of those ideas',[69] it is entirely ineffective if the actuality it causes does not involve *the material alteration of actual nature and the production of a second*.

Having thus demonstrated the material substrate of nature and freedom running like a moebius strip throughout the critical corpus, and forming the basis of the metaphysics of nature *and* freedom, the problem of a physicalist sublime must now be confronted. As we have seen, this problem bears on the power of judgement to select amongst the order of the accidental. *What* is selected is never a particular natural product, but rather a form of productivity, i.e., a causal order. Implicit in the question of the selection of a causal order is the free determinability of temporal sequencing. However, one of the great physical themes of the third *Critique*, one that has secured far less critical scrutiny than has, for example, the biological basis of teleology, puts precisely the free determinability of temporal sequences into question in an open confrontation between first-natural revolutions and second-natural productivity. The problem of geology thus articulates the prospect of a physicalist sublime in nature, outlining the stakes of geophilosophy as Kant, through the Deleuzoguattarian lens that brought this theme initially to light, conceives them.

In the *Critique of Judgement*, Kant calls the 'archaeology of nature' what since the mid-nineteenth century has been called palaeontology.[70]

He reports the horrific findings of this branch of the 'theory of the earth' in the *Opus postumum*:

> How many ... revolutions (including, certainly, many ancient organic beings no longer alive on the surface of the earth) preceded the existence of man, and how many (accompanying perhaps a more perfect organisation) are still in prospect, is hidden from our enquiring gaze – for, according to Camper, not a single example of a human being is to be found in the depth of the earth.[71]

The stark horror of the manifest elimination of once existent species from the earth, and the creation of newer species, amongst which humanity figures, reveals the demoniacal prospect of the earth become 'wasteland, gratuitous and without final purpose'.[72] Without teleology, the particular beings that, because their particularity cannot be deduced *a priori* from the principles of mechanics,[73] make up the 'order of the accidental',[74] merely await extinction, without purchase on the mechanical, necessitarian organism – the 'all-producing globe'[75] – that spawned them. Simultaneously, however, the sketch of a 'chiliastic' or 'eudaimonistic' teleology is apparent in this mechanical speculation.[76] What will be that 'more perfect organisation' still in prospect? Will it count as humanity's 'preservation, quite different in kind' or its elimination, the production of another species?[77]

With the annihilation of humanity goes the annihilation of purpose. This stark presentation of the problem is ultimately a denial that the earth can be considered an organic form, insofar as *if it were*, it would necessarily manifest a 'natural purpose'. It is the problematic conception of 'natural purposes' that enables reflection to judge – rather than the understanding to determine – a natural product to be 'an organized and self-organizing being'.[78] The conception is problematic since, although Kant insists on circumscribing the applicability of natural purpose to reflection alone, the very formulation of a *natural* purpose points immediately beyond the self-limiting realm of critical reflection. Noting, in apparent contravention of the limits of reflective judgement, that 'matter can get more and other forms than it can receive from mechanism',[79] Kant writes, concerning causality according to natural purposes:

> That cause [we] can [find] only in [our] idea [of it]. And yet here the result which conforms to that idea (i.e., the product itself) is given in nature. [Hence] the concept of a causality of nature which implies that nature is a being acting according to purposes seems to turn the idea of a natural purpose into a principle that is constitutive of the natural purpose.[80]

The congruence of the idea of purpose and manifest purposiveness in nature, however – the *harmony* of the powers and presentational capacities of human neurophysiology familiar from judgements of beauty – cannot rule out the prospect of purposes that remain inscrutable for merely human judgement, an idea driving the powers to a sublime dissonance or incongruence, unless *reflective* judgement is to become *determinant*. This prospect cannot be determinantly eradicated for two reasons. Firstly, the 'product itself' is inherently particular, admitting of more and other forms than reflection can supply, unless it is to become a transcendental, thus necessary and *a priori*, determination of that product. Secondly, the transcendentalising move would place determinant restrictions upon mechanism's 'unlimited authority',[81] restrictions that cannot be placed upon it since 'without mechanism we cannot gain insight into the nature of things',[82] and since without this, 'there can be no natural science at all'.[83] Despite this, Kant does rule out inscrutable purposes attaching to natural products. Inveighing against the then current Neptunist school of geology, he writes:

> [W]e cannot regard water, air and earth as means for the accretion of mountains, because there is in fact nothing whatever in mountains that would require that their possibility have a basis in terms of purposes.[84]

From the standpoint of a reflective judgement, however, neither can it be *determined* that mountains do or do not possess intended purposes (or even 'will', as the geological *Naturphilosoph* Henrich Steffens would shortly argue),[85] nor that intentions have mechanistic causes. Since here reflective judgement has far exceeded its critical bounds,[86] it has in effect become transcendently (not transcendentally)[87] constitutive as regards the sorts of natural products that *do not* qualify for the ascription of purposes. The earth is judged therefore to qualify only as a mechanical product, and one that therefore admits only of mechanical explanation.

It is the business of reflection to judge which natural products may be selected for the manifestation of purposes, and explicitly, with neither theoretical nor critical justification, to exclude some of those products. Thus it is perhaps extraordinary that Kant should support one side against the other in the Neptunist-Vulcanist debates in late eighteenth-century geology when the earth has not only been deselected as a purposive being, but is also presented, through the agency of its revolutions, as the enemy of purposive organisation. Seeking to derive the origins of the globe as it is from the movements and silt-depositing processes of an

original 'aqueous solution', Neptunist geology 'dealt with the origins of
the habitable globe' *as it is now*. That is, it belongs to descriptive natural
history.[88] Moreover, since the Neptunist account considered contempo-
raneously observable phenomena (floods), it was conceivable that the
earth had been formed within a relatively short span of time, according
with the biblical story of the flood. In so doing, Neptunism committed
two errors. Firstly, to mechanical processes it superadded a God inferred
from the 'description' of natural purposes in order to explain those purposes,[89] turning physical *teleology* into physical *theology*.[90] Secondly, in an
important sense which will later become apparent, it removed from geological consideration the prospect of 'immeasurable time'.[91] Whereas
physioteleology in general is an attempt by reason to infer, from empirical evidence, a supreme cause of nature 'behind the machinery of this
world',[92] a moral teleology would, by contrast, attempt to infer that
cause 'from the moral purpose of rational beings in nature'[93]: from 'sublime ... freedom ... [as] an original cause'.[94]

Such rational beings are, of course, contingently to be found only in
humanity, so that we can infer that nature's purpose in producing a creative being capable of purposive reasoning and action, is the production
of humanity. Thus, without humanity, 'all of creation would be a mere
wasteland, gratuitous and without final purpose'.[95] Such a wasteland
had indeed been discovered by the Dutch 'natural archaeologist' Petrus
Camper who, following a 'meticulous examination of the traces of ...
natural devastations' had proven to Kant's satisfaction 'that man was not
included in those revolutions'.[96]

Thus Kant sides with the awesome horror of Camper's catastrophist
version of geological events, which insisted, with the Vulcanist geologist
James Hutton, that in 'the economy of the world' there was 'no vestige
of a beginning, – no prospect of an end'.[97] This version of geology is
strictly mechanical, denying the very idea of teleological causation in
nature. The question here has ceased to be the *critical* one of how far
mechanical and teleological explanations of natural products retain their
legitimacy, and has become the practical one of what purchase the mere
concept of natural purpose can have on nature's manifestly mechanical
revolutions, as revealed by Camper's discovery. Thus, the dilemma is:
either there is no finality in nature whatever (since 'the sphere of developed nature is incessantly busy in expanding itself');[98] *or*, if there is to
be, it must be produced. While in epistemological terms, an arbitrary
product is selected from the order of the accidental to explain all other
products, the stakes of Kant's catastrophism are practical: the selection

from the order of the accidental operated through reflective judgement must be realised in nature.

Kant's geological catastrophism therefore entails not merely the epistemic ordering of nature's products, but also that this ordering in effect constitutes a causality irreducible to the mechanical, although grounded in it. It is only at this point that teleological causation becomes instantiated, 'by remote analogy with our own causality in terms of purposes',[99] in organised bodies. But there is another basis for this instantiation than the epistemologically convenient. While Kant is a catastrophist in the archaeology of nature, he is a gradualist in natural history. 'The different animal genera', he writes,

> approach one another gradually: from the genus where the principle of purposes seems to be borne out most, namely, man, all the way to the polyp, and from it even to mosses and lichens and finally to the lowest stage of nature discernible to us, crude matter. From this matter, and its forces governed by mechanical laws, seems to stem all the technic that nature displays in organised beings and that we find so far beyond our grasp that we believe we have to think a different principle [than mechanism] to account for it.[100]

Just as the archaeology of nature poses the problem of an unpresentable time, so natural history displays such gradual continuity that it seems beyond reason not to infer a purposive arrangement on the part of nature. Camper's failure to decipher the least trace of human life from the depths of nature, however, pits a catastrophist archaeology against this gradualist natural history, subjecting purpose to material contingency. In nature's revolutions, therefore, the order of mechanical time confronts that of teleological time. If the sublime is to supply a basis for the preservation of purposive beings different in kind from that prepared by mechanical nature, that basis must be premised on the triumph of purpose over archaeological catastrophism *and* speciation's gradualism.

The third *Critique* poses the mathematical sublimity of phenomena that are unpresentable within a single intuition in purely spatial terms, as phenomena that are 'large beyond all comparison',[101] a magnitude such as 'an earth diameter'.[102] The sublime revelation of rational purposiveness in the nonsensible substrate uniting nature and freedom, by contrast, 'is large *beyond any standard of sense* [*über allen Maßstab der Sinne groß ist*]'.[103] Having exemplified the mathematical sublime only by way of spatial phenomena, however, the implication is that the 'large beyond any standard of sense' is similarly spatial. The problem of an unpresentable time, therefore, remains unexemplified in the Analytic of the Sublime.[104] Such a sublime, however, haunts geology. As the suspicion grows amongst eighteenth-century 'oryctologists'[105] and geologists that the post-deluvian, Mosaic geology of the physicotheologists offers too brief a timespan for the earth to have developed, the prospect of immeasurable time, large beyond any standard of sense, opens up. Even the uniformitarian methodological appeal only to 'presently active forces' as admissible into natural archaeology conceals an equally invalid natural historical assumption: that things have always been as they are now.[106] In other words, such an hypothesis exports the givens of synchronic natural history to the diachronic archaeology of nature, conflating a spatial with a temporal order, inferring temporal sequences from a contingent uniformity. Hence Kant's catastrophism, profoundly influenced by Buffon's thesis that species may devolve as well as evolve. Camper's failure to locate the merest trace of humanity amidst the ruins of nature's most ancient revolutions, and the general discredit into which Scheuchzer's 'discovery' of *Homo diluvii testis* had fallen even by the mid-eighteenth century,[107] combine to suggest an open, catastrophist field, unbounded by physicotheological timescales.

Such an unpresentable time, large beyond any standard of (inner) sense, provokes a geological sublime, a sublime stimulated by the archaeology of nature. It robs inner sense of any standard of time and, with the evident violence of nature's most ancient revolutions having obliterated whole species, it impels the powers to a productivity that reorients the *Grundkraft*, just as the imagination is compelled to produce a second nature 'out of the materials actual nature gives it'.[108] If, however, 'second nature' is produced from materials in accordance with another, spontaneous materially synthetic causality, the powers cannot salve the open horror of nature's revolutions with these givens of natural history. If, in confronting nature's present violence, the powers are impelled to make something of that present nature, then the stakes of the geological sublime must consist not of a spatial, but a temporal production. With no valid hypotheses by which to export the current to the most ancient or the farthest future, the powers must invent another causality, another temporal ordering, in accordance with the nonsensible, spontaneous productivity they acquire through the sublime. In concrete terms, what this means is that, rather than allowing nature's geohistorical revolutions to usurp the position of humanity at the apex of current natural production, the 'more perfect organization' to the presentation of which the productive imagination is driven must be actualised: to defeat nature's revolutions and maintain purposiveness, the metaphysics of nature and freedom necessitates the production of new species.

In the late eighteenth century, 'physics' did not yet denote a specialised field of study. Physics was simply the study of 'physical things', so that, for example, one could talk of 'vegetable physics', as Kielmeyer does as late as 1807. Just as the substrate uniting nature and freedom, rather than being located in a supersensible *realm*, is inaccessible to sense (*übersinnlich*) precisely insofar as it marks the point of transition between sensibility and production, so, for Kant, the metaphysical is neither a realm, nor reducibly ideational. Rather, it marks the point at which the cognitively legislated *description* of physical nature is conjoined with the latter's transformation in accordance with the spontaneous causality of freedom and the desiring-production of actuality. Wherever we look in Kant, it is the same thing: a productive and a receptive usage of the powers, the former always inaccessible to sense, the latter always inert. In this sense, the metaphysics of nature *is* the science of transition, the philosophical transformation of the physical, including the constitution of nervous systems (wherever located). From this perspective, the sublime is not reducibly an aesthetic experience, but rather a purposive selector operative in *thinking matter*. What a mistake ever to have called the sublime a matter of aesthetics alone, since precisely what always gets deselected in the sublime is sensibility. Given that the earth's contingency hangs over all its inhabitants, all that remains is *what selects*. Kant thinks he has done all he can to keep the human species at the top of the heap, but the sublime necessitates that to survive the natural revolutions rumbling in the abysses of deep time, all of nature must be remade. *What is thus 'preserved' by the understanding, if all of nature, including the nature in man, has been remade?* This, the true scale of the Kantian revolution, is what the *Opus postumum* was in search of, and why it was never finished. The enormity of the stakes of the metaphysics of nature – the production of another causal order – has meant that there have been more deaths than completed works in pursuit of its realisation. The real challenge of a philosophy of nature – the *naturphilosophische* challenge – as the Kantian metaphysics of nature lays it down, is not species preservation, but *how to select otherwise than 'human', i.e., philosophically*; and the stakes of this philosophical selection are *the production of new species*.

Notes

1 Kant, *UNH*, p. 170; *Ak*.I: 334.
2 Kant, *UNH*, p. 151; *Ak*.I: 309.
3 Gilles Deleuze and Félix Guattari, *What Is Philosophy?*, trans. Hugh Tomlinson (London: Verso, 1994), p. 85.
4 Deleuze and Guattari, *What Is Philosophy?*, p. 91. In a review of *What is Philosophy?*, Jean-Jacques Lecercle mistakenly suggested that the chapter on 'Geophilosophy' (ibid. pp. 85–113) lay outside the systematic construction of that work (Jean-Jacques Lecercle, 'The Pedagogy of Philosophy', *Radical Philosophy* 75 (1996) 44–6; p. 46). However, Deleuze and Guattari's geophilosophy is not merely lexically a continuation, therefore, of *A Thousand Plateaus* – specifically of the chapter '10,000 B.C.: The Geology of Morals (Who Does the Earth Think It Is?)' (Gilles Deleuze and Félix Guattari, *A Thousand Plateaus*, trans. Brian Massumi (London: Athlone, 1988), pp. 39–74). Rather, as they signal throughout *What is Philosophy?*, the concept of 'Thought-nature' they there develop constitutes an attempt to conjoin the virtual and nature – artifice and physics – to form a 'philosophy of nature' that had been an implicit component of their work since *Anti-Oedipus* (Gilles Deleuze and Félix Guattari, *Anti-Oedipus*, trans. Robert Hurley, Mark Seem and Helen R. Lane (Minneapolis: University of Minnesota Press, 1983)). See also Gilles Deleuze, *Negotiations*, trans. M. Hardt (New York: Columbia University Press, 1995), p. 155.
5 Kant, *CPR*, Aviii–ix.
6 Kant, *CPR*, Axx.
7 Kant, *CPR*, Axxi.
8 Kant, *CJ*, p. 35; *Ak*.V: 195.
9 Kant, *Op.p.*, p. 142; *Ak*. XXII: 496.
10 'Is it not much more proper, or better, is it not necessary to represent the very essence of creation as it ought to be, to be a witness of that power which can be measured by no yardstick?' (Kant, *UNH*, p. 151; *Ak*.I: 309; t.m.). Such descriptions recur throughout *UNH*, and lend credence to the prospect of a physicalist sublime.
11 Deleuze, *Negotiations*, p. 155: 'Guattari and I want to get back to our joint work and produce a sort of philosophy of nature, now that any distinction between nature and artifice is becoming blurred.'
12 Kant, *CJ*, p. 7; *Ak*.V: 170.
13 Kant, *Op.p.*, p. 41; *Ak*.XXI: 476.
14 Kant, *UNH*, p. 186; *Ak*.I: 355.
15 Thus, for example, Reil's Von der Lebenskraft used Kant's first *Critique* to construct a 'vital materialism' (Johann Christian Reils, Von der Lebenskraft, *Archiv für die Physiologie* vol. 1 issue 1 (Halle, 1795)). See LeeAnn Hansen, 'Metaphors of mind and society: the origins of German psychiatry in the revolutionary era', *Isis* 89 (1998) 387–409. Kant criticised Reil's

materialist tenets, since such work 'considers understanding dependent on the body and produced by the workings of the brain' (Kant, *CF*, p. 155; *Ak*.VII: 73). This is not to imply that Kant considered Reil descriptively wrong, but that the unilinear causality by which such descriptions are furnished ignores the natural basis of the metaphysics of freedom, or, otherwise put, substitutes the physics for the metaphysics of nature. For general background on the roots of contemporary neuroscience in Enlightenment and Romantic philosophy, see Edwin Clarke and L. S. Jacyna, *Nineteenth Century Origins of Neuroscientific Concepts* (Berkeley: University of California Press, 1987).

16 Kant, *UNH*, p. 187; *Ak*.I: 356; t.m.

17 Kant, *CPR*, A86/B118.

18 Kant, *CJ*, p. 7; *Ak*.V: 170.

19 Kant, *CJ*, p. 300; *Ak*.V: 415; t.m.

20 Kant, *CJ*, p. 295; *Ak*.V: 410; t.m.

21 Kant, *CF*, p. 199; *Ak*.VII: 109.

22 Kant, *AS*, *Ak*.XII: 33; m.t.

23 Kant, *Ak*.XII: 33; m.t.

24 Kant, *Ak*.XII: 34; m.t. On the effect of Lavoisier's 'chemical revolution' on Kant's philosophy of science, see Michael Friedmann, *Kant and the Exact Sciences* (Cambridge, MA: Harvard University Press, 1985), pp. 264–90.

25 Kant, *RT,* p. 84; *Ak*.VIII: 413–14.

26 Kant, *Anth.*, p. 3; *Ak*.VII: 119.

27 Kant, *CJ*, p. 295; *Ak*.V: 410.

28 Kant, *CJ*, p. 296; *Ak*.V: 411.

29 Kant, *CPR*, A15/B29.

30 Kant, *CPR*, A649/B677.

31 This research programme, explicitly derived from Kant, currently shapes historians of science's approach to the late eighteenth and early nineteenth centuries, and has been designated 'vital materialism' or 'teleomechanism' by Timothy Lenoir, 'Kant, Blumenbach and vital materialism in German biology', *Isis* 71 (1980) 77–108. Especially relevant in the above context is Hansen, 'Metaphors'. Phillip Reid Sloan has also argued for the importance of the Kantian programme in the formation of biology in his introductory essay, 'On the edge of evolution', to Richard Owen, *The Hunterian Lectures in Comparative Anatomy, May and June 1837*, ed. Phillip R. Sloan (London: Natural History Museum, 1992), pp. 15–34. The current programme is most marked by its continuation of the later nineteenth century's vitriolic hostility towards so-called 'idealist' *Naturphilosophie*, veering towards Kant as a safe harbour. I attempt to show here that the critical island offers only a delusory security, and elsewhere, that the oceans of nature-philosophical (*naturphilosophisch*) speculation are physicalistic. See Iain Hamilton Grant, *On an Artificial Earth: Schelling,* Naturphilosophie

and Absolute Empiricism (London: Athlone, forthcoming).

32 Hansen,'Metaphors', p. 397.

33 Marcus Herz, *Versuch über den Schwindel* (Berlin: Voss, 1791).

34 Herz, *Versuch*, p. 61; cited in Hansen, 'Metaphors', p. 398n.

35 Dr John Brown's physiological researches became the subject of heated debate following their German translation in 1795. Eckart Förster offers a balanced account of Kant's relation to Brunonianism in a long note to the translation of *Op.p.*, pp. 270–1, where, despite introducing doubt as to whether Kant was or was not an adherent of that system in both philosophical and empirical terms, and despite using the Brunonian terminology in which the *Anthropology* couches its examination of affects in the 'natural machine', Förster neither looks for nor indicates the possibility of more wide-ranging researches on this matter. Kant's constant references to Stoic virtue, for instance, are merely exemplars of Brunonian prescriptions regarding the maintenance of health, an application of these virtues that is clear both in the *Anthropology* and in the third of the *Conflict of the Faculties*.

36 Strictly speaking, Reil's is a *chemism* rather than a *mechanicism*, as Ayrault puts it: 'Reil's thought is a tributary of Kantianism: to it, matter is the sum of the manifestations that our senses record as an object in space; it reduces the idea of force to a "subjective" relation between the effects that are the manifestations of these causes. But Reil's "chemism" is also consistent with this; and as opposed to traditional "chemism", it attributes no other knowable causes to the fact of life than the properties of matter.' Raymond Ayrault, *La Genèse du romantisme allemand*, 2 vols. (Paris: Montaigne, 1976), II p. 303.

37 Reil, 'Von der Lebenskraft', p. 44; cited in *Friedrich Wilhelm Joseph Schelling, Historisch-kritische Ausgabe. Reihe 1, Ergänzungsband zu Werke Band 5 bis 9: Wissenschaftlicher Bericht zu Schellings naturphilosophischen Schriften 1797–1800*, eds. Hans Michael Baumgartner, Wilhelm G. Jacobs and Hermann Krings (Stuttgart: Frommann-Holzboog, 1994), p. 554.

38 Kant, *CPR*, A86–7/B119.

39 Kant, *AS*, *Ak*.XII: 34–5; m.t.

40 Kant drew out the distinction between chemical and mechanical action in the 'Metaphysical Foundations of Dynamics': 'The action of moved bodies on one another through the communication of their motion is called mechanical; but the action of matters at rest insofar as they change the combination of their parts *reciprocally by their own forces* is called chemical.' (Kant, *MNS*, p. 87; *Ak*.IV: 530; my emphasis).

41 On Stahl and the history of chemistry, see Bernadette Bensaude-Vincent and Isabelle Stengers, *A History of Chemistry*, trans. Deborah van Dam (Cambridge, MA: Harvard University Press, 1996), pp. 57–61. On Stahlian chemistry and Kant, see Friedmann, *Kant and the Exact Sciences*,

pp. 265–8 ff.

42 Kant, *CPR*, Dxii–xiii, t.iii. Kemp Smith's translation of Kant's *Kalken* by 'oxides' effectively misrepresents Stahl's view as Lavoisier's. See Friedmann, *Kant and the Exact Sciences*, p. 265 n67.

43 In consequence, Stahl's vitalism stems from the thesis that since the physical complexity of vital bodies entailed more mixts than aggregates, it followed that life as such could not be reduced to mechanism.

44 Bensaude-Vincent and Stengers, *A History of Chemistry*, pp. 57–9.

45 Kant, *CPR*, Bxxi.

46 Kant, *CPR*, A86–7/B119.

47 Kant, *CPR*, A78/B103.

48 Kant, *CPR*, A87/B119.

49 Kant, *UNH*, p. 189; *Ak*.I: 359.

50 Charles Lyell, *Principles of Geology* (1830–3), ed. James A. Secord (Harmondsworth: Penguin, 1997), p. 16.

51 Georges Louis de Buffon. *Histoire de la nature*, vol. v (Paris: de L'Imprimerie Royale, 1756), p. 62.

52 See Lenoir, 'Kant, Blumenbach'.

53 That science was simultaneously so named in 1802 by Gottfried Reinhold Treviranus, in *Biologie, oder Philosophie der lebendigen Natur*, 6 vols. (Göttingen: Rower, 1802–22), and by Jean Baptiste de Lamarck, in *Recherches sur l'organisation des corps vivants* (Paris: published by the author, 1802).

54 Kant, *Anth.*, p. 3; *Ak*.VII: 119.

55 Kant, *CJ*, p. 121; *Ak*.V: 261.

56 Kant, *RT*, p. 84; *Ak*.VIII: 414.

57 Kant, *MNS*, p. 3; *Ak*.IV: 467.

58 Kant, *CJ*, p. 100; *Ak*.V: 246.

59 Kant, *CJ*, pp. 120–1; *Ak*.V: 261.

60 Kant, *CJ*, p. 260; *Ak*.V: 380.

61 Kant, *CJ*, p. 287; *Ak*.V: 404. I have used Edward Caird's translation of '*Gesetzlichkeit des Zufälligen*' (which Pluhar gives as 'lawfulness of the contingent') due to its more empirical emphasis on accidental products as constituting an order, rather than following a law. Edward Caird, *Kant's Critical Philosophy*, 2 vols. (Glasgow: James Maclehose, 1889), pp. 482–3.

62 Kant, *CJ*, p. 99; *Ak*.V: 246.

63 Kant, *CJ*, p. 118; *Ak*.V: 260.

64 '[Nature] demonstrates her richness in a kind of waste', writes Kant in a Bataillean dithyramb from *UNH*. More pertinently, he writes, 'Man ... is not exempted from this law'. Kant, *UNH*, p. 158; *Ak*.I: 319.

65 Kant, *Op.p.*, p. 226; *Ak*.XXI: 20.

66 Kant, *CJ*, p. 121; *Ak*.V: 261.

67 Kant, *CJ*, p. 127; *Ak*.V: 268.

68 Kant, *CJ*, p. 182; *Ak*.V: 314.

69 Kant, *CPrR*, p. 9n; *Ak*.V: 9n; and *CJ*, pp. 16–17 n18; *Ak*.V: 177n. This thesis is foreshadowed in Preface B of the first *Critique*, where practical reason as a whole is defined, in contradistinction to the conceptual determinations of speculative reason, as what *'actualizes'* (Kant, *CPR*, B ix–x).

70 Kant, *CJ*, p. 315 n20; *Ak*.V: 428n. Although Cuvier and Lamarck had developed the relevance of the study of fossils for natural history, the term 'palaeontology' was coined by Cuvier's successor to the chair of comparative anatomy at the Museum National d'Histoire Naturelle, Ducrotayé de Blainville, in 1834. See William Coleman, *Biology in the Nineteenth Century* (Cambridge: Cambridge University Press,1977), pp. 63ff; Toby A. Appel, *The Cuvier-Geoffroy Debate: French Biology in the Decades before Darwin* (New York: Oxford University Press, 1987), p. 212; and W. N. Edwards, *The Early History of Palaeontology* (London: British Museum, 1976), pp. 40–1.

71 Kant, *Op.p.*, p. 67; *Ak*. XXI: 214–15.

72 Kant, *CJ*, p. 331; *Ak*.V: 442.

73 'What the critical Kant wanted was a metaphysics of nature….What he really got was only the idea of a possible nature', writes George di Giovanni, in 'Kant's Metaphysics of Nature and Schelling's *Ideas for a Philosophy of Nature*', *Journal for the History of Philosophy* 17 (1979) 197–215, 214. This effectively parallels Carl Friedrich Kielmeyer's argument in *Über Kant und die deutsche Naturphilosophie*, in *Natur und Kraft: Carl Friedrich Kielmeyers gesammelte Schriften*, ed. F. H. Köhler (Berlin: Kieper, 1938).

74 Kant, *CJ*, p. 287; *Ak*.V: 404.

75 Kant, *Op.p.*, p. 66; *Ak*.XXI: 213.

76 Kant, *CF*, p. 145; *Ak*.VII: 81.

77 Kant, *CJ*, p. 121; *Ak*.V: 261.

78 Kant, *CJ*, pp. 252–3; *Ak*.V: 373–4.

79 Kant, *CJ*, p. 296; *Ak*.V: 411.

80 Kant, *CJ*, p. 288; *Ak*.V: 405.

81 Kant, *CJ*, p. 303; *Ak*.V: 417.

82 Kant, *CJ*, p. 295; *Ak*.V: 410.

83 Kant, *CJ*, p. 304; *Ak*.V: 418.

84 Kant, *CJ*, p. 312; *Ak*.V: 425.

85 Henrich Steffens' *Beyträge zur innern Naturgeschichte der Erde* (Freiberg, 1801) took from Schelling the idea that all of nature must be thought as the divergent products of a single, living, 'fundamental form', and from A. G. Werner, the founder of the Neptunist school of geology, the evidence that the earth was in continual movement, to suggest that this movement constituted the 'will' that reached its highest expression in man. For Steffens' comments on the *Beyträge*, see the single volume abridgement of his ten volume autobiography, entitled *Lebenserinnerungen* (Jena: Eugen

Diederichs, 1908), pp. 175–6.

86 'Teleology as a science does not belong to any doctrine, but belongs only to …the critique of…judgement' (Kant, *CJ*, p. 302; *Ak*.V: 417).

87 'We shall entitle the principles whose application is confined entirely within the limits of possible experience, *immanent*; and those, on the other hand, which profess to pass beyond these limits, *transcendent*.' (Kant, *CPR*, A295–6/B352).

88 Charles Coulston Gillespie, *Genesis and Geology*, 2nd edn. (Cambridge, MA: Harvard University Press, 1996), p. 46. For a Hegelian geological take on the 'Neptunist-Vulcanist' debates in the late eighteenth century, see Timothy H. Levere, 'Hegel and the earth sciences', in *Hegels Philosophie der Natur: Beziehungen zwischen empirischer und spekulativer Naturerkenntnis*, eds. Rolf-Peter Horstmann and Michael J. Petry (Stuttgart: Klett-Cotta, 1986), pp. 103–21.

89 Kant, *CJ*, p. 302; *Ak*.V: 417.

90 Kant, *CJ*, p. 324; *Ak*.V: 436.

91 Kant, *CF*, p. 161; *Ak*.VII: 89.

92 Kant, *CJ*, p. 327; *Ak*.V: 439.

93 Kant, *CJ*, p. 324; *Ak*.V: 436.

94 Kant, *Op.p.*, p. 226; *Ak*.XXI: 20.

95 Kant, *CJ*, p. 331; *Ak*.V: 442.

96 Kant, *CJ*, p. 316; *Ak*.V: 428.

97 James Hutton, 'Theory of the earth; or an investigation of the laws observable in the composition, dissolution and restoration of land upon the globe', *Transactions of the Royal Society of Edinburgh* 1 (1788) 304. See also Lyell, *Principles of Geology*, pp. 16–17.

98 Kant, *UNH*, p. 154; *Ak*.I: 319.

99 Kant, *CJ*, p. 255; *Ak*.V: 375.

100 Kant, *CJ*, p. 304; *Ak*.V: 418–19.

101 Kant, *CJ*, p. 103; *Ak*.V: 248.

102 Kant, *CJ*, p. 111; *Ak*.V: 254.

103 Kant, *CJ*, p. 112; *Ak*.V: 255.

104 Although the collapse of successive presentations of sense into a single instant is described as the imagination 'do[ing] violence to the inner sense' (Kant, *CJ*, p. 116; *Ak*.V: 258–9), these successive presentations are still measured against objects that cannot be presented within a single presentation due to their spatial proportions.

105 This is the late eighteenth-century term for what has been known, since the mid-nineteenth century, as palaeontology. See Edwards, *The Early History of Palaeontology*, p. 41.

106 D. J. Depew and B. H. Weber, *Darwinism Evolving: Systems Dynamics and the Genealogy of Natural Selection* (Cambridge, MA: MIT Press, 1997), p. 97.

107 Johann Scheuchzer, *Homo diluvii testis* (Tiguri, 1726). The Swiss naturalist
    Scheuchzer was an early defender of the view that fossils were relics of
    formerly living creatures, and published *Herbarium Diluvianum*, a record of
    fossilised plants supposedly dating from the deluge, in 1709. Thus, in
    Homo diluvii testis, he published a paper entitled 'An account of the
    remains of a man who had witnessed the Deluge', containing an illustration
    of 'the bony skeleton of one of those infamous men whose sins brought
    upon the world the dire misfortune of the deluge' (cited in Humphrey
    Davy, *On Geology* (Madison: University of Wisconsin Press, 1982), p. 128).
    Georges Cuvier later showed the skeleton to be that of a salamander. See
    Edwards, *The Early History of Palaeontology*, pp. 12–14.
108 Kant, *CJ*, p. 182; *Ak*.V: 314.

4

A 'Sacred Thrill': Presentation and Affectivity in the Analytic of the Sublime

Jim Urpeth

Some of the main sources of recent interpretations of the Analytic of the Sublime have been readings from Heideggerian and deconstructive perspectives.[1] I shall argue that essential aspects of AS cannot be adequately addressed from an HD perspective and require instead a Nietzschean or genealogical critique. From such a perspective the alterity manifest within AS is *material* and *affective* in nature. It is the *impersonal* affectivity associated with a de-anthropomorphised materiality that provokes Kant's vociferous assertion of the sublimity of 'reason' which, he argues, distinguishes 'man' in kind from nature. The 'trace' of this material alterity in AS is the notion of 'raw nature' (*die rohe Natur*).[2] To read AS genealogically is to insist that the most fundamental presuppositions of Kant's conception of the sublime lie in a régime of theologico-humanist value which eluded his critique of metaphysics.

I

In the HD readings of AS the main concern is, as Nancy states, the 'question of presentation'.[3] Such interpretations detect an affinity between Kant's consideration of the sublime and Heidegger's thematisation of being. Librett describes this as the relation between 'two forms of the thought of what exceeds representation'.[4] Similarly, Lacoue-Labarthe conjoins Kant and Heidegger in the claim that, 'the *sublime is the presentation of this*: *that there is presentation*'.[5] The HD readings of AS demonstrate its status as a text concerned with the disclosure of the unobjectifiable process of presentation *per se*. Kant's sublime is akin to Heidegger's ontological difference as both are concerned, in Librett's words, with 'the gift of a measureless measure'.[6]

For HD readings Kant's account of the role of the imagination in AS is interpreted in ontological terms insofar as, operating at the limits of presentation, it discloses an excess to the *a priori* presentational powers of the mind. Escoubas encapsulates these readings when she claims that the imagination, as the 'faculty of the reality of the real',[7] is the 'Kantian name for Being'.[8] Kant's insistence that the sublime, given the limitations of the imagination, can only be invoked 'negatively' is an aspect of AS of central significance to HD readings of it.[9] Kant describes the imagination's futile attempt to present the 'indemonstrable' ideas of reason.[10] Lyotard demonstrates the radicality implicit in the imagination's endeavour to 'present the unpresentable'.[11] As he states, 'the distress of the imagination becomes the sign of the intelligible in the sensible'.[12] The HD readings' interpretation of the 'metaphysical' motif of 'negative presentation' relates Kant's conception of an excess to presence to that found in the texts of Heidegger and Derrida.[13]

The HD readings' insistence on the non-dialectical nature of Kant's conception of the 'negative presentation' of the sublime is commendable. Lyotard argues that AS is concerned with a 'differend of feeling' that is intrinsically irresolvable.[14] Similarly, Sallis insists that AS describes 'a disclosure within the sensible of the very difference between the sensible and supersensible'.[15] That Kant's insistence that the relation between the imagination and reason in the sublime underwrites 'subjective purposiveness' is not to be read in terms of dialectical resolution is confirmed by Sallis when he states that, 'the supervenient purposiveness does not eliminate the discord; it does not simply dissolve it but rather *is* precisely a purposiveness *of* that very discord'.[16]

Kant's references in AS to an 'abyss' also appeal to HD interpreters.[17] Kant does not, however, accord this notion a primordial ontological status. That the abyss the imagination encounters in the sublime only challenges the empirically compromised powers of the mind and leaves reason and its relation to the infinite unscathed is clearly stated by Kant:

> If a [thing] is excessive for the imagination ... [it] is ... an abyss in which the imagination is afraid to lose itself. Yet ... for reason's idea of the supersensible [this same thing] is not excessive but conforms to reason's law to give rise to such striving by the imagination.[18]

Sallis characterises the role of reason in relation to the abyss as described in this passage as,

> a guardrail that protects and preserves ... the self-disclosure that is achieved in the judgment of the sublime. ... It prevents one's ever deci-

sively losing oneself in the abyss; it guarantees self-recovery, assures that self disclosure is self recovery.[19]

The HD readings show how AS resonates with the theme of the limits of presentation that such an interpretative perspective identifies with the overcoming of metaphysics. Yet such readings largely ignore the genealogical question concerning the extent to which Kant remains committed in AS to the evaluative and affective constitution of the hierarchical oppositions it critically refashions. The exclusively ontological approach of the HD readings of AS is illustrated in Escoubas' conception of the theme of 'raw nature':

> The *rohe Natur* ... indicates that the imagination, the faculty of the beautiful and sublime, is thematised as the faculty of ontological difference, as the faculty of the "*is*" in "it is beautiful" or "it is sublime."[20]

Such a response to Kant's encounter with natural processes resistant to anthropomorphisation covertly avoids any critical interrogation of the triumphant reassertion in AS of the Platonic-Christian tradition's negative evaluation of dysteleological materiality and the affectivity it presupposes, namely pessimism. These readings do not interrogate the most fundamental import of the self-disclosure the sublime offers to human beings – namely, an insight into the ultimate transcendence of material nature provided by their determination by reason which, for Kant, cannot be conceived in naturalistic terms.

II

In its themes of 'violence', 'resistance', 'sacrifice' and, above all, 'negative pleasure', AS provides a disclosure of the affective and evaluative economy that constitutes Platonic-Christian metaphysics. To subject these aspects of AS to critique requires a reading attuned to the values pre-critically endorsed in AS and the affective-libidinal investments underlying them. The task of such a genealogical reading consists in the assessment of the 'type of will' manifest in AS. The rhetorical gestures of AS are conceived as a 'sign-language' symptomatic of an anonymous libidinal-affective economy. Kant's text is interpreted as an interrelation of material forces, a configuration of the *will to power*. The task is to ascertain the balance of reactive or active forces within AS, to assess the degree to which a healthy or life-affirming rather than a sick or life-denying perspective predominates within it.

A genealogical reading of AS must reflect the subtlety of Nietzsche's evaluation of the 'ascetic ideal'.[21] It thus consists of two interrelated phases. The first critically interrogates the evaluative economy underlying the rhetoric of AS. This supports an initially oppositional critique of Kant's text based on a negative assessment of the degree to which AS can be conceived in terms of the 'affirmation of life' understood in terms of the primacy of becoming. The second, more radical, phase of a genealogical critique of AS uncovers in Kant's text a libidinally invested appropriation of the ascetic ideal that cannot be interpreted simply in terms of the 'denial of life'. On this level an immanent critique of AS is possible in which its response to 'raw nature' is revealed to be erotic rather than moral. Kant's text is thereby shown to undermine its seemingly moral stance through the valorisation of an affective economy in which pleasure and asceticism are no longer opposed. The interpretation of AS as a moral text is supplanted by an affirmative critical assessment of the pleasures it recommends. The affective-libidinal type manifest in AS is not interpreted in terms of denial but as the affirmation of pleasures reason takes in the humiliation of the finite dimensions of the mind. The critical task arising for such a reading of AS is the evaluation of the relative health or sickness of the libidinal economy of AS, the quality of the type of will manifest within it.

III

For Kant, the aesthetic feeling evoked by the sublime is induced by an experience of nature as 'unbounded' or 'formless'.[22] As he states, 'it is … in its chaos that nature most arouses our ideas of the sublime … in its wildest and most ruleless disarray and devastation'.[23] The Kantian sublime concerns an encounter with 'raw nature' which displays an 'utter lack of anything leading to particular objective principles and to forms of nature conforming to them'.[24] The theme of 'raw nature' marks a rare occasion on which the critical system addresses an incompliant nature beyond the reach of transcendental legislation, a non-mechanistic and dysteleological materiality that interrupts the *a priori* processes which constitute nature as a law-governed field of phenomena.[25]

In accord with the task Kant sets himself of thematising aesthetic feeling in general in terms of the *a priori* principle of 'subjective purposiveness',[26] the feeling of the sublime stimulated by the 'contrapurposiveness' (for the imagination) of 'raw nature' is ultimately shown to be purposive from the perspective of the *'whole vocation'* of the mind'.[27]

For Kant, aesthetic judgement concerns the feelings of pleasure and displeasure associated with a bonding exercise between the *a priori* powers of the mind which underscores the coherence of the rational-moral subject. As with the beautiful, the 'subjective purposiveness' of the sublime consists in the indeterminate relation it engenders between the imagination and another *a priori* power of the mind which, in the case of the sublime, is reason. In the sublime such purposiveness resides in the *discord* between the powers of the mind and only remains so insofar as this discord is *sustained* and not dialectically resolved. As Kant states, 'imagination and reason here give rise to such a purposiveness by their *conflict*'.[28]

The feeling of the sublime induced by 'raw nature' is thus teleological insofar as the appropriate relation between the imagination and reason is underwritten. The sublime is purposive in that the critically disciplined relation between the empirical and transcendent dimensions of the mind is reinforced. The sublime discloses a rift between the powers of the mind which binds it together, a schism that integrates insofar as it is not resolved. It is a purposive mental conflict that characterises the relation between the imagination and reason in those who can legitimately lay claim to belong to humanity in Kant's sense.[29]

It is this conception of a purposiveness without specific conceptual determination (i.e., 'without a purpose') that, for Kant, is the source of the value of aesthetic feeling and secures its role in his critical defence of the theologico-humanist values he inherits. Hence the feeling of the sublime, 'raise[s] the soul's fortitude above its usual middle range',[30] and thereby discloses the 'subjective purposiveness' which, in Kant's view, is the basis of the *a priori* status 'pure judgments of taste' can legitimately claim.

Kant identifies two kinds of sublime feeling related to the theoretical (the mathematical) and practical (the dynamical) roles of reason as these are exercised in response to nature's 'magnitude' and 'might' respectively. He argues that the imagination is 'inadequate' to the demands made of it by reason in response to the 'contrapurposiveness' of 'raw nature'. The inherent limits of the presentational power of the imagination and the order of inner sense are thereby disclosed.[31]

In the mathematical sublime the 'inadequacy' of the imagination's finite powers indirectly discloses the transcendent order of reason which contains a 'nonsensible standard that has … infinity itself under it as a unit'.[32] Hence, Kant argues, a distinguishing criterion of being human is thereby disclosed insofar as reason grants man, 'a superiority over nature itself in its immensity'.[33] In the dynamical sublime the imagination is seen to fail when the demand is placed upon it in response to the forbidding 'might' of 'raw nature' to present the moral and religious themes of practical reason through which the supersensuous subject is able to 'resist' the 'might' of nature, which is thereby denied any ultimate 'dominion' over the human. The feeling of the dynamical sublime, Kant claims, enhances human beings' 'self-estimation' (*Selbstschätzung*),[34] enabling them to 'discover ... an ability to resist ... which gives us the courage [to believe] that we could be a match for nature's seeming omnipotence'.[35]

Hence, for Kant, it is the realisation of the very 'inadequacy' of the *a priori* presentational powers of the mind which underscores the supremacy of reason and thereby discloses the sublimity of the subject as the natural being uniquely endowed with a relation to transcendent ideas. The aesthetic feeling of the sublime reminds the human subject of the attributes that elevate it above nature, in particular, the awareness of its essential 'freedom' from natural determination. The sublime is an event of aesthetic self-disclosure through which human beings retrieve their obligation to consider themselves as autonomous *persons* rather than heteronomous *things*.[36]

For Kant it is an error to predicate sublimity to nature. As he states, 'the vast ocean heaved up by storms cannot be called sublime'.[37] To ascribe sublimity to nature is to commit the fallacy of subreption.[38] As Kant states, 'the object is suitable for exhibiting a sublimity that can be found in the mind',[39] and,

> an object of nature ... makes intuitable for us the superiority of the rational vocation of our cognitive powers over the greatest power of sensibility.[40]

Kant argues that judgements of the sublime only concern, 'what *use* we can make of our intuitions of nature so that we can feel a purposiveness within ourselves entirely independent of nature.'[41] Hence for Kant, whilst it is appropriate within certain critical restrictions to judge nature to be beautiful, we can never legitimately describe it as sublime; as he insists, '[f]or the beautiful in nature we must seek a basis outside ourselves, but for the sublime a basis merely within ourselves'.[42] Sallis notes that the sublime is even more 'withdrawn' into the subject than the beautiful.[43] The feeling of the sublime induces the mind to 'abandon sensibility'.[44] Thus Kant is discussing 'a way of thinking that introduces sublimity into our presentation of nature'.[45]

It is the critique of this alleged sublimity of the human in relation to the natural order which lies at the heart of a Nietzschean interrogation of AS. Its task is to uncover and challenge the desire which produces the aesthetic sensibility that interprets 'raw nature' teleologically in terms of theologico-humanist values. In the following passage Kant expresses some of the core values his critique of metaphysics sought to defend,

> [W]e found in our mind a superiority over nature itself in its immensity … though the irresistibility of nature's might makes us, considered as natural beings, recognize our physical impotence, it reveals in us at the same time an ability to judge ourselves independent of nature….This keeps the humanity in our person from being degraded.[46]

It would be straightforward to construct an oppositional Nietzschean critique of the theologico-humanist values endorsed in this passage which seem clearly indicative of the 'sickness' and 'pessimism' of the 'slave' perspective that yearns to escape 'this world'. Rejecting the 'anti-nature' of the values underpinning AS, Nietzsche exposes the *ressentiment* that lies at the source of any desire on the part of humanity to consider itself as distinct in kind from the natural order. From the perspective of the merely oppositional form of a Nietzschean critique of AS, Kant's view in the passage cited above, that a naturalistic account of the human as a whole entails 'degradation', would be taken as key indicator of the nihilism he uncritically shares with the Platonic-Christian tradition.

Hence the first phase of a Nietzschean critique of AS finds it to be dominated by life-denying values insofar as it unequivocally valorises the transcendent. Kant defines the boundaries of the human by prescribing 'a feeling that the mind has a vocation that wholly transcends the domain of nature (namely, moral feeling)'.[47] In oppositional mode Nietzsche would condemn Kant's appropriation of aesthetic feeling in general for the anthropocentric project of reinforcing the values that constitute the rational-moral subject.

However, as suggested above, such an oppositional critique seriously underestimates both the radicality of AS and an alternative Nietzschean critique of it. From such a non-oppositional critical perspective a Nietzschean reading of AS identifies it as a clear example of the appropriation of the 'ascetic ideal' for the self-preservation (rather than 'denial') of a particular affective-libidinal economy.[48] This possibility must now be explored.

IV

The second phase of a Nietzschean reading of AS seeks to expose and critically assess the perspectival régime of values operative in AS interpreted as the expression of a particular affective-libidinal economy. A key theme for such a critique of AS is the primacy Kant claims for the *a priori* principle he identifies as the basis of aesthetic judgement, namely, 'subjective purposiveness'. It is through this notion that Kant undertakes his critically disciplined teleological appropriation of aesthetic feeling. In contrast, Nietzsche's critique of the value of metaphysical values rests on the affirmation of the primacy and irreducibility of dysteleological material processes (i.e., the Dionysian) in which the human is, *in toto*, inextricably embedded. A critical reading of AS from such a perspective challenges Kant's teleological appropriation by reason of the encounter with 'raw nature' in terms of the 'feeling of our supersensible vocation'.[49]

The significance of the notion of 'subjective purposiveness' is reinforced through its relation to another crucial theme in Kant's text, namely, the 'feeling of life' (*Lebensgefühl*).[50] AS contains a remarkable transcendental energetics of aesthetic feeling. For Kant, whilst the 'subjective purposiveness' of the play of the imagination and understanding in the beautiful is a 'feeling of life's being furthered',[51] the interaction of the imagination with reason in the sublime consists of a simultaneous feeling of attraction and repulsion.[52] The sublime is 'the feeling of a momentary inhibition of the vital forces followed immediately by an outpouring of them that is all the stronger.'[53]

Kant's conception of the 'feeling of life' uncritically assumes, albeit in relation to the supersensuous dimensions of the human, the primacy of self-preservation. For Kant, the instincts eliminate the 'disinterestedness' necessary for pure judgements of taste. Thus the natural phenomena which evoke the feeling of the sublime can only do so 'provided we are in a safe place'.[54] Yet self-preservation in relation to the rational-moral dimensions of the subject is strangely excluded by Kant from a similar criticism. A Nietzschean critique of AS challenges Kant's conception of the self-preservation of the supersensuous subject as 'disinterested'.

The connections between the themes of the 'feeling of life', 'subjective purposiveness' and 'self-preservation' are apparent in the following passage:

> [A] superiority over nature…is the basis of a self-preservation [*eine Selbsterhaltung*] quite different in kind from the one that can be assailed and endangered by nature outside us … it calls forth our strength (which does not belong to nature [within us]).[55]

In this passage Kant aligns the sublime with the 'self-preservation' of the rational-moral subject and insists on a non-naturalistic account of it. It is the non-naturalistic origin of reason that guarantees salvation from the otherwise crushing disclosure of the insignificance and vulnerability of the human in comparison to the 'contra-purposiveness' of 'raw nature'.

Kant clearly tends to identify the 'interests', both sensuous and super-sensuous, of human life with those of life *in general*, even to the extent of developing a teleological appropriation of the dysteleological (i.e., 'raw nature'). This represents an, albeit critically constrained, anthropo-morphism that Kant attempted to legitimise. From a Nietzschean per-spective Kant merely seeks an overcoming of empirical interests and leaves intact the noumenal interests of the rational-moral subject, the value of which is excluded from critique. Kant does not develop a con-ception of disinterestedness that departs from a merely anthropocentric perspective in order to affirm the dysteleological trajectories of a non-anthropomorphic life. That Kant's conception of disinterestedness is limited to a merely anthropocentric perspective is rhetorically asserted when he asks incredulously, 'how can we call something by a term of approval if we apprehend it as in itself contrapurposive?'[56]

V

Kant's project of a critique of aesthetic feeling is concerned to justify the claim to 'universal assent' which, he argues, pure judgements of taste can legitimately claim. From the perspective outlined here, Kant's claims for the 'universality and necessity' of the type of aesthetic feeling he valorises are contested. A Nietzschean perspective rejects such uni-versalism by contrasting a 'noble' and 'slave' *sensus communis*. In the case of the sublime, reason can legitimately demand, Kant argues, that all who claim the title 'human' will share its response to the plight of the *a priori* presentational powers of the mind when overwhelmed by the 'contrapurposiveness' of 'raw nature'. To disagree with a pure judge-ment of taste is to remain mired in the sensuous, which Kant reductively construes in terms of egoic interest, and so to forfeit a place in the *sensus communis*. In the case of the sublime, the affective condition which Kant argues can be legitimately universalised is 'negative pleasure'.[57] This pleasure, which reason derives from the displeasure felt by the imagina-tion when confronted by 'raw nature', can be described as a type of tran-scendental *Schadenfreude*. A Nietzschean reading of AS denies the claim to 'universality and necesssity' which Kant makes for this 'negative pleasure' in that it is identified merely as the aesthetic sensibility of a particular type of will. Contemporary thought can no longer ignore the interlocking dimensions of power and value that lie behind Kant's construction of the *sensus communis*. The HD interpreters' focus on the 'question of presentation' marginalises the normative violence of AS, its covert censorship of alternative aesthetic sensibilities incommensurable with its project of constructing and legitimising moral personhood.

From a Nietzschean perspective Kant's conception of the sublime in terms of 'negative pleasure' is a more fundamental theme in AS than that of 'negative presentation', the key theme for HD readings of the text. This is because a genealogical interpretation of a text accords primordial ontological status to the libidinal-affective economy manifest in its valorisations. Such a reading evaluates the libidinal type manifest within a text.[58]

In describing the sublime feeling of 'negative pleasure' Kant offers a revealing glimpse into the nature of the libidinal affectivity of the Platonic-Christian tradition. AS describes an increasingly remote affective condition, namely, 'a feeling that we have a pure and independent reason'.[59] Kant's celebration of 'negative pleasure' is a seminal expression of the erotic genius of the West, namely, the intense pleasures that stem from 'self-denial', the libidinal dynamics of which are the ('extra-moral') source of the 'ascetic ideal'.

To pursue this perspective on AS presupposes an appreciation of Nietzsche's libidinal interpretation of the 'ascetic ideal' in which it is conceived as the West's principal 'technique of ecstasy'. From this perspective the 'ascetic ideal' is not an essentially moral phenomenon but a device employed in the pursuit of the pleasures that characterise the Platonic-Christian libidinal type. That this libidinal economy pursues intensificatory processes that entail the 'denial' of some sources of pleasure (i.e., the body) in order to maximise the yield from other erogenous zones (i.e., the rational-moral) should not be misinterpreted as a moral phenomenon.[60]

The relish with which Kant valorises 'negative pleasure' cannot be accounted for within a moral interpretation of it. Kant's endorsement of the pleasure reason gains through the torments endured by the imagination is couched in a highly charged rhetoric that barely conceals the essentially erotic heart of the sublime. As Kant states, 'raw nature' is 'violent to our imagination, and yet we judge it all the more sublime for that.'[61]

In contrast to Kant's vision of the pure origins of reason Nietzsche describes it thus:

> the misunderstanding of passion and reason, as if the latter were an independent entity and not a system of various passions and desires; as if every passion did not possess its quantum of reason.[62]

From the perspective of this passage, AS is read economically in terms of competing libidinal forces. The specific type of libidinal-affective state celebrated in AS is encapsulated by Nietzsche thus:

> [M]an is the cruellest animal towards himself; and with all who call themselves "sinners" and "bearers of the Cross" and "penitents" do not overlook the sensual pleasure that is in this complaint and accusation.[63]

The pleasure of the sublime as 'a pleasure that is possible only by means of a displeasure',[64] is an example of the development of the 'festive joy' in cruelty which characterised the 'ancients'.[65] For Nietzsche, the ascetic techniques Kant deploys to discipline the body differ only in degree from those epochs in which 'mankind felt no shame towards its cruelty'.[66] Nietzsche discusses morality in terms unimaginable to Kant,

> the moral conceptual world ... began with a thorough and prolonged blood-letting, like the beginning of all great things on earth. And may we not add that this world has really never quite lost a certain odour of blood and torture?[67]

In seeking to illustrate this claim Nietzsche immediately evokes Kant, 'even in good old Kant: the categorical imperative smells of cruelty'.[68] Given that Kant, particularly in the dynamical sublime, insists on the mutually reinforcing nature of the moral and aesthetic spheres, it can be claimed that an abattoirial odour also pervades the 'negative pleasure' of AS. The HD readings of AS seem strangely blind to its darker themes of violence, sacrifice and their gruesome genealogy.[69]

Hence the oppositional Nietzschean stance towards AS has to be modified once it is appreciated that Kant does not pursue the project of moralisation for moral reasons. Rather, he non-repressively valorises the pleasures that characterise the Platonic-Christian libidinal-affective economy. Nietzsche describes the Platonic-Christian eroticism which, I suggest, marks AS, thus:

> there is an ... over-abundant enjoyment of one's suffering ... of making oneself suffer – and wherever man allows himself to be persuaded to self-denial in the *religious* sense, or to self-mutilation ... or in general to desen-

sualization, decarnalization, … he is secretly lured and urged onward by his cruelty, by the dangerous thrills of cruelty directed *against himself*.[70]

Hence, Kant's sublime is, arguably, an example of what Nietzsche termed the 'ever-growing intellectualization and "deification" of cruelty, which runs through the whole history of higher culture (and indeed, constitutes it in an important sense)'.[71] Nietzsche encapsulates this libidinal interpretation of the Platonic-Christian tradition thus: '[F]undamentally … everything sublime up to the highest and most refined thrills of metaphysics, derives its sweetness solely from the ingredient of cruelty mixed in with it'.[72]

Kant compellingly advocates the pleasures he identifies as a 'voluptuousness [of] the mind'.[73] AS is a febrile text which speaks of a 'vibration' (*Erschütterung*) that convulses the mind in the cross-currents of pleasure and pain flowing between the imagination and reason in the sublime.[74] Kant speaks of the 'sacred thrill' (*der heilige Schauer*) that arises from the 'sacrifice' of the imagination, and therewith nature.[75] Such passages describe a transcendental libidinal state beyond the pleasure/pain opposition.

A radical Nietzschean reading excavates in AS a non-moral problematisation of the pleasures of the body which are condemned on libidinal grounds as diminished intensities in comparison to the pleasures of reason, especially when accessed through the humiliation of the finite powers of the mind. In Foucault's terms, human beings are constitutively enmeshed within such *'perpetual spirals of power and pleasure'*.[76]

From the most radical Nietzschean perspective it is not the site of pleasure (i.e., mind or body) that is at question in a critical reading of AS but the assessment of the intensity and quality of the pleasures it valorises. Hence AS is not necessarily the expression of a 'slavish' type of will simply because it endorses the 'ascetic ideal'. Not all manifestations of the 'ascetic ideal' are, as Nietzsche insisted, necessarily to be condemned, nor are all 'sensualisms' to be affirmed. Such a dismissal of the pleasures AS extols would underwrite the very oppositional thinking that makes possible the metaphysical notion of a de-libidinised reason. The radical, immanent Nietzschean critical perspective demonstrates that such an ascetic conception of reason plays no part in AS.

VI

CJ seeks to universalise a particular affective-libidinal economy. In AS

Kant uninhibitedly affirms the pleasures of the rational-moral subject. From a Nietzschean perspective, the universalist pretensions of AS remain problematic, given Kant's equalisation of human beings expressed in the claim that, 'we presuppose moral feeling in man'.[77]

A revealing moment in Kant's rhetorical defence of the 'healthy' human type he promotes is the condemnation of the 'unrefined' or 'uncultured' individual *(der rohe Mensch)*.[78] This type is 'lacking in the development of moral ideas',[79] and thus unable to experience the pleasures of the sublime. When confronted by the 'contrapurposiveness' of 'raw nature' which leads the morally cultivated to experience the sublimity of reason, the 'uncultured' individual is only able to conceive 'nature's destructive force' pessimistically. This is due to their utilitarian outlook which entails that they can only interpret nature's indifference to the human in terms of 'hardship, danger, and misery'.[80]

Kant's opposition between the 'moral' and 'unrefined' types' response to 'raw nature' is part of a cultural-political agenda that asserts criteria for being human. This construction of the 'healthy' human tacitly excludes an aesthetic sensibility which affirms 'raw nature' as the occasion for the dissolution of the man/nature opposition AS institutes. Kant's critical teleological appropriation of aesthetic feeling excludes the, in Nietzsche's sense, 'noble' perspective which affirms the 'contrapurposiveness' of 'raw nature' as that which interrupts the theoretical and practical projects of man. Such a type has an affective-libidinal economy which feels pleasure on those occasions when it is disclosed that the primary processes of nature do not offer the slightest teleological support for the rational-moral ideals Kant valorises. Beyond the 'optimism' of the morally cultivated and the 'pessimism' of the morally retarded, Nietzsche celebrates the sublimity of the dissolution of 'man' through the affirmation of the Dionysian, or 'raw nature'.[81]

For Kant, a feeling for the sublime is 'prepared through culture'.[82] It is helpful here to recall Nietzsche's distinction between culture and civilisation,

> the high points of culture and civilization do not coincide: one should not be deceived by the abysmal antagonism of culture and civilization. The great moments of culture were always, morally speaking, times of corruption; and conversely, the periods when the taming of the human animal ("civilization") was desired and enforced were times of intolerance against the boldest and most spiritual natures. Civilization has aims different from those of culture –perhaps they are even opposite – .[83]

From this perspective AS is overwhelmingly concerned with the project of 'civilisation' rather than 'culture', with the task of containing the instinctual and material bases of human life.[84] Yet this apparently moral problematisation of the pleasures is undercut by Kant's engagement with the libidinal economy of the type he seeks to universalise. AS offers a libidinal critique of the pleasures of the 'uncultivated' type. It is not their lack of morality that Kant bemoans but rather the limited palette of pleasures available to them.

A Nietzschean *transvaluation* of Kant's aesthetics requires the affirmation of an aesthetic sensibility that does not share the goals of civilisation Kant pursues but which cannot be simply classified as 'uncultured'. The existence of an aesthetic feeling that is cultured but not civilised, that cultivates pleasures other than those of moralisation, undermines the universality Kant claims for the aesthetic sensibility he promotes. Hence even though Kant describes his conception of the sublime as 'noble',[85] from a Nietzschean perspective he could be said to be describing the aesthetic sensibility of the 'slave', characterised by a *ressentiment* against 'raw nature'. AS is thereby interpreted as a critical defence of the aesthetic sensibility of the 'slave' that insists on the 'subjective purposiveness' of aesthetic feeling rather than a 'noble' affirmation of radically dysteleological processes.

These contrasting evaluations of 'raw nature' are the expressions of radically different affective-libidinal types that pursue incommensurable pleasures, namely 'negative pleasure' (Kant) and 'tragic joy' (Nietzsche). The difficult task arising from the second, more radical, form of Nietzschean critique is that of the evaluative comparison of these qualitatively different affective-libidinal sensibilities.

A 'noble' aesthetic sensibility is thus absent from AS as the former rejects the value of the rational-moral subject and seeks to reverse the Kantian teleological trajectory by cultivating a type assimilable to 'raw nature' that does not resist its dysteleological trajectory. A 'tragic' cultural politics arises in which the absence of any hint of teleology in nature is taken as a comforting deflation of man, the re-engulfment of the human in an anonymous excess. Kant's sublime has no place for the aesthetic response to nature that aligns it with a 'becoming-other' in the sense of the dissolution of man into the sublimity of the impersonal material flux of the 'sea of forces flowing and rushing together'.[86] It is this 'extra-moral' sublimity that unmasks the anthropocentrism of the fallacy of subreption,[87] and provides the 'noble' libidinal-affective sensibility with its distinctive 'sacred thrill'.

Notes

1   Many examples are found in J.-F. Courtine et al, *Of the Sublime: Presence in Question*, trans. J. S. Librett (New York: SUNY Press, 1993). Hereafter *SPQ*. In the following I also consider further texts by Derrida, Lyotard and Sallis. There are, of course, many differences between these readings of AS. Nonetheless they share many assumptions about the nature of the reading AS requires today. I describe this approach as the 'Heideggerian-deconstructive' reading. Hereafter HD.

2   Kant, *CJ*, p.109, t.m.; *Ak*.V: 253.

3   Nancy, in Courtine et al, *SPQ*, p. 2.

4   Librett, in Courtine et al, *SPQ*, p. 194.

5   Lacoue-Labarthe, in Courtine et al, *SPQ*, p. 96.

6   Librett, in Courtine et al, *SPQ*, p. 207.

7   Escoubas, in Courtine et al, *SPQ*, p. 60.

8   Escoubas, in Courtine et al, *SPQ*, p. 69.

9   See Kant, *CJ*, pp. 107–14; *Ak*.V: 251–7.

10 Kant, *CJ*, p. 215; *Ak*.V: 342.

11 Jean-François Lyotard, *Lessons on the Analytic of the Sublime*, trans. E. Rotenberg (Stanford: Stanford University Press, 1994), p. 141. See also pp. 150–3, 210–15, 233–4. For HD readings of this theme that contrast with Lyotard, see Jean-Luc Nancy, *SPQ*, pp. 36ff and Escoubas, *SPQ*, p. 63.

12 Lyotard, *Lessons*, p. 141.

13 Of course, Heidegger's and Derrida's critique of metaphysics entails the overcoming of the supersensuous/sensuous and infinite/finite oppositions that structure AS (albeit in a critically delimited way) and which are presupposed by the notion of 'negative presentation'. For an excellent discussion of this theme see Philipe Lacoue-Labarthe, 'Sublime Truth', in *SPQ*, pp. 71–109.

14 See Lyotard, *Lessons*, pp. 147–53, 234.

15 John Sallis, *Spacings – of Reason and Imagination in Texts of Kant, Fichte, Hegel* (Chicago: Chicago University Press, 1987), p. 115.

16 Sallis, *Spacings*, p. 119.

17 See Kant, *CJ*, pp. 115, 124, 130; *Ak*.V: 258, 265, 270.

18 Kant, *CJ*, p. 115; *Ak*.V: 258.

19 Sallis, *Spacings*, p. 130.

20 Escoubas, Courtine et al, *SPQ*, p. 62.

21 I discuss this issue in '"Noble" Ascesis: Between Nietzsche and Foucault', *New Nietzsche Studies* 2:3/4 (1998) 65–91.

22 Rudolf Makkreel notes that for Kant the absence of form is not a necessary condition of the sublime. See Rudolf Makkreel, *Imagination and Interpretation in Kant: The Hermeneutical Import of the Critique of Judgment* (Chicago: University of Chicago Press, 1990), p. 85. However, it is clearly the aesthetic response to the 'formless object' (Kant, *CJ*, p. 98; *Ak*.V: 244) that is

Kant's main concern in AS.

23   Kant, *CJ*, pp. 99–100; *Ak*.V: 246.

24   Kant, *CJ*, p. 99; *Ak*.V: 246.

25   Derrida considers the theme of 'raw nature' but does not challenge Kant's response to it in the way I develop here. See Jacques Derrida, *The Truth in Painting*, trans. G. Bennington and I. McLeod (Chicago: University of Chicago Press, 1987), pp. 123, 127, 132, 143. Kant's notion of 'raw nature' in AS is, in many respects, akin to what Bataille terms 'base matter'. Both thinkers link the encounter with such a radically unassimilable materiality with the sublime but offer very different evaluations of it. Nonetheless, from the immanent Nietzschean perspective I outline in this paper the difference between Kant's and Bataille's conceptions of the sublime cannot be viewed as a contrast between a 'moral' and a 'transgressive' thinker. Indeed, from such a perspective it becomes highly questionable as to which account of the sublime is the more erotically charged. For Bataille's conception of the relation between 'base matter' and the sublime see Georges Bataille, *Visions of Excess: Selected Writings 1927–39*, ed. A. Stoekl (Minneapolis: University of Minnesota Press, 1985), pp. 15–16, 51, 142.

26   Kant, *CJ*, p. 115; *Ak*.V: 258.

27   Kant, *CJ*, p. 116; *Ak*.V: 259. For an excellent account of this aspect of AS see Makkreel, *Imagination and Interpretation in Kant*, pp. 78–87.

28   Kant, *CJ*, pp. 115–16; *Ak*.V: 258.

29   The barely concealed normativity of Kant's account of the 'subjective purposiveness' of the relation between the faculties in the sublime does, occasionally, become explicit. An example is the discussion of the 'fanaticism', 'delusion', 'madness' and 'mania' (Kant, *CJ*, pp. 135–6; *Ak*.V: 275) that ensues if the proper relation between the imagination and reason is violated.

30   Kant, *CJ*, p. 120; *Ak*.V: 261.

31   Lyotard, *Lessons*, pp. 19–26, 141–6 and Makkreel, *Imagination and Interpretation in Kant*, pp. 67–77, 86, offer contrasting accounts of how the domain of inner sense as described in *CPR* is exceeded in the sublime. A key focus for these commentators, and others such as Sallis (see *Spacings*, p. 127), is Kant's account of the 'regress' of the imagination and 'aesthetic comprehension' in the 'mathematical sublime' (Kant, *CJ*, p.116; *Ak*.V: 258-9). The most ambitious claims for the radicality of this aspect of AS are made by J. Rogozinski in 'The Gift of the World', *SPQ*, pp. 133–56.

32   Kant, *CJ*, p. 120; *Ak*.V: 261.

33   Kant, *CJ*, p. 120; *Ak*.V: 261.

34   Kant, *CJ*, p. 121; *Ak*.V: 262.

35   Kant, *CJ*, p. 120; *Ak*.V: 261.

36   See Kant, *CJ*, p. 121; *Ak*.V: 262.

37   Kant, *CJ*, p. 99; *Ak*.V: 245.

38 Kant,*CJ*, p. 114; *Ak*.V: 257.
39 Kant, *CJ*, p. 99; *Ak*.V: 245.
40 Kant, *CJ*, p. 114; *Ak*.V: 257.
41 Kant, *CJ*, p. 100; *Ak*.V: 246.
42 Kant, *CJ*, p. 100; *Ak*.V: 246.
43 See Sallis, *Spacings*, p. 99. For an interesting discussion of Kant's account of the distinction between the beautiful and the sublime in terms of being 'at home in nature' rather than 'not at home in nature' see Howard Caygill, *Art of Judgment* (Oxford: Blackwell, 1989), pp. 339–47.
44 Kant, *CJ*, p. 99; *Ak*.V: 246.
45 Kant, *CJ*, p. 100; *Ak*.V: 246.
46 Kant, *CJ*, pp. 120–1; *Ak*.V: 261.
47 Kant, *CJ*, p. 128; *Ak*.V: 268.
48 I refer here to Nietzsche's exposure of the 'paradox' inherent in proponents of the 'ascetic ideal'. See Friedrich Nietzsche, *On the Genealogy of Morality*, trans. C. Diethe (Cambridge: Cambridge University Press, 1994), III: 11–13, pp. 89–94. Hereafter *GM*.
49 Kant, *CJ*, p. 115; *Ak*.V: 258.
50 For an excellent analysis of this theme see Makkreel, *Imagination and Interpretation in Kant*, pp. 88–99. See also J. H. Zammito, *The Genesis of Kant's Critique of Judgment* (Chicago: University of Chicago Press, 1992), pp. 292–305.
51 Kant, *CJ*, p. 98; *Ak*.V: 244
52 Kant, *CJ*, p. 98; *Ak*.V: 245.
53 Kant, *CJ*, p. 98; *Ak*.V: 245.
54 Kant, *CJ*, p. 120; *Ak*.V: 261.
55 Kant, *CJ*, pp. 120–1; *Ak*.V: 261–2.
56 Kant, *CJ*, p. 99; *Ak*.V: 245.
57 Kant, *CJ*, p. 98; *Ak*.V: 245.
58 Such a reading does not offer a psycho-sexual biographical or personalist analysis insofar as the libidinal-affective processes it thematises are anonymous.
59 Kant, *CJ*, p. 116; *Ak*.V: 258.
60 In general terms I apply to AS the Nietzsche-inspired insights of Foucault's 'critique of the repressive hypothesis'. See Michel Foucault, *The History of Sexuality: Volume One*, trans. R. Hurley (Harmondsworth: Penguin, 1981), pp. 15–49.
61 Kant, *CJ*, p. 99; *Ak*.V: 245.
62 Friedrich Nietzsche, *The Will to Power*, trans. W. Kaufmann and R. J. Hollingdale (New York: Random House, 1967), no. 387, p. 208. Hereafter *WP*.
63 See Friedrich Nietzsche, *Thus Spoke Zarathustra*, trans. R. J. Hollingdale (Harmondsworth: Penguin, 1969), p. 235.

64   Kant, *CJ*, p. 117; *Ak*.V: 260.
65   Nietzsche, *GM*, II: 6, p. 45.
66   Nietzsche, *GM*, II: 7, p. 46.
67   Nietzsche, *GM*, II: 6, p. 45.
68   Nietzsche, *GM*, II: 6, p. 45.
69   For an exceptional discussion of these themes in AS see Nick Land,
     'Delighted to Death', *Pli: Warwick Journal of Philosophy* 3:2 (1991) 76–88.
     See also J. Protevi, 'Violence and Authority in Kant', *Epoché* 2:1 (1994)
     65–89.
70   Friedrich Nietzsche, *Beyond Good and Evil*, trans. R. J. Hollingdale (Har-
     mondsworth: Penguin, 1973), pp. 140–1. Hereafter *BGE*.
71   Nietzsche, *GM*, II: 6, p. 46. See also Nietzsche, *BGE*, p. 140; *GM*, II: 18,
     pp. 63–4; III: 11, 12, pp. 89–92.
72   Nietzsche, *BGE*, p. 141.
73   Kant, *CJ*, p. 167, t.m.; *Ak*.V: 300.
74   Kant, *CJ*, p. 115; *Ak*.V: 258.
75   Kant, *CJ*, p. 129; *Ak*.V: 269.
76   Foucault, *The History of Sexuality*, p. 45.
77   Kant, *CJ*, p. 125; *Ak*.V: 266.
78   Kant, *CJ*, p. 124; *Ak*.V: 265.
79   Ibid.
80   Ibid.
81   I outline a conception of a Nietzschean sublime in '"A Pessimism of
     Strength": Nietzsche and the Tragic Sublime', in *Nietzsche's Futures*, ed. J.
     Lippitt (London: Macmillan, 1999), pp. 129–48.
82   Kant, *CJ*, p. 124; *Ak*.V: 265.
83   Nietzsche, *WP*, no.121, p. 75. Similarly Nietzsche claims that, 'culture is
     destroyed by belief in morality', *WP*, no.151, p. 95.
84   See Kant, *CJ*, pp. 163–4, 188; *Ak*.V: 296–7, 319.
85   Kant, *CJ*, p. 133; *Ak*.V: 272.
86   Nietzsche, *WP*, no.1067, p. 550.
87   Kant, *CJ*, p. 114; *Ak*.V: 257.

5

Life and Aesthetic Pleasure

Howard Caygill

The ubiquity of the concept of life in Kant's *Critique of Judgement* has been accompanied by a striking absence of critical discussion.[1] Not only is 'life' put under direct and sustained scrutiny in the largely ignored *Critique of Teleological Judgement* – but it also directs, or rather disrupts, the progress of the argument in the *Critique of Aesthetic Judgement*. Pleasure in the beautiful is there defined in terms of the 'feeling of life' or 'a feeling of the furtherance of life'.[2] The critical neglect of Kant's concept of life not only obscures many aspects of his account of aesthetic pleasure but serves also to mask a fundamental shift in the critical philosophy between the first and the third *Critiques*, one that Kant himself was reluctant to acknowledge. This involved the movement away from the representational model of consciousness that dominated the first *Critique* to the more dynamic and corporeal model that emerges episodically in the third. It is a shift signalled by a change in the conduct of the critical argument from a juridical concern with the legitimacy of representations to what might be described as an economic concern with the distribution (promotion and hindrance) of the forces that constitute life. This shift entailed the extension of the dynamic concept of matter to life itself and, while providing a solution to the riddle of aesthetic pleasure, raised for Kant the spectre of hylozoism and the death of philosophy.

Kant's growing realisation that the concept of life troubled the representational model of consciousness can be traced through the pre-critical *Lectures on Metaphysics*, but it is only in the third *Critique* that he admits its full implications. Yet even here the concept emerges episodically alongside and in competition with the representational model, occasionally even grafting itself on to and scrambling the language of representation. This process of interruption and scrambling is most evident in Kant's discussions of aesthetic pleasure, where the nature of the experience described most resists the representational model of consciousness. Kant's analysis of aesthetic pleasure has always provoked problems for the understanding of the critical philosophy, seeming to point to an experience that resists formalisation, but which nevertheless can be broken down into an analogue of the table of categories. It will be suggested that the difficulty with aesthetic pleasure stems from the relationship Kant insists upon between it and a non-representational concept of life.

Three important *loci* in the *Critique of Judgement* for the alignment of aesthetic pleasure and life are to be found in §§ 1, 23 and 29. The first, at the very beginning of the Analytic of the Beautiful (§1), offers a fine example of Kant's scrambling of the language of representation by a concept of life that exceeds it. Kant begins by distinguishing between the cognitive representation of a 'regular, purposive building' and the 'conscious representation' of it attended by 'a sensation of delight.'[3] His analysis of the latter – the debut of aesthetic pleasure – constitutes one of the most obscure sentences in the third *Critique*. In it the non-cognitive representation at issue 'is tied [*bezogen*] wholly to the subject, indeed to the feeling of life itself, under the name of the feeling of pleasure and displeasure.'[4] The latter feeling 'grounds a quite particular capacity for distinguishing and estimating' that compares 'the given representation in the subject with that whole capacity for representations of which the *Gemüt* in feeling its state, becomes conscious.'[5] The transfers carried out in this passage by means of the conjunctives 'tied', 'founds' and 'compares' are dizzying: the representation is referred to the subject and the feeling of life, the latter to the feeling of pleasure and displeasure and this in turn to a capacity of discrimination that returns the original representation to a comparison with the 'capacity' of representation of which the *Gemüt* (a term inconsistently translated as 'mind' or 'soul' but having a far more complex meaning that will emerge below) becomes conscious when feeling its condition.

Before referring this movement of representation to an aporetic reflexivity it would be well to look at the other passages aligning life and aesthetic pleasure. In §23, the first section of the Analytic of the Sublime, Kant distinguishes between the satisfaction provided by the beautiful and the sublime in terms of a dynamics of vital forces. While the beautiful 'directly brings with it a feeling of the furtherance of life,' the sublime provokes an 'indirect' pleasure in 'the feeling of a momentary checking of the vital powers and a consequent stronger outflow of them'.[6] The difference in the modality of the pleasures arises from the immediate promotion of the feeling of life produced by the beautiful and the interruption and subsequent reactivation of the vital forces by the sublime. What remains unexplained is the feeling of life or vital force itself and what it might mean for it to be promoted or hindered.

The term 'feeling of life' is common to both §1 and §23, but it is not used in the same sense in the two passages. In the first passage it is couched in the language of representation and aligned with terms such as 'subject', 'faculty of distinction', 'whole faculty of representations',[7] while in the second it is inseparable from the language of dynamics. While a linking argument between the two passages might be contrived in terms of the feelings of pleasure and pain and direct/indirect pleasure this would not fully explain the operations of the feeling of life and thus leaves unexplained the very aesthetic pleasure that is the focus of the analysis.

The chase of the 'feeling of life' is sent off in yet another direction by the reference in §29 where Kant explores the different effects sensible and intelligible representations can have on 'the feeling of life'. Referring ambiguously to Epicurus, he concedes that 'all *gratification* or *grief* may ultimately be corporeal' for the reason that 'life without a feeling of bodily organs would be merely a consciousness of existence, without any feeling of well-being or the reverse, i.e. of the furthering or the checking of the vital powers.'[8] Here life is tied to the bodily organs and the feeling of corporeal well-being to the promotion of the vital powers. Kant continues with the intriguing definition that 'the *Gemüt* is by itself alone wholly life (the principle of life itself), and hindrances or furtherances of it must be sought outside it and yet in man, consequently in union with his body.'[9] The *Gemüt* is identified with life, but the dynamic of life is located inside and outside man, consequently in the body which for Kant seems to be simultaneously interior and exterior.

The third passage adds to the previous pair the thoughts that the *Gemüt* is life and that promotion and furtherance of it involves the body. From this it may be seen that the *Gemüt* forms the link between the discussion of representation in §1 and that of vital dynamics in §§23 and 29. In the former, when the *Gemüt* is affected by its condition it becomes aware of the whole faculty of representations. This awareness permits a given representation to be compared with the whole faculty through the discriminations provided by the feeling of pleasure and pain. Yet these in their turn are but the name given to the 'feeling of life'. If the results of §§23 and 29 are factored into this account the result is even more confusing: in these the *Gemüt* is life, and pleasure and pain the effect of its promotion or hindrance. Perhaps pleasure and pain are diagnostic aids for assessing the impact of a given representation on the life of the organism, but this would require a very special concept of representation which would be governed less by its relation to an object than to the feeling of life in general. If not, there seems no obvious way of reconciling the accounts founded in representation and in vital dynamics.

It is hard to avoid the suspicion that the difficult linkage between the concept of life and aesthetic pleasure indicates a fault line running across Kant's philosophy. The suspicion is both confirmed and complicated by an analysis of the origins of these concepts and arguments in Kant's earlier work. The pre-occupations that surface in the third *Critique* may certainly be traced to the lectures on anthropology and theology,[10] but more revealingly to the *Lectures on Metaphysics*, appearing in an already developed state as early as *Metaphysik L₁* from the mid-1770s.[11] From this and later transcripts of Kant's *Lectures on Metaphysics* it can be shown that the discussions of life in terms of representation and dynamics emerged from different parts of the lecture course and were set in different argumentative contexts and directed to very different ends. The tension between them was intensified when they were brought into proximity with each other as in the analyses of aesthetic pleasure.

Kant lectured on metaphysics according to Baumgarten's *Metaphysics*, a text officially approved for instruction in the Prussian universities.[12] Baumgarten was a follower of the influential early Enlightenment philosopher Christian Wolff, and was orthodox in most respects except in his view of the relationship between reason and sensibility. In this he was closer to Leibniz than to Wolff, maintaining a continuum between sensibility and reason and claiming that sensible knowledge is not simply the corruption of rational knowledge but has its own *aesthetic* perfection. Baumgarten illustrated these laws by means of the example of art in his *Reflections on Poetry* (*Meditationes philosophicae de nonnullis ad poema pertinibus*; 1735) and his incomplete *Aesthetica* (1750–8).[13] In the *Metaphysics* he largely follows the Wolffian architectonic established in Wolff's *Rational Thoughts on God, the World and the Human Soul as well as Things in General* (originally published in 1719),[14] which organised the materials of metaphysics according to the headings of ontology ('things in general'), cosmology ('the world'), empirical and rational psychology ('the soul') and theology ('God'), a pattern that persisted into Kant's first *Critique*. The main discussions of life and aesthetic pleasure are to be found in the commentaries on empirical and on rational psychology. The former consists of a description of the parts and functions of the representational power of the human soul according to cognition and appetition while the latter considers rational attributes of the soul such as its relation to the body and its immortality. The character and extent of Kant's discussion of empirical as opposed to rational psychology shows his preference for the former, as does his carrying over of much of its material into his lectures on anthropology and theology.

The extended commentary on Baumgarten's discussion of the appetitive faculties and functions of pleasure and displeasure,[15] recorded in *Metaphysik L₁* (mid-1770s) and later transcripts such as *Metaphysik Mrongovius* (1782–3) and *Metaphysik Vigilantius* (1794–5),[16] can be identified as the matrix of the link between pleasure, representation and life established in §1 of the *Critique of Judgement*. The transcript of the *Lectures on Metaphysics* from the 1770s anticipates the *Critique* in proposing a 'faculty for distinguishing things according to the feeling of pleasure and displeasure, or of satisfaction and dissatisfaction' apart from the faculty of cognition.[17] It serves as a supplementary faculty insofar as it is interested in the affective sense of representations already given by the cognitive faculty – as a faculty of sense it relies on the cognitive faculty for its representations: 'All pleasure and displeasure presupposes cognition of an object'.[18] However, the predicates pleasure and displeasure do not refer to the object of representation, but rather to 'the faculty in us for being affected by things.'[19] At this point Kant insists on departing from Baumgarten's view that pleasure is the outcome of the sensible perception of a perfection, thus establishing the position presented over a decade later in §1 of the *Critique of Judgement*.

In *Metaphysik L₁* the intent of Kant's disagreement with Baumgarten and the motivation of his original position on pleasure is much more apparent. The difference between his and Baumgarten's position is stated in terms of quality and modality: Baumgarten's aesthetic rests on the quality of an object (its perfection) while Kant's concerns the relation of an object to the subject, in his terms, its modality: 'With pleasure and displeasure what matters is not the object, but rather *how* the object affects the mind.'[20] The faculty of pleasure and displeasure, he continues, distinguishes objects 'not [according to] what is met with in themselves, but rather [according to] how the representation of them makes an impression on our subject, and how our feeling is moved there by [sic]'.[21] While the stress upon the modal operation of the faculty illuminates the passage in the third *Critique*, it does not solve the problems of the vital sources of pleasure and displeasure or the nature of the judgement couched in terms of life.

Kant attempts to clarify the modality of pleasure in the next paragraph of *Metaphysik L₁*. He states that representations are 'two-fold' – of the object or the subject – which means that they are comparable 'either with the objects or with the entire life of the subject.'[22] The two-fold character of the representation is asymmetrical, with objects on the one side and 'the entire life of the subject' on the other. Kant gives an important clue to the modal character of pleasure when he describes pleasure and displeasure as the 'subjective representation of the entire power of life for receiving or excluding objects' or again 'for either most inwardly receiving them or excluding them.'[23] The movement of reception into the power of life, or exclusion from it, mirrors Kant's understanding of matter in terms of the forces of attraction and repulsion.[24] The power of life either attracts and is attracted to the object – so much so that it would incorporate it – or it is repulsed by the object. At this point Kant disappointingly announces that '[m]ore cannot be said of this here',[25] only to go on and, indeed, to say more, but prefaced by a cautionary elision of objective and subjective cognition with Baumgarten's theory of logical and aesthetic perfection.

In the following two paragraphs of the lectures Kant gives an extended development of what will become the compressed thought of §29 of the *Critique of Judgement*, namely that the *Gemüt* is the life principle. He begins by defining life as the 'inner principle for acting from representations' then modulates it first into the 'principle of life' and then into 'the entire power of the *Gemüt*'.[26] If a given representation 'harmonizes' with this principle/power of life/*Gemüt* 'then this is *pleasure*'; if, however, it 'resists' the principle/power then 'this relation of conflict in us is *displeasure*'.[27] The account of pleasure here suppresses a stage in the argument revealed in that of displeasure. This is the stage of the receptivity of the representation by life/*Gemüt* which produces harmony and then pleasure just as the resistance and exclusion of a representation produces conflict, and this displeasure. Yet the movement of representation – reception/exclusion – harmony/conflict – pleasure/displeasure remains difficult to follow, given the lack of definition of life itself. Kant replays the argument in reverse: objects are not intrinsically beautiful but only '*in reference to living beings*', a phrase he repeats in order to fix the ground of the predicate '*in the living being*' or that faculty in the living being 'for perceiving such properties in objects.'[28] The *explanandum* – the peculiar faculty of discrimination – has now become the *explanans*, only for it in its turn to be once again explained in terms of the 'agreement or ... conflict of the principle of life with respect to certain representations or impressions of objects.'[29]

The peculiar circularity in the argument between faculty of discrimination, the affects of pleasure and displeasure and the principle of life seems to arise from treating the life principle as a state with which a representation can harmonise or come into conflict rather than as a dynamic movement of attraction and repulsion. If life is a given state – as it is whenever the *Gemüt* is described in terms of the faculties of intuition, imagination, understanding and reason – then there is need of a faculty to adjudicate whether a given representation does or does not accord with the organisation of the life principle into faculties. However, Kant repeatedly undermines this understanding of life by returning to the view that it is a dynamic process of reception and expulsion.

Such a return is evident in the subsequent paragraph where Kant attempts to sharpen the dynamic view of life already intimated. He begins with another definition. Instead of the earlier definition of life as the 'inner principle for acting from representations' which privileges representation and implicitly objectivity, he now defines life as simply 'the inner principle of self-activity' without privileging representation. Self-activity is governed by an inner principle, and while Kant concedes that this must 'act according to representations', this conformity is now secondary to the dynamics of life.[30] The principle at issue is no longer thought in terms of representation, but in terms of an immanent self-activity which might involve representation, but is not defined by it. Kant examines this 'inner principle' more closely, rephrasing the modality of this self-activity – earlier described in terms of reception/expulsion – as the promotion or hindrance of life. While in the earlier paragraph the representation remained important as the spur to the activity of life – it could either be received or expelled – now it simply supplements an existing movement, either promoting or hindering the activity of the life principle. From this point of view the 'feeling of the promotion of life is pleasure, and the feeling of the hindrance of life is displeasure.'[31] From this he moves to the more audacious claims, first that pleasure and displeasure are grounds of activity and the hindrance of activity, and then that pleasure 'consists in desiring', displeasure 'in abhorring.'[32] With the introduction of desire the receptive/exclusive movement returns, but this time not in terms dictated by the digestive movement of reception/exclusion but in terms of a promotion/hindrance of life which is ultimately determined by the future continuation or cessation of the activity of life itself.

At this point in the development of his argument Kant breaks off and turns to an illuminating discussion of the three forms of life: animal, human and spiritual, which he maps on to the distinctions between the agreeable, the beautiful and the good, later to become prominent in the architectonic of the third *Critique*. While this discussion offers some fascinating insights into the motivation underlying the argument of the Analytic of the Beautiful, it is notable that in the latter the discussion of life *per se* all but disappears. It persists in terms of the grades of activity provoked by the agreeable, the beautiful and the good, but the issue of the vital sources of the pleasure so distributed remains shelved. The concept of life will return later in the lecture series in the context of a discussion of death in the section on rational psychology.

The discussion of life and aesthetic pleasure provoked by the commentary on Baumgarten's empirical psychology moved beyond the confines of aesthetic perfection but did not provide a full and satisfactory account of Kant's alternative. Pleasure and displeasure are referred to life, but the concept remains undeveloped. *Metaphysik L₁*, however, shows that Kant's views on the subject of life were already highly developed before the critical philosophy. There the discussion moved from the comparison by a faculty of discrimination of a representation with a static vital principle to a working of the vital principle, first according to a modality of reception/expulsion, and then to one of promotion/hindrance. It is the latter, the second dynamic model, that persists into the third *Critique*, evident both in §§23 and 29, where it supplements the version founded in representation based on a problematic faculty of discrimination proposed in §1.

Kant's position on life and aesthetic pleasure does not show signs of having developed substantially in the subsequent transcripts of his comments on empirical psychology in his *Lectures on Metaphysics*. In *Metaphysik Mrongovius* from 1782–3 (after the publication of the *Critique of Pure Reason* in 1781), the discussion of life is largely avoided, reduced to one cryptic reference. The assumption that this reflects a change in the content of Kant's lectures rather than the quality of Mrongovius' note-taking is supported by the usually reliable and exhaustive character of Mrongovius' transcript and the omission of the discussion from the transcript of 1790–1, the *Metaphysik L₂*.[33] The transcript from 1794–5, *Metaphysik Vigilantius*, shows evidence of the results of the third *Critique* in its distinction between sensible gratification/pain and reflective pleasure/displeasure, but it avoids the problem of determining the ground of reflective aesthetic pleasure. As in the third *Critique*, so here too Kant refers reflective aesthetic pleasure to the harmony of the *Gemütskräfte* or the notorious free-play of the imagination and the lawfulness of the understanding,[34] which here, as also on occasions in the third *Critique*, masquerades as an *explanans* rather than an *explanandum*. Yet it was already evident in *Metaphysik L₁*, as also throughout the *Critique of Judgement*, that there is a level of explanation for aesthetic pleasure and displeasure anterior to the harmony of the *Gemütskräfte*.

The development of this level of argument is to be found in the *Lectures on Metaphysics* during Kant's reflections on rational psychology, but here the dynamic conception of life appears in a context quite distinct from that of the empirical psychology. In his comments on Baumgarten's paragraphs on the state of the soul after death,[35] which address the question of whether the soul will continue to live after the death of the body, Kant offers some fascinating clarifications of his concept of life, but in abstraction from the particular problem of the nature of aesthetic pleasure and displeasure.

Kant's discussion of life in the context of rational psychology is consistent with the discussion earlier in the lecture course of pleasure and displeasure, characteristically clarifying and extending it in some ways while complicating it in others. Life is initially defined as 'a faculty for acting from an *inner* principle, from spontaneity.'[36] This faculty or 'source' that 'animates the body' is described as an *actus*. The *actus* of life animates the matter of the body which is itself 'lifeless' and indeed serves as a 'hindrance to life that opposes the principle of life.'[37] Here matter serves the same function as the displeasurable representation earlier in the empirical psychology, that is, of hindering life. Life itself is an *actus* independent of the body. While the soul is the principle of life, the body is its tool or *organon*. The discussion of rational psychology in the lectures deriving from pre-critical, critical, and post-critical stages of Kant's authorship remains faithful to the broad project of Baumgarten's metaphysical textbook. Their rational psychology departs from the *a priori* distinction between two substances – soul and matter – and seeks to combine them in a *commercio*.

Kant's fidelity to the rational metaphysical tradition goes as far as describing the corporeal *organon* as a cart and the *commercio* between soul and body as analogous to that of 'a human being … fastened to a cart.'[38] Even given the parody of Plato's *Phaedrus*, the latter analogy is rather surprising, since it might be expected for the soul to occupy the position of the driver rather than the horse, but Kant's analogy is ruthlessly consistent. The cart's motion proceeds from the human being who

pulls it: best for that human would be liberation from the cart, but failing that, the lot of the human horse would be improved if 'the wheels on
the cart [were] greased'.[39] The effects of greasing or not greasing the
wheels are described in terms, familiar to us from another context, of
the promotion or hindrance of life: 'if the soul is once bound to the body,
then the alteration of the hindrances is a promotion of life; just as
motion is easier when the wheels on the cart are greased, although it
would be even easier upon liberation from the cart.'[40] Life, or the *actus*
of the soul, becomes the motive power of the body, which as 'lifeless
matter ... is a hindrance to life' and for which 'a good constitution of the
body is also a promotion of life'.[41] In this view, death is the maximum
promotion of life, being 'not the absolute suspension of life, but rather
a liberation from the hindrances to a complete life.'[42]

Although Kant destroyed the foundations of rational psychology in
the Transcendental Dialectic of the *Critique of Pure Reason*, he continued to teach the analogy of the human horse and cart. In *Metaphysik
Mrongovius* (1782–3), the unfortunate human is even 'welded' to the
cart and its death described as the 'promotion of the life of the soul',[43]
while in *Metaphysik K$_2$* from the early 1790s (that is, after the publication of the *Critique of Judgement* in 1790) the human is still welded to the
cart, but the latter is now significantly described as a 'support' of life and
not simply an obstacle to it.[44] This modification is taken further in *Metaphysik Vigilantius* (1794–5), reflecting a change in Kant's understanding
of life provoked by the composition of the third *Critique*.

Before looking more closely at these changes it is necessary to review
the tension between the accounts of life given in the two parts of the
Lectures on Metaphysics and their persistence into the third *Critique*. The
work of the pleasant representation in promoting life in the empirical
psychology is undertaken in the rational psychology by the application
of grease to the body/cart that must be dragged forward by the soul.
Given the linkage between aesthetic pleasure and the promotion of life
pursued in the third *Critique*, the implication here is that the work of art
serves as the grease for lubricating the *commercio* between soul and
body. This is an intriguing implication, with its possible intimation of a
'materialist aesthetics', but it is not entirely consistent; nor is the further
implication that the representation which most promotes life is the one
that ends it, although this is admittedly a position not far removed from
the characterisation of the sublime in the third *Critique*.

The view of promotion and hindrance of life in the lectures on empirical psychology rested on a movement of reception and expulsion wholly

inconsistent with the analogy of a rickshaw used in the lectures on rational psychology. The former view implied that this movement is internal to life itself, that life relates to matter in terms of an immanent movement or *actus* of incorporation and expulsion but not in terms of the interaction or *commercio* of distinct substances. The view of life as immanent movement fundamentally questions the opposition between life partaking of the spontaneity of the soul in opposition to the dead materiality of the body, and its corollary that the two substances may enter into *commercio* only through representation. While the concept of life developed in the empirical psychology brings together corporeality and consciousness in an expanded *Gemüt*, that of the rational psychology opposes soul to matter.

Kant sketches an outline of his expanded concept of *Gemüt* in the passage from §29 of the *Critique of Judgement* that identifies *Gemüt* and an immanent life principle and suggests that its hindrance and promotion is to be sought 'outside it and yet inside man, consequently in union with his body'.[45] The body is no longer external dead materiality, fit only to be expelled by life, but the site of the movement of life in receiving and expelling, a movement distributed topologically in terms of an identical inside/outside. While further specification of this concept of the *Gemüt* must be sought outside of the *Critique*, in the *Lectures on Metaphysics* from the 1790s, it is clear that it is quite distinct from any view of the representational 'mind' or 'soul' as the site of *commercio* between opposed material and intelligible substances.

The move towards a corporeal concept of life announced in a preliminary way in §29 of the third *Critique* is developed a little further in *Metaphysik K$_2$* with the notion of the body as a support for the soul, but most fully in *Metaphysik Vigilantius*. Here Kant qualifies the tenets of rational psychology by first rehearsing the demonstration that life may be hindered by matter and then moving to a fundamental distinction between '*the principle of life*' and the '<*actu*> *of life itself*'.[46] The *actus* is inseparable from the body, not in the sense of being 'welded' to it as its ineluctable adversary, but as a corporeal manifestation of life – or, to use Kant's word, as *Gemüt*. The co-operation of the body with the *actus* of life 'visibly manifests itself' – makes what is internal external – 'through sensation as the consequence of these actions of life'.[47] Appropriate to the context, Kant's examples are largely negative, involving the 'sacrifice of powers', such as fatigue,[48] but the argument also holds for other sensations of life, such as pleasure. In this, too, the *actus* of life visibly manifests itself through the medium of the body, a movement implied in the pleasure of the aesthetic judgement of taste. Here the beautiful representation promotes the actualisation of life by a homeopathic dose of the hylozoic union of soul and matter.

In *Metaphysik K₂* Kant described hylozoism as 'the death of all philosophy', but this in a context that already foresaw a qualification of the lifeless materiality of the body.⁴⁹ The latter only holds if opposed and complemented by a 'principle of life', and not if life is thought as an *actus* or *Gemüt* that for Kant is both inside and outside the body. The externality of the *actus* of life to matter is thus qualified in a way that makes sense of the relation between life and pleasure but at the cost of abandoning the basic platonic structure of the 'philosophy' that would meet its end through hylozoism. This problem tormented the *Opus postumum* where Kant distinguished between matter and living or organic bodies, mainly in terms of the presence of ends and thus of desire in the latter. Yet time after time in the late notes Kant confronts the forces of attraction and repulsion that govern matter with the forces of life, or the movement of organic bodies, only to resist any transition from the first to the second through the interplay or transposition of forces. He insists on viewing living bodies as absolutely spontaneous and governed by ends given by means of representation. The emphasis on the representation of ends necessary to protect philosophy from hylozoism is ultimately destructive of pleasure, perversely locating the promotion of life in death. Even at the end of Kant's authorship, and in spite of his most astute intuitions, the experience of pleasure and its link to the concept of life remained a question that could not be explicitly answered.

Notes

1 All references to the *Critique of Judgement* (*CoJ*) in this paper are to the translation by J. H. Bernard (New York: Hafner Press, 1951).

2 Kant, *CoJ*, p. 38 and p. 83; *Ak*.V: 204 and 244.

3 Kant, *CoJ*, p. 38, t.m.; *Ak*.V: 204.

4 Kant, *CoJ*, p. 38, t.m.; *Ak*.V: 204.

5 Kant, *CoJ*, p. 38, t.m.; *Ak*.V: 204.

6 Kant, *CoJ*, p. 83; *Ak*.V: 244–5.

7 Kant, *CoJ*, p. 38; *Ak*.V: 204.

8 Kant, *CoJ*, p. 119; *Ak*.V: 277–8.

9 Kant, *CoJ*, p. 119, t.m.; *Ak*.V: 278.

10 See ch. 4 in Howard Caygill, *Art of Judgement* (Oxford: Basil Blackwell, 1989).

11 Kant, *Metaphysik L₁* (mid-1770s), in *Lectures on Metaphysics* (*LM*), pp.

17–106; *Ak*.XXVIII: 195–301.

12   See the selections from the *Metaphysica*, in A. G. Baumgarten, *Texte zur Grundlegung der Ästhetik*, ed. Hans Rudolf Schweizer (Hamburg: Felix Meiner Verlag, 1983).

13   A. G. Baumgarten, *Reflections on Poetry: A. G. Baumgarten's Meditationes philosophicae de nonnullis ad poema pertinibus*, trans. Karl Aschenbrenner and W. B. Holther (Berkeley and Los Angeles: University of California Press, 1954); and *Aesthetica,* in *Ästhetik als Philosophie der sinnlichen Erkenntnis*, trans. Hans Rudolf Schweizer (Basel and Stuttgart: Schwabe & Co, 1973).

14   Wolff, *Rational Thoughts on God, the World and the Human Soul as well as Things in General*, in *Metafisica Tedesca*, ed. Raffaele Ciafardone (Milan: Rusconi, 1999).

15   Baumgarten, *Metaphysica*, §§ 655–62.

16   Kant, *Metaphysik Mrongovius* (1782–3), in *LM*, pp. 107–286; *Ak*.XXIX: 747–940; and *Metaphysik Vigilantius* (K$_3$)(1794–5), in *LM*, pp. 415–506; *Ak*.XXIX: 943–1040.

17   Kant, *Metaphysik L$_1$, LM*, p. 62; *Ak*.XXVIII: 245.

18   Kant, *Metaphysik L$_1$, LM*, p. 62; *Ak*.XXVIII: 246.

19   Kant, *Metaphysik L$_1$, LM*, pp. 62–3; *Ak*.XXVIII: 246.

20   Kant, *Metaphysik L$_1$, LM*, p. 63; *Ak*.XXVIII: 246.

21   Kant, *Metaphysik L$_1$, LM*, p. 63; *Ak*.XXVIII: 246.

22   Kant, *Metaphysik L$_1$, LM*, p. 63; *Ak*.XXVIII: 247.

23   Kant, *Metaphysik L$_1$, LM*, p. 63; *Ak*.XXVIII: 247.

24   See Kant, *The Metaphysical Foundations of Natural Science*.

25   Kant, *Metaphysik L$_1$, LM*, p. 63; *Ak*.XXVIII: 247.

26   Kant, *Metaphysik L$_1$, LM*, p. 63, t.m.; *Ak*.XXVIII: 247.

27   Kant, *Metaphysik L$_1$, LM*, p. 63; *Ak*.XXVIII: 247.

28   Kant, *Metaphysik L$_1$, LM*, p. 63; *Ak*.XXVIII: 247.

29   Kant, *Metaphysik L$_1$, LM*, p. 63; *Ak*.XXVIII: 247.

30   Kant, *Metaphysik L$_1$, LM*, p. 63; *Ak*.XXVIII: 247.

31   Kant, *Metaphysik L$_1$, LM*, pp. 63–4; *Ak*.XXVIII: 247.

32   Kant, *Metaphysik L$_1$, LM*, p. 64; *Ak*.XXVIII: 247.

33   Kant, *Metaphysik L$_2$* (1790–1791?), in *LM*, pp. 297–354; *Ak*.XXVIII: 531–94.

34   Kant, *Metaphysik Vigilantius* (K$_3$), *LM*, p. 481; *Ak*.XXIX: 1011.

35   Baumgarten, *Metaphysica*, §§ 782–91.

36   Kant, *Metaphysik L$_1$, LM*, p. 94; *Ak*.XXVIII: 285.

37   Kant, *Metaphysik L$_1$, LM*, p. 94; *Ak*.XXVIII: 285.

38   Kant, *Metaphysik L$_1$, LM*, p. 95; *Ak*.XXVIII: 286.

39   Kant, *Metaphysik L$_1$, LM*, p. 95; *Ak*.XXVIII: 287.

40   Kant, *Metaphysik L$_1$, LM*, p. 95; *Ak*.XXVIII: 287.

41   Kant, *Metaphysik L$_1$, LM*, pp. 95–6; *Ak*.XXVIII: 287.

42   Kant, *Metaphysik L₁, LM*, p. 96; *Ak*.XXVIII: 287.
43   Kant, *Metaphysik Mrongovius, LM*, p. 278; *Ak*.XXIX: 913–14.
44   Kant, *Metaphysik K₂* (early 1790s), in *LM*, pp. 393–413; *Ak*.XXVIII: 753–75; p. 403; *Ak*.XXVIII: 763.
45   Kant, *CoJ*, p. 119, t.m.; *Ak*.V: 278.
46   Kant, *Metaphysik Vigilantius* (K₃), *LM*, p. 504; *Ak*.XXIX: 1039.
47   Kant, *Metaphysik Vigilantius* (K₃), *LM*, p. 504; *Ak*.XXIX: 1039.
48   Kant, *Metaphysik Vigilantius* (K₃), *LM*, p. 504; *Ak*.XXIX: 1039.
49   Kant, *Metaphysik K₂, LM*, p. 405; *Ak*.XXVIII: 765.

6
The Joy of Judgement

Andrea Rehberg

[W]here beings are not very familiar to man and are scarcely and only roughly known by science, the openedness of beings as a whole can prevail more essentially [*wesentlicher walten*] than it can where the familiar and well-known has become boundless.[1]

[E]ven the purest Θεωρια has not left all moods behind it.[2]

What is it that opens up any given phenomenon for philosophical discussion? On what grounds does such a discussion open itself to a phenomenon? And if the phenomenon in question is itself a philosophical text? Such questions are no doubt capable of provoking a wide variety of possible responses. Here only a very particular response is called for, namely one which relates the possible richness of a philosophical text to the issue of its essential ambiguity. Hence the richness of a text is a measure of the extent to which it does not coincide with itself, the extent to which it differs from itself, so that this differing itself chimes through and moulds the text. Thus the assumption underlying the present paper is that the play of the text's self-differing and the interpretation, similarly unable to coincide with itself, which responds to this play, form a restless process of ongoing productivity ever anew.

Even this preliminary answer might go some way towards explaining why Kant's texts continue to attract and fascinate a wide range of readers. The last decade has seen a blossoming of outstanding texts on the *Critique of Aesthetic Judgement* in particular, which have shed new light on the significance of the beautiful and the sublime, the imagination and pre-conceptual judgement, both for Kant's own critical project and beyond. This has generally resulted in a more tempered view of Kant, so that this 'civil servant of reason' could at the same time emerge as a precursor of the thought of a more profound relation to things than that afforded in representational thinking.

Does this also mean that the *Critique of Teleological Judgement*, which has attracted far less *philosophical* interest, is simply a less richly ambiguous text in the sense indicated, and therefore less deserving of philosophical attention (as opposed to scholarly attention in the manner of a history of science or of ideas)? Is it perhaps the complete absence from the *Critique of Teleological Judgement* of the very terms which have attracted philosophical readers to the *Critique of Aesthetic Judgement* which has banished the former text into the shadow of its more illustrious companion piece? If this were the case it would imply a great hermeneutic poverty, which would be tantamount to fetishising certain central terms, even if it were for the purposes of a profound textual rupture. But, conversely, neither can it be a fruitful procedure to introduce alien terms into the register of any given text and thereby to subdue the specifics of its textuality. Instead, we must presume that it is not certain terms, thoughts, concepts or any such textual *items* which make possible the reinvigoration of a received text, but a more profound *movement* of thought between them, in which a text cannot come to rest with/in itself, strains against itself, and so keeps on growing and shrinking, bearing tendencies towards both life and death, like all living things. This paper is predicated on the assumption that *CTJ*, too, harbours a rich polyphony and the task it thereby sets itself is to draw out and make audible this diversity of voices. Needless to say, it is impossible here to run through the entire gamut of notes sounded by *CTJ* – even if this were theoretically possible – but some of the more surprising concords and discords in the text will be allowed to resonate a little more distinctly.

Some of the most revealing points one can make about *CTJ* concern its relation to the *Critique of Pure Reason*. This is not meant to throw open the great debate as to whether *CJ* bridges the 'immense gulf' between the first and the second *Critique*,[3] between the phenomenal and noumenal aspects of subjectivity. But both *CPR* and *CTJ*, in their significantly different ways, look to nature for an answer to the basic question of 'what is a thing?'– which for Kant has to be rendered as something like 'how do the *a priori* faculties respond to, i.e., transcendentally and hence formally produce, a given thing, as part of nature'? Or, to put it another way, how is the systematic experience of nature called science possible, what are the conditions of possibility of this experience? An implicit assumption of Kant's enquiries into these issues is of course that knowledge, truth as correspondence, is the fundamental way in which human being as subjectivity relates to the natural world as objectivity. By contrast, the present essay is written against the backdrop of a number of critiques of representational thinking, above all those of Heidegger and of French Heideggerians.

The issues which *CTJ* discusses in great detail had already arisen briefly in the chapters of *CPR* collectively entitled Appendix to the Transcendental Dialectic,[4] but on the basis of questions regarding any possible use of the ideas of pure reason for the theoretical knowledge of nature. The connection between these two texts has far-reaching implications for the comprehension of the role which *CTJ* plays in the critical system, although for the purposes of this paper only the most salient points of the connection between the Appendix and *CTJ* need to be indicated.

The attempts of speculative metaphysics to use the ideas of reason – immortality, freedom and God – *constitutively* had been the prime object of the critique of reason, as executed in the Dialectic of *CPR*. But in the Appendix Kant asks whether there could be a *regulative* use for the ideas of reason in the field of theoretical knowledge, and if so, to what effect. Greatly abbreviated, and re-ordered for the sake of simplicity, his argument runs as follows: What is sought is empirical but systematic knowledge about nature, i.e., science. The only sufficient criterion of empirical truth lies in the coherent use of the understanding, but the understanding itself does not provide systematic unity. Hence the particular, diverse and essentially unconnected judgements of the understanding need to become the objects of a higher integrating power, namely reason, whose positive function is precisely to look for and to impose unity. But in order to secure the truth of our empirical statements about nature we must *presuppose* the systematic unity of nature as objectively valid and necessary, even though it is not given, so that at the same time we can never find such unity in nature itself, i.e., arrive at it *a posteriori*.[5] For these reasons Kant calls this idea of the systematic unity of nature one of the *maxims* of reason, that is to say, a 'subjective' – yet, importantly, still transcendental – principle which is not derived from the nature of the object but which reason must give to itself for the regulative and heuristic use of its ideas in the field of knowledge so that such maxims are treated as if they were objectively valid.[6]

Here we see the same turn as that later developed more fully in *CTJ*, with two important differences. Firstly, while writing *CPR*, Kant still takes it that the idea which provides the transcendental principle for the

unification of heterogeneous statements about nature is that of systematic unity, as an idea of reason; whereas in *CTJ* the transcendental principle which is said to fulfill this function is that of purposiveness, as a
principle of the faculty of judgement. Secondly, as already indicated,
what leads Kant to postulate the transcendental principle starts from a
different point in the critical project in each case, namely from the question of the possibility of the regulative use of the ideas of reason in the
first *Critique*, and from the aspiration to systematic knowledge of the
particular forms and laws of nature in *CTJ*. Hence the two texts may be
said to start from opposite ends of the transcendental-empirical, or uni-
versal-particular scale, even though they concur in many of their central
conclusions and are formally analogous in many respects.

As in both previous *Critiques*, Kant's starting point in *CTJ* is that philosophy (or metaphysics as science) has only two parts, namely a theoretical and a practical part,[7] whose objects are nature and freedom,
respectively. Each of these parts is in need of a critical grounding to cir-
cumscribe its legitimate derivation, scope and application – as opposed
to the illegitimate, transcendent field in which speculative metaphysics
entangles itself. Both parts relate to their respective objects through synthetic *a priori* judgements, i.e., judgements which neither merely analyse
the content of the concepts with which they operate nor simply relate
knowledge gained *a posteriori*. For Kant, the objective reality of a synthetic *a priori* judgement is guaranteed by involving the combination of
two *a priori* faculties. Any such judgement must be based on the *a priori*
principles intrinsic to a faculty and brought into play by it in such judgements. Hence *CTJ* must discover the faculties which underlie judgements about organic nature and it must discover the *a priori* principles
by means of which these faculties generate such judgements. This is one
of the tasks to which *CTJ* must respond and it is in this respect that it
completes the critical consideration of natural science and hence of the
theoretical part of critical philosophy.[8]

But more than the continuity, it is the discontinuity between these two
texts and their respective conceptions of nature that is of interest here.
What, then, has changed from the first to the third *Critique* and in what
ways does Kant respond to the development his thought has undergone
in the interval? The nature envisaged in *CPR* was 'nature in general', all
possible objects of experience as constituted by the faculties under the
rule of the *mechanical* laws of the understanding. The contiguity of concerns Kant seeks to establish between mathematics, physics and metaphysics[9] stems largely from the dominance accorded to the

understanding as the chief productive faculty in these sciences. Whilst Kant does not abjure the basic account of nature given in the first *Critique* (apart from anything else, to do so would undermine the most fundamental critical insights), this account is no longer sufficient to explain transcendentally that aspect of nature which, by the time of the third *Critique*, had forced itself on his thought, namely the very materiality of nature, its qualities as organic.

To put it in more Kantian terminology, the question which *CTJ* seeks to address is that of the transcendental conditions of possibility of the knowledge held in the life sciences. Like physics, they aim at a systematic knowledge of empirical nature, but in contrast to physics they are not content to explain their objects, namely the products and empirical laws of material nature, in terms of mechanism alone but must in addition aim to theorise the functions of organisms in terms of purposes. The rival claims of mechanism and teleology to explain sufficiently the phenomena of nature give rise to the problem of the antinomy, dealt with in the Dialectic of *CTJ* (although the debate continues as to where, and indeed whether, Kant offers a solution).[10]

But this fairly uncontentious account of some of the central technical issues of *CTJ* may be complemented by a more 'suspicious' reading of the forces which contributed to its construction. One of the implications of the above account is that Kant came to realise that there was a kind of nature, namely its particular organic products, or a certain understanding of nature, which threatened to escape the all-encompassing grasp of reason and that *CTJ* was his attempt to reinforce or to impose universal rationality on what most eluded it, even if the means by which this was accomplished appeared rather convoluted or even far-fetched at times.

But it is not just on the level of the matter of individual organisms that disintegration is perceived as a deep threat to the organising powers of reason. The empirical laws derived from the observation of nature, too, could harbour such a diversity as to defy reason's capacity to weld them into a coherent whole. Kant writes of the 'worrying boundless heterogeneity [*Ungleichartigkeit*] of empirical laws and heterogeneity [*Heterogeneität*] of natural forms',[11] and he elaborates:

> The diversity and heterogeneity of empirical laws could be so great that it might be partially possible for us to connect perceptions according to occasionally discovered particular laws, but never to bring these empirical laws themselves into the unity of affinity under a common principle if, as is

intrinsically possible (at least as far as the understanding can make out a priori), the diversity and heterogeneity of these laws ... were infinitely large and presented to us *a raw chaotic aggregate* and not the least trace of a system, although we nevertheless *must* presuppose such a [system] according to transcendental laws.[12]

Again, this is an exemplary passage, in that the last clause announces the willed response ('we *must* presuppose') to the threat envisaged in the first part of the sentence, namely that nature might possibly escape or defy the efforts of rational thought to bind it into coherence and thus even retroactively destabilise the entire critical project, as Kant hints could happen if the critique of teleology were to fail.[13] What this demonstrates is the ambiguity which fuels and drives *CTJ*, in that, on the one hand, this text is based upon the – however fleeting – recognition of a possible outside of reason, even a multiplicity of outsides of rational philosophy, yet, on the other hand, it responds to them by means of ever more elaborate conceptual constructs. Having briefly gestured towards the edges of our text's consciousness, where threats of disintegration lurk, we turn next to a gap in the composition of the faculties themselves which the faculty of teleological judgement is designed to make good.

The understanding makes in principle possible the cognition of objects of sense and it does so because it contains *a priori* constitutive concepts and principles. But this constitutive capacity only reaches as far as the formal aspects of an object. Consequently, there comes a point where the understanding, as faculty of cognition, runs up against its own limitations, for it can not of course constitute the material aspect of objects (only an intellectual intuition would be capable of this, but this for Kant is a limit concept, like the thing in itself).

Yet experience (always constituted *a priori* by the understanding) presents it with objects whose materiality displays a certain regularity and lawfulness. The understanding (as faculty of cognition) presents to cognition (as understanding) certain objects, namely organisms and the empirical laws observable in them, whose regularity and lawfulness are not explicable in terms of the understanding (as faculty of *a priori* concepts).[14] When faced with organic nature, the understanding realises its deficiency because it discerns 'a lawfulness in things which to understand or to explain, the understanding's universal concept of the sensible no longer suffices'.[15] In other words, the understanding is cast in the role of both subject and object of cognition and also as exceeding its own limitations precisely at the point of realising them and hence deferring to the faculty of judgement for their (temporary) resolution.[16] At this point the faculty of judgement is mobilised to make up for the deficiency of the constitutive understanding as regards organisms, or we might say that it is the limitation of the constitutive understanding in this respect which creates an opening for a freer activity of the faculty of judgement than was possible in the context of *CPR*.

The faculty of judgement (*Urteilskraft*) is fundamentally the faculty of subsumption. In the constitutive judgements investigated in *CPR*, the universal (as *a priori* concept of the understanding) is given and the particular (empirically given intuitions) will be subsumed under it. But when faced with organic nature, only the particular (organisms) is given empirically (although still, as objects of experience, constituted by the understanding) and the universal (law or concept) must be found for it. As indicated, the universal (concept) which is to explain the lawfulness of organisms cannot be derived from the understanding, for it only reaches as far as the formal conditions of objects. Hence, if the subsumption of the particular under the universal is to occur – failing which, as we saw, chaos looms – the universal (concept) will have to be provided from elsewhere. The faculty of judgement, unlike the understanding and reason, does not itself contain any concepts. It can only, in the broad sense, synthesise between what is empirically given and what it produces *a priori*. What the faculty of teleological judgement does in response to this dilemma is to borrow a concept from and of reason, namely that of a purpose. In this act of borrowing, by directing its economy towards reason, it also betrays or foreshadows the final orientation of teleological thought, namely towards speculative rational ideas. But at the same time it is still the case that concepts of reason are only ideas and any attempt to apply them constitutively to objects of nature results inevitably in the transcendent use of reason, characteristic of dogmatic metaphysics and wholly unacceptable to the critical propaedeutic to metaphysics *as* science, and the metaphysics *of* science.

This means that when the faculty of judgement applies the concept of a purpose to organisms and their empirical laws, and then takes this purposiveness to be objective and material, it does so on the understanding that it cannot claim to know these objects as so constituted but only gives a law for the investigation of material nature to itself, merely as a heuristic principle.[17] Hence what we find in the subsumptive act of the teleological faculty of judgement is that the empirically given particular is a product of the understanding but the *a priori* universal under which it must be subsumed is a concept of reason. In this regard it is sharply distinguished from the subsumption which occurs in *CPR*, namely of sensibility to understanding. In *CTJ*, only the understanding and reason are directly involved. Although this appears to weight it heavily towards solely conceptual operations, teleological judgement also opens up a quite different possibility.

In order to explain the peculiar act of the faculty of judgement in which it gives a concept (borrowed from reason, for the non-constitutive application to natural products) to itself, Kant invokes the notion of heautonomy.[18] In this heautonomous act, the faculty of judgement gives a law, 'neither to nature nor to freedom, but solely to itself'.[19] We might say that on the occasion of an encounter with material nature, and given that the constitutive understanding has ceded this field of knowledge, the faculty of judgement legislates to itself in an act of virtual, if still conceptual, auto-affection. Although the faculty of teleological judgement negotiates a difficult path between the understanding (which provides the initial object as empirical knowledge) and reason (which lends the idea on which the *a priori* principle of teleological judgement is based), the use of these materials by the faculty of judgement is ultimately self-given or autogenous.

Now, although this is still an act of (self-)legislation, it nevertheless at the same time marks a moment of the emancipation of thinking from the all-encompassing legislation of the concepts of the understanding which dominated knowledge, as witnessed in the Analytic of the first *Critique*. Hence it demonstrates that a flaw or failure in the workings of the faculties (the insufficiency of the concepts of the understanding to constitute natural products and the incapability of a concept of reason to determine them), far from threatening the collapse of the critical system, may give rise to the liberation of thought from its conceptual determination even if, as is also the case here, Kant himself seeks to repair this imminent rupture by means of yet more law-giving.

A teleological judgement is based on the concept of purposiveness which the faculty of judgement gives to itself, both between and apart from the two other higher faculties of understanding and reason, in order to account for the lawfulness of heterogeneous organic nature. This concept, on which the *a priori* principle for the faculty of teleological judgement is based, is considered by the understanding as objectively contingent but for the faculty of judgement it is fully transcendental, i.e., not derivable from, but necessary for experience – here taken as the systematic 'experience' (i.e., science) of material nature – which is why Kant calls it transcendental purposiveness.[20]

But – and this is the thought which will dominate the rest of this paper – this is a peculiar transcendentality, because unlike the transcendentality of the *a priori* concepts found in the other *Critiques*, it can be traced still further back. In fact, the basis on which this 'transcendental' concept rests is as yet thrice removed and so we must burrow deep, through two further intermediate stages, into the ultimate ground of the purposiveness which a teleological judgement about natural products poses to itself. And at each stage, there emerges a sense of the conflicting directions in which the text pulls and to which a hermeneutics of suspicion, or a hermeneutics of difference, can point.

Kant's concept of teleology is unquestionably indebted to the Aristotelian notion of telos.[21] But as a consequence of the Copernican turn the emphasis necessarily shifts from objects themselves towards the state of the faculties or, more accurately, to the necessary relation between the active faculties and the objects which stir them into activity. And it is precisely this relation on which Kant draws in one of his earliest explanations in *CJ* as to how purposiveness is to be understood in this text, when he writes of 'the purposiveness [*Zweckmäßigkeit*] or appropriateness [*Angemessenheit*] of nature to our capacity of the faculty of judgement'.[22] Although this appropriateness can quite bluntly be heard as a form of adequacy, *adaequatio*, it is alternatively possible to sharpen our ears to the measure (*Maß*) which lies at the core of it, and which, together with its several cognates, forms one of the major tones to sound repeatedly through the entire text.[23]

When the faculty of judgement posits to itself the concept of a purposiveness or appropriateness, in which nature is thought as standing in a measured relation to the faculty of judgement (notice again the autogenous character of this positing), it does so not because it dreamily or wilfully ignores the question whether rational judgement really has the capacity to measure up to material nature. On the contrary, it does so precisely because no such correspondence is ultimately possible for reason. Throughout the Dialectic of *CPR* Kant had explained innumerable times the fundamental insight that there can be no objective reality, no empirical objects, which correspond to any of the ideas of reason. In fact, it is the impossibility of any such correspondence which is the cornerstone of the critique of speculative metaphysics and hence, in a sense, the founding insight of the critical system. In other words, it is *because of* the inadequacy or incommensurability (*Unangemessenheit*) of rational judgement to the excessive heterogeneity of nature, that a rational judgement about nature as heterogeneous (diversity of products and empirical laws) has to introduce or presuppose this measured relation which it acknowledges at the same time to be a mere idea.[24] The following passage, in which Kant evokes the reason why the faculty of judgement *must* adopt purposiveness as its transcendental principle, may illustrate this play of incursion into and recursion from the excessive heterogeneity of nature:

> *It is quite conceivable* that ... the specific differences [*Verschiedenheit*] in the empirical laws of nature ... might ... be so great that it would be impossible for our understanding to discover in nature a graspable [*faßbare*] order ... and to make a coherent experience from a matter [*Stoff*] which is for us so confused, really [*eigentlich*] only infinitely diverse and *not* adequate [*nicht angemessen*] to our capacity to grasp it [*Fassungskraft*].[25]

In response to this possibility Kant appeals to the two facets of measure, 'purposiveness or appropriateness' (*Zweckmäßigkeit* or *Angemessenheit*), to plug the gap opened by the abyssal possibility that there is *no* measure in which reason and organic nature become commensurable and that empirical nature is *not* adequate to our higher faculties. This layer of measure forms the first stage of our descent into the underworld, the ground of *CTJ*.[26]

Apropos this register of *Maß* we are led to recall Heidegger's 1951 essay 'Poetically Dwells Man',[27] which marks one of his many encounters with the poetry of Hölderlin. The poem which begins 'In lovely blue ...' contains the verses:

> [A]s long as friendliness still
> In the heart, the pure, lasts, measures
> Man not unhappily himself
> With the Godhead. Unknown is God?
> Is he revealed as the heaven?
> ... Of humans the measure it is
> ... poetically dwells
> Man on this earth ...
> Is there on earth a measure? There is
> None.

Heidegger's interpretation of these lines centres on the play between heaven and earth, God and Man, God as unknown and as revealed, revealed as unknown, and, between each of them, the measure which keeps them apart, thereby granting meaning and being in this interval, and which simultaneously chains them to each other, so that their differing is suppressed in favour of their (related) identities. In short, Heidegger reads the measure in terms of, even *as*, the ontological difference. But why then is there no measure on the earth, given that ontological differing is very much an event or process of the earth? Heidegger's answer is that the measure *is* the 'there is' (*es gibt*), so that the giving cannot give itself but must withdraw itself in order to give (beings). Ontological differing cannot be the object of representation or, as Hölderlin has it, the God only reveals himself as unknown.

I would suggest that there is a formal similarity between Kant's and Heidegger's reflections on measure. Kant uses the register of measure to compensate for the measurelessness or incommensurability which the critique of speculative reason revealed to exist between the ideas of reason and nature as purposive. To put it in the starkest terms, it is precisely the non-correspondence between reason in its demand for unificatory purposiveness in nature and nature's purposiveness as mere idea which demands the introduction of a transcendental measure to plug the gap left by the unattainability of any objective measure. This is broadly analogous to Heidegger's reading of Hölderlin's 'Is there on earth a measure? There is/None' as the withdrawal of being (the unknown God) whose withdrawal (as unknown) opens up (reveals as unknown) the distance (measure) between heaven and earth in which both, and Man as suspended between them, may come to be. Whilst Kant's concerns in *CTJ*, and the terms in which he expresses them, are of course very different from those of Heidegger, the above account of 'Poetically Dwells Man' can be read back into Kant's text to uncover a broadly similar dynamic of thought.

We approach the second stage of our reading via one of the elaborations of the transcendental principle of the faculty of judgement offered by Kant, where he characterises it as the 'harmony [*Zusammenstimmung*] of nature to our cognitive faculty' which the faculty of judgement 'presupposes a priori'.[28] As we saw in the preceding paragraphs, what the heautonomous *a priori* principle of the faculty of judgement (i.e., purposiveness) does, is to establish a profound, if only 'pragmatic', measure or harmony between what is essentially a 'boundless' heterogeneity in empirical nature and the systematic demands of the faculty of teleological judgement under the sway of an idea of reason. This autogenous or self-given harmony is traced throughout *CJ* by a particular register, namely that of '*stimmen*', '*Stimmung*' and related terms.[29]

Prior to examining this register a little further, it needs to be remembered that Kant never ceases to emphasise that the judgements made by the faculty of teleological judgement are not determinative (*bestim-*

mend) but merely reflective.[30] Hence the register of '*stimmen*' etc. can be seen to have the double function of marking the difference and distance from the determinative (*bestimmende*) judgements central to the first *Critique* and yet, at the same time, of harking back to the stem of the verb found in the earlier type of judgements. This parallels the way that *CTJ* itself both distances itself from *CPR* – namely in the more complex ways it conceives and constitutes its object – and yet builds on the crucial critical insights won in the earlier text.[31]

Perhaps one of the most modest claims Kant makes for the scope of the concept of purposiveness, and one of the most important instances of his use of the '*Stimmung*' register, can be seen in the following passage:

> The [merely] thought harmony [*Übereinstimmung*] of nature in the manifoldness of its particular laws with our need to find universality of principles for it must, according to all our insight, be judged as contingent, yet nevertheless as indispensable for the needs of our understanding, hence as purposiveness through which nature harmonises [*übereinstimmt*] with our aim, though *only* directed towards cognition.[32]

What is most remarkable about this passage is the use of 'only' in conjunction with the term 'cognition', given that the possibility and the scope of the cognition of nature in its particular laws is precisely what *CTJ* investigates or seeks to establish. The paragraph which begins with this passage closes by stating again the necessity of attributing to nature a purposiveness, by means of the faculty of judgement, *because* the understanding is unable to prescribe laws to its empirical manifoldness.[33] This is tantamount to saying that we *must* cognise material nature as purposive (through the faculty of judgement) because we *cannot* cognise it as purposive (through the understanding). Aside from being delightfully paradoxical, this also decisively limits the aspirations of cognition and opens the path towards a very different understanding of human being's relation to its world, one which finds explicit expression some one hundred and thirty years later, when we read:

> *Mood [Stimmung] has, in each case, already disclosed being-in-the-world as a whole and makes possible, first of all, a directedness towards.*[34]

This remark occurs in §29 of *Being and Time*, where Heidegger elaborates mood (*Stimmung*) or being-attuned (*Gestimmtsein*) as the ontic aspect of the ontological disposition (*Befindlichkeit*) of Dasein. Heidegger's phenomenology of Dasein's pre-theoretical relatedness to its world, or being-in-the-world, is relevant to this reading of *CTJ* insofar as the latter can be read as already containing certain strands or elements which break the ineluctable bonds of knowledge between *reason* and nature (or world) which *CPR* had established as the primary mode of transcendentality. It is not of course being suggested here that *BT* functions as anything like a commentary on Kant's text, nor indeed that *CTJ* precisely foreshadows Heidegger's phenomenological analysis of Dasein. But the obtrusiveness of the register of *Stimmung* in *CTJ* makes it possible to question Kant's hitherto unshakeable belief in rationality and its theoretical 'attitude' because it suggests what Heidegger later shows as the true import of mood, namely that 'the possibilities of disclosure which belong to cognition reach far too short a way compared with the primordial disclosure belonging to moods',[35] that 'ontologically we must leave the primary discovery of the world to "bare mood"',[36] and finally that 'ontologically mood is a primordial kind of Being for Dasein'.[37] As these remarks show, for Heidegger, mood, or being-attuned, is an originary form of transcendence, neither subjective nor objective and certainly not to be heard on a merely psychological level.[38] This is made clear when he writes, 'A mood comes upon us. It comes neither from the "outside" nor from the "inside", but arises as a way of being-in-the-world from out of it itself'.[39]

Kant does not of course discuss heautonomy, as the quality of a certain kind of judgement, in terms of mood. Nonetheless, this concept shares some formal characteristics with the kind of pre-theoretical relatedness described by Heidegger, insofar as both mark a space between objectivity and subjectivity that is irreducible to either of them but instead exceeds both and thereby makes them possible in the first place. I would also suggest that, insofar as Kant calls the transcendental *a priori* principle of purposiveness which first of all makes possible any (albeit still chiefly theoretical) relation to the world of material nature *Zusammenstimmung* and *Übereinstimmung*, i.e., different modalities of *Stimmung*, mood, his thought was beginning to glimpse transcendence as no longer containable within the limits of reason alone, but instead as an immanent beyond, in short, as alterity, later explicitly developed as such by Heidegger.[40]

Having completed the penultimate stage of the enquiry into the ultimate grounds of teleological judgement, from such judgements to the positing of a measure between the faculty of judgement and nature, and hence to the idea of a transcendental, pre-theoretical attunement between the faculty of judgement and nature, it only remains to ask what sustains the entire series of assumptions which have to be in place to make a teleological judgement possible. The title of section VI of the second Introduction to *CJ*, 'Of the Connection of the Feeling of Pleasure [*Lust*] with the Concept of the Purposiveness of Nature' already hints at some of the astonishing observations in it.[41]

In this section Kant states that 'the attainment of that aim [namely, to bring unity of principles into the particular laws of nature by means of the concept of purpose] is connected with the feeling of pleasure [*Lust*]'.[42] However, he is under no illusion that the other kind of subsumption, that of perceptions under categories (as found in *CPR*), could effect any pleasure, because there the operation of subsumption is 'automatic', insofar as the understanding acts spontaneously. But, by contrast, he observes that the 'discovered unifiability of two or more empirical heterogeneous laws of nature under one principle which comprehends them both [is] the reason for a very noticeable pleasure [*Lust*]',[43] whereas, he claims, we would balk at the representation of nature in which we would only meet with the heterogeneity of its laws without being able to integrate them into ideal purposive systems.[44] On the one hand, this is no doubt an example of Kant's 'irrational' prejudices in favour of the necessary systematicity of thought and in favour of a very traditional model of the life sciences.

But the other, more advanced strain which cautiously emerges here, albeit on an as yet rather simplistic model, could be understood as something like a gesture towards the libidinal ground of all thought, the *Lust*, pleasure or joy, which may provoke and produce certain thoughts. In the course of section VI, Kant also allows himself a highly unusual moment of quasi-genealogical speculation, when he writes:

> It is true that we no longer feel any noticeable pleasure in the graspability of nature and the unity in its division into genera and species ... but this pleasure was no doubt there at one time and it is only because even the most common experience would not be possible without it, it has gradually been mixed with mere cognition and has not been especially noticed any longer.[45]

It seems that this is a partial or fleeting recognition of the fact that it is not the project of cognition which fuels the life of thought but rather something like an originary, transcendental affect or pre-individual desire, which can be the object of description or speculation but which cannot be analysed further. It would even seem that Kant glimpsed this enigmatic 'ground' of thought when he called the relation of the *a priori*

principle of the faculty of teleological judgement to the feeling of pleasure or unpleasure (*Lust und Unlust*) 'the mysterious' (*das Rätselhafte*).[46]
And so, what we are left with at the end of our descent into Kant's critical teleology is something like the inexplicability or mysteriousness at
the core of teleological judgements, in Kant's case wedded to the ideal
of systematic unity, but ripe for reinscription, the beginnings of a joyful
science.

Notes

1   Martin Heidegger, 'On the Essence of Truth', in *Basic Writings*, trans.
    David Farrell Krell (San Francisco: Harper Collins, 1993), p. 129.
2   Martin Heidegger, *Sein und Zeit*, 16th edn. (Tübingen: Max Niemeyer
    Verlag, 1986). Hereafter *SZ*. Martin Heidegger, *Being and Time*, trans. John
    Macquarrie and Edward Robinson (Oxford: Blackwell, 1995), p. 177.
    Hereafter *BT*.
3   Kant, *CJ*, p. 14; *Ak*.V: 175.
4   Kant, *CPR*, A642–704/B670–732.
5   Kant, *CPR*, A651/B679.
6   Kant, *CPR*, A666/B694.
7   Kant, *CJ*, First Introduction, sec.s I and II; *Ak*.XX: 195–206.
8   See Kant, *CJ*, p. 18; *Ak*.V: 179; and especially, *CJ*, p. 35; *Ak*.V: 195.
9   As when he asks the three guiding questions of *CPR*, 'How is pure mathe-
    matics possible?', 'How is pure science of nature possible?', 'How is meta-
    physics, as science, possible?' (Kant, *CPR*, B20–2).
10 See Gary Banham, *Kant and the Ends of Aesthetics* (Basingstoke: Macmillan
    Press, 2000), ch. 8, 'The Antinomy of Reflective Judgment Re-treated', for
    a discussion of some of the most important recent contributions to this
    ongoing debate and for a very careful consideration of the enormously
    complex issues involved.
11 Kant, *CJ*, First Introduction, sec. IV, p. 398, t.m.; *Ak*.XX: 209.
12 Kant, *CJ*, First Introduction, sec. IV, p. 397–8, t.m., emphases added;
    Ak.XX: 209.
13 Kant, *CJ*, p. 5; *Ak*.V: 168.
14 It should be emphasised again, as mentioned in passing in the opening
    paragraphs of this essay, that the productive imagination, unlike in *CPR*
    and *CAJ*, does not play any part in the account of teleological judgements
    as given in *CTJ*. Any discussion of the significance of this omission must be
    left for another occasion.
15 Kant, *CJ*, p. 7, t.m.; *Ak*.V: 169.
16 Although it might be provocatively, and too simplistically, Hegelian to put
    it like this, this issue of a split or multiple understanding looms in *CTJ*. The

chief difference between Kant and Hegel is that for the latter all differences are thematised as oppositions internal to a rationality ultimately on the way to self-identity whereas the former allows a reading to gesture towards non-oppositional differences and/as the ongoing deferral of identity.

17 See for instance Kant, *CJ*, p. 295, First Introduction, sec. II, p. 394; *Ak*.V: 410–11, *Ak*.XX: 205.

18 Kant, *CJ*, p. 25, First Introduction, sec. VIII, p. 414; *Ak*.V: 186, *Ak*.XX: 225.

19 Kant, *CJ*, First Introduction, sec. VIII, p. 414; *Ak*.XX: 225.

20 See for instance Kant, *CJ*, p. 25; *Ak*.V: 185. Kant defines a transcendental principle as that 'by which is represented the universal a priori condition under which alone things can become objects of our cognition' (Kant, *CJ*, p. 20, t.m.; *Ak*.V: 181).

21 See for instance Book II of the *Physics*. Aristotle, *Physics*, Books I–IV, trans. Philip H. Wicksteed and Francis M. Cornford (Cambridge, MA: Harvard University Press and London: William Heinemann, 1980).

22 Kant, *CJ*, First Introduction, sec. II, p. 393 n., t.m.; *Ak*.XX: 204 n.

23 See for instance *Ak*.XX: 208, 214, 215, 234, *Ak*.V: 186, 188, 189.

24 See for instance Kant, *CJ*, First Introduction, sec. II, p. 394; *Ak*.XX: 205.

25 Kant, *CJ*, p. 25, t.m., emphases added; *Ak*.V: 185.

26 The closely related issue of the 'technique of nature', which views nature as art, cannot be discussed here because it leads into the problem – central to *CJ* – of how *CAJ* and *CTJ* belong together.

27 Martin Heidegger, '…dichterisch wohnet der Mensch', in *Vorträge und Aufsätze* (Pfullingen: Neske, 1985). All translations from this essay, including Hölderlin's poetry, are my own.

28 Kant, *CJ*, p. 24, t.m.; *Ak*.V: 185.

29 Such as: *zusammenstimmen/Zusammenstimmung* (Kant, *Ak*.XX: 212, 220, 230, 232, 233, 243, *Ak*.V: 185, 190); *übereinstimmen/Übereinstimmung* (Kant, *Ak*.XX: 210, 217, 233, *Ak*.V: 180, 186, 191, 192); *einstimmig/Einstimmigkeit* (Kant, *Ak*.XX: 214, 233, *Ak*.V: 187).

30 See especially Kant, *CJ*, First Introduction sec. V; *Ak*.XX: 211–16 and §69; *Ak*.V: 385–6.

31 Jean-François Lyotard, in his reading of the *sensus communis* of *CAJ*, finds not primarily a harmony (*Einstimmung*) but a voice (*Stimme*), pre-individual and impersonal, in which 'the subject gives voice to itself "before" it sees itself or conceives of itself', i.e., is ready for cognition. Although Lyotard's points to some extent converge with those I attempt to make here, he takes them in a rather different direction. Jean-François Lyotard, 'The Subject in *statu nascendi*', in *Who Comes After the Subject?*, eds. Cadava, Connor, Nancy (London: Routledge, 1991), p. 226.

32 Kant, *CJ*, p. 26, t.m., emphasis added; *Ak*.V: 186.

33 Kant, *CJ*, p. 26; *Ak*.V: 187.

34   Heidegger, *SZ*, p. 137, *BT*, p. 176, t.m.
35   Heidegger, *SZ*, p. 134, *BT*, p. 173.
36   Heidegger, *SZ*, p. 138, *BT*, p. 177, t.m.
37   Heidegger, *SZ*, p. 136, *BT*, p. 175.
38   See Heidegger, *SZ*, §10 and p. 134, *BT*, p.1/2.
39   Heidegger, *SZ*, p. 136, *BT* 176, t.m.
40   In her reading of the sublime, Éliane Escoubas finds *Stimmung* to be one of the pivotal terms on which both the Analytic of the Beautiful and of the Sublime in *CAJ* turn. See Éliane Escoubas, 'Kant or the Simplicity of the Sublime', in *Of the Sublime: Presence in Question*, J.-F. Courtine et al, trans. J. Librett (Albany: SUNY Press, 1993), especially pp. 58–60.
41   Kant, *CJ*, p. 26, t.m.; *Ak*.V: 186.
42   Kant, *CJ*, p. 27, t.m.; *Ak*.V: 187.
43   Ibid.
44   Kant, *CJ*, p. 27–8, t.m.; *Ak*.V: 188.
45   Kant, *CJ*, p. 27, t.m.; *Ak*.V: 187.
46   Kant, *CJ*, p. 7, t.m.; *Ak*.V: 169.

7

Kant's Joke (Or, On Continuing to Use the Word 'God')

Paul Davies

For those disinclined by sentiment or training either to become Nietz-sche scholars or to consider themselves Nietzschean philosophers, his texts are experienced, if at all, in the form of a dilemma. The nimble and lightly worn learning of the thinking akin to dancing Nietzsche admires and encourages, and to which he always opposes the ponderous systemat-ics of 'old Kant',[1] never quite tells us what we would do or become if we accepted either the vision or the diagnosis. For us, Nietzsche names a question always explicitly to Kant, but also implicitly and crucially to the question Kantian critique embodies, the question of the possibility of philosophy as such. Ponderously then, on my part, Nietzsche is expe-rienced as a question to the question of the possibility of philosophy, a question to the effectiveness of this critical reconsideration. Nietzsche's work becomes the exemplar of a writing that resists being fully re-appro-priated by even the most preparatory of philosophies. To repeat: Nietz-sche's various challenges to Kant are thus always also challenges to philosophy itself, to its possibility and to the possibility of its *continuing*. This essay is an attempt to meet one of them.

I

We can, following Heidegger, call it Kant's thesis about being. It remains one of the most famously successful, if cryptic, passages in modern phi-losophy, and comprises: a negative claim ('"Being" is obviously not a real predicate'); a clarification of that claim ('that is, it is not a concept of something which could be added to the concept of a thing'); and a con-cluding positive claim ('It is merely the positing of a thing, or of certain determinations, in and of themselves').[2] It is said to show that any argu-ment which would move from the analysis of a concept to a conclusion asserting necessary existence must be invalid. The drawing out of the implications of this effectively transcendental argument is, for Kant, the only contribution philosophy can make to 'ontotheology'. In the context of the *Critique of Pure Reason*, the critical undermining of a constructive rationalism not only signals the end of the attempt to formulate onto-logical arguments but also raises the issue of what philosophy is to do with those words and concepts traditionally protected by the assump-tion that such arguments are intelligible.

Kant's objection to the ontological argument is neither to the major premise which he accepts, where God is defined as the greatest or most perfect conceivable being, nor to the conclusion which he believes, where God's existence is asserted, but rather to the minor premise where 'existence' is said to be inherent in the very meaning of 'the great-est or the most perfect conceivable being'. Predication never guarantees or bestows existence. In the first *Critique*, the statement that being is not a real predicate both marks the limits of legitimate theoretical specula-tion on the nature and existence of God and restricts subsequent philo-sophical usage of the word 'God' to reflections on the (moral and practical) efficacy of 'God' as a transcendental and regulative idea. Although, since Kant, there have been attempts either to suggest that existence is easily formalisable as a real predicate or to indicate the rel-atively uncontroversial use of existence proofs in, say, mathematics, the success of Kant's thesis can be discerned from the fact that no major philosopher has sought to retrieve a straightforward Anselmian or Cartesian proof of God's existence. This success has often been won by way of an implicit revising of the thesis: thus for Frege, 'exists' is analysed as a second-level predicate and the 'is' asserting existence is fully and logically expressed by the existential quantifier; and, for Hei-degger, to say that being is not a real predicate is to affirm the ontologi-cal difference, to say that being is not a being. Each of these interpretations focuses on the negative claim; each has a rather ambigu-ous relation to the positive claim. On a Fregean reading, the positive claim either means no more than the negative claim or it is evidence of a lamentable slide back into psychologism, conflating the meaning of 'exists' with the action (the act of positing) of a subject. On a Heideg-gerian reading, the positive claim might be seen as just one more attempt to theorise being and so as a forgetting of the difference briefly and profoundly glimpsed in the negative claim. But whether it be read in its Fregean or Heideggerian paraphrase the implications of Kant's thesis for an ontological argument are upheld.

Even where issue is taken with the content of Kant's negative thesis, there need be no unequivocal return to a positive ontotheology. For Hegel, Kant is not wrong to assert that being is not a real predicate, but he does not examine thoroughly enough the consequences of this assertion for both our understanding of 'reality' and our understanding of 'our understanding of "reality"'. Ironically, it is in the ontological argument itself, especially in its Anselmian version, that Hegel detects a genuine insight into the meaning of 'God' and into God's becoming concept. The argument demonstrates that there is in God, necessarily, a speculative identity of the real and the conceptual. Kant's critical thesis about being is to be completed by retrieving the ontological argument it would have consigned to a pre-critical philosophical past; but it is a retrieval that reflects and completes the historical alteration of theism (of God and of the concept of God). Anselm and Kant, in their respective contexts and fashions, provide insight into what we might call God's self-realisation in and as thought and history. Hegel's supplement to Kant's critique of ontotheology attempts to disclose something like the philosophical meaning of theism. His retrieval of the ontological argument does not entail going back to endorsing a pre-Kantian philosophical theism. As with Kant so with Hegel, their critical and historical reflections on theism entail a straightforward assertion of neither God's existence nor God's non-existence. What, for Kant, marks the logical limits of ontotheology, for Hegel marks or demonstrates ontotheology's historical accomplishment. In such a way Hegel, as well, can be said to underwrite the success of Kant's thesis.

To all of this, however, one might be tempted to a less sanguine response. Why has Kant's treatment of the ontological argument met with such a friendly reception? Indeed why should it have succeeded at all? Even if it is clear what Kant meant by 'real predicate', why should the fact that 'exists' is or is not one have any effect on the logical basis of theism? Surely the conclusions of ontological arguments, whether valid or not, are indifferent to the philosophico-grammatical status of the predicate. Moreover, if even on his own terms the outcome of Kant's ontotheology acknowledges the theoretical *possibility* of God's existence, then does it not leave room for explicitly modal ontological proofs (i.e., an argument, closer to Anselm's than to Descartes', from its possibly being the case that actually God exists to its being the case that actually God exists)? Although this might have been a feasible objection in the pre-critical *The One Possible Basis for a Demonstration of the Existence of God* (the *Beweisgrund*), where one finds the first complete formulation of Kant's thesis, it cannot or ought not to be the case in the *Critique of Pure Reason* given the *Critique*'s technical construing of 'possibility'.⁵ The critical context of the claim that being is not a real predicate is supposed to prohibit any further theoretical speculation by drawing attention away from the content of the thesis itself and towards its status, to what it tells us of the one, that finite rational being, for whom it demonstrates the impossibility of their ever being able to reach a substantive conclusion. For some philosophers, however, this can only look like a renewed dogmatism. If Kant would situate all future philosophical use of the word 'God' solely in the moral and practical sphere, he can do so only by stipulation. And why should anyone agree to that?

It is in this context that Nietzsche's idiosyncratic response can make itself felt. Nietzsche would applaud the philosophers who remain baffled by Kant's success, seeing them at least as honestly seeking either to sustain a robust theism or to admit an equally robust atheism. To such full-blooded content, Kant's critique merely provides a reflective and 'gentle moralism'.⁴ Nietzsche does not want simply to re-engage with the logical debate about God's existence, but he does want to present Kant's successful circumscribing of that debate in a very different light, one that will permit it to have done with theistic philosophy altogether. Something happens to theism in Kant's thesis or, better, something that has happened to theism is expressed in Kant's thesis; but the success of the thesis, rather than perpetuating another, more anodyne 'moral' theism, ought to be aligned with the insight that the only definitive refutation of the arguments for theism must be historical rather than putatively transcendental. Thus:

> In former times, one sought to prove that there is no God – today one indicates how the belief that there is a God could *arise* [*entstehen*] and how this belief acquired its weight and importance: a counter-proof that there is no God thereby becomes superfluous. – When in former times one had refuted the "proofs of the existence of God" ["*Beweise vom Dasein Gottes*"] put forward, there always remained the doubt whether better proofs might not be adduced than those just refuted: in those days atheists did not know how to make a clean sweep.⁵

If the theoretical conclusion still allows that God's existence is possible, then it suffices to encourage the search for better and more valid proofs. Accordingly, if Kant's thesis about being is really to do the critical work it set out to do, it must relinquish: firstly, the demand that theoretical philosophy accept the possibility of God's existence; secondly, all talk of discovering transcendental 'conditions of possibility', the means by which critical philosophy claims to be able to step back from traditional metaphysical disputes; and, thirdly, the continued philosophical use of the word 'God'. There is something absurd, for Nietzsche, in Kant's defence of each of these, a defence amounting to little more than a presumption.

Nietzsche, in the penultimate section of *The Anti-Christ*, considers or fantasises about an earlier missed opportunity:

> I behold a spectacle at once so meaningful and so strangely paradoxical it would have given all the gods of Olympus an opportunity for an immortal roar of laughter – *Cesare Borgia as Pope.* ... [*T*]*hat* would have been a victory of the only sort *I* desire today – : Christianity would have thereby been *abolished*! – What happened? A German monk, Luther, went to Rome [and] fulminated ... *against* the Renaissance ... Instead of grasping with profound gratitude the tremendous event which had taken place, the overcoming of Christianity in its very *seat* – ...What Luther saw was the *corruption* of the Papacy, while precisely the opposite was palpably obvious.[6]

Luther reformed the Church. And Kant? Would he not somehow stand as both Luther and the Renaissance, reforming scholasticism in the very move that could have robbed it of its mainstay – its theism? Might the thesis about being not serve as his 'Cesare Borgia on the papal throne'?

II

The 'joke' is told or retold by Nietzsche in *The Gay Science*; and it goes like this:

> *Kant's joke* [*Kants Witz*] – Kant wanted to prove, in a way that would dumbfound the common man, that the common man was right: that was the secret joke of this soul. He wrote against the scholars in support of popular prejudice, but for scholars and not for the people.[7]

On first reading, the joke depends on Kant's philosophy being presented as a difficult way of stating the obvious, a precedent perhaps set by Kant himself. Recall the modest reassurance in the B edition Preface where, despite all the changes wrought by the critique of metaphysics, 'the situation remains entirely as favourable as ever with regard to universal human reason', and where whatever loss there is 'affects only the monopoly of the schools; in no way does it affect the interests of the people [*das Interesse der Menschen*]'.[8] Kant, like Luther, *ein Mann aus dem Volke*? For Nietzsche, Kant's is a philosophy that not only significantly changes nothing but also provides a transcendental guarantee or prescription that everything remain and continue as before. The difference Kant's critique of metaphysics makes, its replacement for the *indifferentism* to which philosophy has supposedly succumbed,[9] is no more than a newly and philosophically respectable 'no difference'. Kant's laboriously complex critical architectonic would seem to do no more than pander to and sustain common prejudice. But, so read, the joke would seem to do no more than pander, in its turn and in Nietzsche's hands, to a common, contemporary, and positivistic prejudice about philosophy. The difficulty of Kant's work is deceptive, merely concealing the fact that there is nothing new being said. The people whose beliefs and practices it would support have no need to read it; and the scholars who do read it, those intended readers for whom the philosophical reflection on the science and history that informs and challenges 'common sense' is both important and necessary, will find in it only the most convoluted repetition of that common sense.

Yet for whom is Kant's work being so described? Not, presumably, those who have never read Kant and are unlikely ever to have an interest in reading him. One presumes Nietzsche writes for those likely to have read Kant and likely to want to read Nietzsche. Were the people referred to in Nietzsche's 'Kant's joke' to read it they may be convinced of the fact that there is no need to read Kant. Were the scholars to read it they may think they hear in it a philosophical or scholarly endorsement of a non-philosophical or unscholarly prejudice against philosophy and scholarship. If the 'joke' behind Kant's project is the continuing spread of the very indifferentism that project would combat, how can 'Kant's joke' be any more than the indifferent pointing out of that fact?

But as with so many of the reflexive moments in Nietzsche's texts, one is deceived if one thinks one can stop here. Nietzsche is aware, for example, that his genealogy of moral philosophy not only addresses the same audience and the same concerns as those of moral philosophy itself, but also stems from the same impulse or motivation. Hence the need for a genealogy of genealogy. Nietzsche's genealogical project is a genealogical critique, and as such it is continuous with the critical engagement of philosophy that precedes it. But this admission does not mean that one can straightforwardly replace 'Kant's joke' with 'Nietzsche's joke'. Nietzsche does want the move from Kantian critique to genealogical critique to make a difference: to move *from* the 'no difference' that Kant's critique supposedly makes – and that permits the continuing of both philosophy and non-philosophy in and through that critique – *to* the 'difference' Nietzsche's critique makes when philosophy continues as genealogy. With this transition in mind, the 'joke' acquires a further nuance. It tells of a Kant who, in writing for the scholar, rather than finding a way to refine the critique of common prejudice instead ingeniously conspires to turn the scholar into the common man. Kantian philosophy would be the apotheosis of scholasticism, a scholasticism that succeeds through its spuriously sophisticated trivialisation. The critique of theoretical and practical reason is still too much reason's critique. It is the means by which reason legitimates itself, its knowledge and truth, and so ensures that the critical form of the question (What are the conditions of the possibility of knowledge and truth?) remains in thrall to the pre-critical metaphysical form (What is knowledge? What is truth?). Nietzsche's genealogical question would endeavour to correct or to vitiate this subservience: Where did the desire for truth and knowledge come from?

Later in *The Gay Science*, Nietzsche is again amused by Kant, and in particular by the categorical imperative:

> This term tickles my ear and makes me laugh ... It makes me think of old Kant who had obtained the "thing in itself" *by stealth* ... and was punished for this when the "categorical imperative" crept stealthily into his heart and led him *astray – back* to "God", "soul", "freedom", and "immortality", like a fox who loses his way and goes astray back into his cage. Yet it had been *his* strength and cleverness that had *broken open* the cage.[10]

The categorical imperative, the supposedly non-historical representation of human duties as divine commands,[11] ensures the entire critical project stands as a symptom of a refusal. Everything has changed *theoretically*; but nothing has happened. To Kant's move from the 'thing in itself' back to 'God', we can contrast Nietzsche's own move from the 'thing in itself' as he accepts and radicalises it in, say, the essay 'On Truth and Lies in a Nonmoral Sense',[12] to the perspectivism he outlines fourteen years later in the second edition of *The Gay Science*. The trajectory runs from the thought of the unknowable and unthinkable 'thing in itself' where the thought of the existence of the 'thing in itself' entails perspectivism, there being an infinite number of possible perspectives of and on to what is in and of itself unthinkably non-perspectivisable, to a perspectivist interrogation of the very notion of 'existence' where the name 'the thing in itself' (and the names 'the unknowable', 'the unthinkable' and 'the non-perspectivisable') must be discarded. The introduction of the thing in itself must not be thought to grant anything

to a positive future metaphysics; for such a metaphysics, as Kant unwit-
tingly demonstrates, at least to Nietzsche's satisfaction, will always turn
out to be a way of continuing to deify thought. It will move from the idea
or concept of X to a consideration of the legitimacy of practical or theoretical uses of claims about the existence of X. From the thought of the
thing in itself to the thought that the thing in itself exists; from the
thought of the unknowable to the thought that the unknowable exists –
if neither of these inferences is theoretically valid, it ought to be for two
reasons: (1) No analysis of a concept can yield a positive existence claim:
existence claims are not analytic. (2) The realisation of the impossibility
of such an analysis ought to provoke a thoroughly critical examination
of those concepts whose function and value derived from the assumption of their possibility. Kant's account of what is wrong with the ontological argument provides us with a succinct expression of (1). But, by
itself, it is not enough to prevent, firstly, metaphysical and ontological
speculation about the implications of the unknowability of the thing in
itself and, secondly, the return and the legitimising of a certain philosophical discourse on God, a god who exists. The examination called for
in (2) must thus be a genealogical one. It treats the tendency to ask
about the nature, essence, or being of what is only a concept and, finally,
only a word by inquiring into the origins of the desire for it to be more.
Its strategic conclusion is the acceptance that there is no meaningful
'thought of the thing in itself' or 'thought of the unknowable', the suspicion of intrinsic meaning here having everything to do with the meaning philosophy continues to give to the 'thought of (the existence of)
God'. The persistence of the terms in Kant's texts serves the practical
validation of an 'X exists' which, by stipulation, is able to resist or to be
excused from the theoretical constraint. Kant holds it to be a condition
of the possibility of any future metaphysics that it admit to the mean-
ingfulness and to the content of the judgement 'God exists'. The conclusion of the pre-critical *Beweisgrund* stands: 'It is thoroughly necessary
that one be convinced of God's existence; but it is not nearly so necessary that it be demonstrated.'[13] And if later one is forced – 'critically' –
to conclude that it cannot be demonstrated, the comfort remains: its not
being able to be demonstrated ought in no way to trouble either metaphysics or the rational basis of theism.

We have, then, a fundamental disagreement about the tasks of a critical philosophy. For Kant, a thesis about being entails a critical withdrawal from a theory about God. One of the consequences of this
withdrawal is the acknowledgement of the theoretical possibility of

God's existence. For Nietzsche, a reluctance to engage ever more critically with theism only leads to ever more superficial pronouncements
about being or existence in general. Kant's thesis, once successful, ought
critically to turn on itself, calling into question the ideas of 'real predication' and of a simple and absolute logical 'positing' of a thing and its
determinations. The subtleties involved in distinguishing between a cat-
egorial actuality and possibility on the one hand and a non-categorial
Sein on the other (see note 3 below) are delusive. Ontology is not revi-
talised by refusing a theoretical theism or atheism, but rendered perni-
ciously empty. Its continued and increased influence derives both from
its having nothing to say and from its claiming to have a critical and transcendental justification for its having nothing to say. It continues by sus-
taining the influence of theism in and for a world no longer, practically
or theoretically, convinced by theism. Its silence on this matter is a positive and paralysing one; and what it paralyses is atheism. All of the
inconsistencies Nietzsche attributes to Kant's system have to do with
the refusal to delimit, consistently and atheistically, the concept of God.

There is an irony here, although its philosophical significance is not
immediately apparent. Nietzsche detects in Kant's claim to have
achieved a critical break from traditional ontotheology a means of perpetuating it. The transcendental remarking of certain traditional disputes cannot be logically recognised by the participants in them without
their ceasing, in some way, to be such participants. Thus the thesis about
being, rather than contributing to a debate, shows why no substantive
contribution is possible. But, on Nietzsche's terms, this invokes both a
far too insipid and regulated understanding of what a philosophical
debate is and a dogmatic and violent attempt to be exempted from any
debate. Kant's thesis about being is a move in a philosophical conversa-
tion about the existence or non-existence of God. It is not different in
kind from any other move, and the pretence that it is can only confirm
its continuity with the dogmatically theistic tradition that precedes it.
Nietzsche emphasises the continuity of Kantian discontinuity and in so
doing seeks to achieve a real discontinuity. To Kant's logical discontinuity for the sake of historical continuity, we can contrast Nietzsche's logical continuity for the sake of historical (genealogical) discontinuity.

III

The question is how a Nietzschean 'godlessness' works, of how it serves
a new thought of existence, and of how – and indeed whether – this new

thought can be broached or stated in non-Kantian terms; that is, in terms that permit us, finally and historically, to have done with whatever Kant was trying to accomplish logically in his thesis about being.[14] For the sake of brevity, we will restrict ourselves to an examination of one section from *The Gay Science* in which the Nietzschean trajectory to and from Kant is made quite explicit. It can be read as unfolding in four stages:[15]

(i) Entitled '*Our new "infinite"* [*Unser neues »Unendliches«*]', the section begins by referring to a series of questions that the advocates of perspectivism might reasonably be expected to have to answer, questions concerning:

> [h]ow far the perspective character of existence [*des Daseins*] extends or indeed whether existence has any other character than this; whether existence without interpretation [*Dasein ohne Auslegung*], without "sense" [*ohne »Sinn«*], does not become "nonsense" [*»Unsinn«*]; whether, on the other hand, all existence is not essentially engaged in *interpretation* [*nicht alles Dasein essentiell ein auslegendes Dasein ist*] –

Does perspectivism say only how *we* must think of existence? If so, might there not be something more to existence that we necessarily fail to grasp or to pick out both from our perspectives or in our interpretations and so with our notions of 'perspective' and 'interpretation'? Or are these concerns themselves scarcely legitimate? We seem to have a choice, either concluding that all existence is essentially engaged in interpretation, or concluding that existence not essentially engaged in interpretation is nonsense. This last claim says both that there is existence without sense and that there is nothing we can ever know or think about it. The claim both offers a thought of existence (all existence) and demarcates the line beyond which such a thought cannot go. Nothing follows from the 'There is' of 'There is nonsensical existence'. It is a lesson we would learn were we to hear 'All existence is essentially engaged in interpretation' as 'All existence, for us, is essentially engaged in interpretation'. Nietzsche thus rehearses a critical Kantian move, one that in part accepts the thesis about being: the distinction between existence essentially engaged with interpretation and existence without sense resembles that between an existence for us and an existence, as it were, in itself, and so on Nietzsche's reading that between the phenomenal and the noumenal. Yet in asking whether *all* existence might not be essentially engaged in interpretation, Nietzsche is also warning that these distinctions themselves must on some level be untenable.

(ii) And the response? To declare that everything here is undecidable:

> that cannot be decided even by the most industrious and most scrupulously
> conscientious analysis and self-examination of the intellect; for in the
> course of this analysis the human intellect cannot avoid seeing itself in its
> own perspectives, and *only* in these. We cannot look around our own
> corner: it is a hopeless curiosity that wants to know what other kinds of
> intellects and perspectives there *might* be;

The questions posed in (i) are so exhaustive, it is difficult to see how this
can be an adequate answer. It surely simply restates the perspectivism
under review; and in doing so, rather than leaving the matter undecided,
opts for a particular solution. Everything we say about existence must be
heard in terms of a 'for us', even when we ask about an existence that
would extend beyond it, an existence that 'for us' is not for us. The 'for
us' overwhelms all philosophical talk of *all* existence, just as perspectivism overwhelms each and any attempt to comment on its absolute
status.

(iii) Nietzsche continues with a change of tone:

> But I should think that today we are at least far from the ridiculous immod-
> esty that would be involved in decreeing from our corner that perspectives
> are permitted only from this corner. Rather has the world become "infinite"
> for us all over again, inasmuch as we cannot reject the possibility that *it may
> include infinite interpretations* [*unendliche Interpretationen*].

Here we touch on the paradox at the heart of Nietzsche's project: an
infinity (the world becoming infinite) that, *for us*, removes us from the
centre of things; a non-anthropocentric perspectivism; a perspectivism
that concedes its own perspectival character, but one that discerns in
that concession neither self-refutation nor self-undermining. Note how
Nietzsche insists that the manner in which the world once again
becomes a problem *for us* no longer permits of a critical or transcendental block to the question of the possibility of infinite interpretations. Perspectivism and the problem of the world is the problem of perspectivism
and the possibility of infinite perspectives. In this identification lies the
acknowledgement that with perspectivism there is the return of a
description of the world that could reconfigure it as a problem for us.
And this just is the final version of the problem of the 'for us'. As we
encounter the term in this passage, 'the world' names what demands the
perpetual radicalising of the 'for us'. We can thus never rest secure with
a statement to the effect that 'The world is [or exists] for us'.

(iv) The section comes to its close:

> Once more we are seized by a great shudder; but who would feel inclined immediately to deify [*vergöttlichen*] again after the old manner this monster of an unknown world? And to worship the unknown henceforth as "the Unknown One" [*»den Unbekannten«*]. Alas, too many *ungodly* possibilities of interpretation [*viele **ungöttliche** Möglichkeiten der Interpretation*] are included in the unknown, too much devilry, stupidity, and foolishness of interpretation – even our own human, all too human folly, which we know.

What is to be avoided is an inference from the world's possibly containing infinite interpretations not so much to the thought of its being once again unknown and unknowable, but rather to the thought that the thought of its being once again unknown and unknowable is something more than just one more interpretation. Nietzsche opposes not so much the thought of the limits of the knowable as the thought that such limits legitimise a reverence or uncertainty before the thought of the unknown and unknowable that lies beyond them. The world and the perspectivist 'for us' must be thought atheistically. Neither 'The world exists for us' nor 'The world does not exist for us' adequately expresses Nietzsche's perspectivism. Each may however have a strategic value and function; the former introducing the topic, the latter de-anthropomorphising it; the former implicitly making of all philosophical existence theories and claims, theories and claims of an irreducible existence-for-us, the latter showing how even ontology must be informed by an absolute and infinite indifference; the former always restricting renewed talk of a substantial and theorisable unknown 'it' that exists in and as this indifference, the latter always on hand to counter the confidence even this restriction might encourage – the thought, for example, that it stands as a critical or transcendental delimitation. Nietzsche speaks here of an infinite that is not godly and whose analysis can never break free of the symptomatology that reveals the endlessly human (all too human) attempts at a definitive interpretation.

The tendency or temptation to deify involves positing a perspective (God's) that is not just another perspective, an interpretation (God's) that is not just another interpretation. It is a positing of an unknowable and unthinkable existence – and so of the existence of the unknowable and the unthinkable – that coheres around the name of God and falls under 'his' comprehension. And even though, for Kant, this cannot be said theoretically, on pain of irrationality, its possibility keeps everything and above all the thing in itself in place. Existence outside interpretation and perspective is synonymous with existence outside *our* interpretation and perspective, and finally with existence in and from God's interpretation and perspective. On a Nietzschean reading, Kant's thesis about being ought to conclude with the realisation that existence claims, of whatever sort, are necessarily always interpretations, always perspectival. To treat this realisation as a cause for either epistemological despair (What then can we ever know about what *really* is?) or self-congratulation (And so doesn't everything in the end speak of, to, and for *us*?) is, implicitly, to rely on the traditional devaluing of perspective, interpretation, and evaluation. It is to assume that the partiality of a perspective is a sign of its falling short of an absolute or divine perspective, *one* from which we are perhaps forever excluded but *one* to which we aspire and *one* against which we judge ourselves.

The thesis about being should work to free the thought of being from the grip of ontotheology; but it cannot do so in its Kantian pre-critical or critical contexts; for we 'deify again after the old manner' when we think that the philosophical use of the notion of the unknown or the unknowable provides grounds for the thought that the unknown or the unknowable exists; and we also 'deify again after the old manner' when we introduce a thesis about being to show that, theoretically, such an existence must be judged (evaluated as) possible. Each of these deifications assumes that a certain definition or critique is hereby completed; there being little or no sense to the idea that the necessary existence at issue might be further analysed with regard to other interpretations and evaluations, the perspectives in which it resounds *for us*. Perspectivism requires that we, the world, and its infinite possible interpretations be ungodly: the unknown can have no privileged logical or ontological purchase on the known; it is not *one*.

IV

Nietzsche's perspectivism is announced and refined in such an exact fashion, its aphorisms and styles so deliberately set against what it sees and ridicules as the garrulous pedantry of academic philosophy, that to question it is inevitably to seem unsubtle, dull, essentially incapable of appreciating it. Yet that risk notwithstanding, is there not a suspicion of invulnerability here, the insinuation that Nietzsche's text, at its most ingenious, is a trap for the always culpable reader and that not to accept the triad *perspectivism / atheism / genealogy* is to have succumbed to the very stupidity it has described and isolated? With this suspicion in mind, we conclude with the following questions.

Does the atheism of Nietzsche's genealogical critique consist in the deployment of godlessness or the non-existence of God, not as a metaphysical thesis but as a regulative ideal, that is, as a rule for the advancement of genealogy as a critical and historical thinking? If so, is it not the straightforward counterpart to Kantian critique, advancing both by way of an implicit transcendental argument (the non-existence of God as a condition for the possibility of genealogical critique and indeed for an *active* life) and by the promise of a justification of a certain 'common sense' (genealogy confirming the atheism already assumed, if not yet affirmed, in contemporary life and culture)? Would we have here a moment when the 'critique' in 'genealogical critique' is not entirely constrained by the adjective, when it remains a transcendental and non-historical affair?

Being is not a real predicate: to Nietzschean ears, Kant's thesis is both too modest and not modest enough. It is too modest in that it refuses to affirm its consequences for ontotheology and so to begin the move to an a-theistic ontology; too modest in that it is unable to prevent what should have been a subsequent and thoroughgoing moral critique of the concept of God from collapsing into a godly moralism. It is not modest enough in that it pretends to speak from a positively transcendental viewpoint, one that distinguishes it from previous metaphysics and one that can now be identified as the site and property of critical philosophy. The modesty of Kant's thesis derives from the thought that in commenting on the ontological argument in this critical manner a new sort of philosophical gesture is being employed. Kant's take on the ontological argument is supposedly not akin to, say, Gaunilon's objections to Anselm. Nietzsche challenges this pretension to a new sort of gesture, not because newness is impossible here but because what marks it as new is a critical ineffectuality, a passive appeal for non-participation; Kant's joke being to have propounded a new thesis as a non-event. Thus even in its lack of modesty, the thesis is charged with not going far enough. Nietzsche, like most of those who in part accept the thesis, will make this complaint: it doesn't go far enough; it doesn't clarify the implications for philosophy of this treatment of 'being'; the difference it introduces remains underdetermined. But the Nietzschean accusation is more far-reaching than any other. 'Kant's joke' relies on the self-evidence of the idea that a philosophical thesis must make a difference and that the difference it makes must be historically evaluatable. It is as though the difference Kant invokes, the difference that characterises one version of the step into critique, is not weighty enough, not different or discontinuous enough, to register genealogically. But it would be interesting to ask whether philosophy might not actually need this new and newly underdetermined difference, indeed whether it might only be able to proceed by way of a modest critical capitulation to the thought that it leaves everything as it is, and whether, *contra* Nietzsche, a positive value might not have to be given to what will always be genealogically analysed as a difference that makes no difference, and so to something that, by definition, genealogy always *misses*.

Note an ambiguity in the Nietzschean and perspectivist appropriation of the thesis about being, as we have imagined it, that hints in the direction of such questions. Consider the following two aspects:

(a) Deification of the unknown involves an implicit recourse to an ontological argument. The thesis about being is thus an effective check to such deification. But the thesis in this context is the modest Kantian version. It does not assert that the unknown does not exist; true, nor does it conclude that the existence of the unknown is possible, but in insisting that the unknown be examined with respect to its human possibilities the emphasis, like that in the first *Critique*, is placed firmly on those finite beings who ponder existence and non-existence. To this extent at least, the trajectory of Nietzsche's perspectivism accepts Kant's thesis in its modest achievement.

(b) If Kant's thesis is to endorse atheism, then it would seem that from the claim that 'Being is not a real predicate', Nietzsche must conclude that 'God cannot exist necessarily' and that 'Necessarily God cannot exist'. There need be nothing logically contentious here. The important point is that Nietzsche treats the thesis as a claim not about the incoherence of the predicate when interpreted as 'real' but, firstly, about the historical event of God's non-existence and, secondly, about all the tricks needed for philosophy to continue with theism in the wake of this event (many of these tricks being provided by Kant). So read, the thesis belongs to an argument that *must* effect a change in those theists or agnostics who admit its validity. But doesn't this claim simply contradict what Nietzsche says in *Daybreak*, the very lines we cited earlier: 'today one indicates how the belief that there is a God could arise and how this belief acquired its weight and importance: *a counter-proof that there is no God thereby becomes superfluous*'?[16] Has not historical refutation replaced logical refutation? The crucial word here, however, is 'today' ('*heute*'); for an argument is needed that carries Nietzsche's reader from the logical interest in God's necessary existence and non-existence, that quest for proof and counter-proof, to the current genealogical interest in indicating both how such a logical interest arose and how, for such a long time, it was satisfied. An argument is needed that warrants that 'thereby' ('*dadurch*'). Whereas Kant would seek to demonstrate the theoretical impossibility of proof or counter-proof, Nietzsche would indicate, firstly, the historical significance and function of the proof and, secondly and *consequently*, the superfluity of any counter-proof. In order to avoid Kant's transcendental talk of 'possibility' here, the anaemic and non-historical 'distance' it would ostensibly keep from the tradition, Nietzsche needs to produce or to imagine a context where atheism and the (historical) refutation of theism *must* be acknowledged and where not to acknowledge them reflects back onto the reader, back onto the symptomatic nature of the reader's refusal or inability.

Interestingly at this juncture the rhetorical aim of Nietzsche's writing is not dissimilar to that of Descartes' ontological argument in the Third Meditation. Descartes moves from a definition of God, a clarification of the thought of God, to the claim that God exists; and given the context in which that argument arises (the comfort it brings to the logical solipsist of the Second Meditation and the task it will need to perform in the Fourth Meditation), Descartes implies that it would be wilfully irrational not to accept theism as a result of accepting this argument for it. This is not quite the case with Anselm who does not seem to think that his argument, even if acknowledged to be valid, can in and of itself force anyone to be reconciled with religious theism. It serves rather as an aid to faith. In an age of Christian theism, the understanding need not be insulted by that theism. And it seems uncontroversial to conceive that someone might continue to think, say, a particular (modal) ontological proof valid and its premises true, yet not be himself or herself a believer in God's existence. There is nothing necessarily wrong here; but for Descartes and, I think, Nietzsche there is; and although they have very different assumptions and expectations as to what can stand or work as an argument, for the one it must lead to (actual) theism, for the other, to (actual) atheism. The refusal to accept the event of atheism, the necessity of God's non-existence, must always count for Nietzsche as a further symptom of decadence. A decadent philosopher, we might say, is not only one who *today* is not atheistic but also one who denies that *today* an argument concerning necessary (non-)existence can logically affirm and endorse atheism.

The argument of (a) cannot be that of (b); moreover, if (b) holds then the modest thesis of (a) cannot begin to do its work. Kant's thesis about being takes as one of its targets just that sort of assurance about the productivity of arguments that, in very different ways, Descartes and Nietzsche espouse. The decadent philosopher of (b) may be indebted to the very same modest version of the thesis that succeeded in the formulating of the perspectivism in (a). The assertive and productive version of the thesis in (b) could never arrive at, let alone sustain, that formulation. For Nietzsche, we humans, to whose evaluations and interpretations philosophy must turn, ought not to think of (evaluate, interpret) ourselves as necessarily theists; for Kant, we ought so to think of ourselves. This is not the dispute that concerns us in the present paper. For Nietzsche, the analysis of interpretation and evaluation cannot properly begin until released from the taint of necessary theism; for Kant, the means by which such release would be won run counter to the modest ruling of the thesis about being. Here, broadly stated, is the relevant disagreement; and there is no getting beyond it. Either, with Nietzsche, philosophy learns to laugh at the self-evidently ludicrous idea of Kant's continuing and of our continuing today with Kant – Kant's continued theism simply amplifying the obviousness of the joke; or, remembering how Nietzsche supplements perspectivism by aligning the thesis about being with a pre-Kantian confidence in the effects of arguments concerning necessary (non-)existence, philosophy continually indicates the way in which this anti-Kantian usage falls vulnerable to the thesis itself, to the permutations of the supposedly ludicrous difference that makes no difference, to this new and always almost *critical* summary. If there is no getting beyond the disagreement – in the end perhaps it does come down to inclination, to sentiment or training – it may nevertheless open up a space in which a certain philosophy learns to continue and learns that it must continue, a continuing that neither theism nor atheism guarantees and that is itself neither theistic nor atheistic; and if such a philosophy should come to admit to the *possibility* of theism or atheism that admission in its non-participation only indicates that philosophy's critical task lies elsewhere. Even in their most familiar surroundings, Kant's reflections on the ontological argument show the subtlety of the call to a critical caution, a modesty just modest enough:

> The concept of a supreme being is in many respects a very useful idea. But this idea, precisely because it is merely that, is quite incapable of allowing us to expand, by means of it alone, our cognition regarding what

exists. Even as regards possibility the idea is unable to teach us anything further.[17]

If genealogy or perspectivism is necessarily atheistic, philosophy is never necessarily synonymous with genealogy or perspectivism. Can we go further? If genealogy or perspectivism is necessarily atheistic, it may even be that necessarily philosophy is not synonymous with genealogy or perspectivism. And there will always be a sense to its continuing in and as that difference.

Notes

1 Friedrich Nietzsche, *The Gay Science*, trans. Walter Kaufmann (New York: Random House, 1974), sec. 335, p. 264.

2 Kant, *CPR*, A598/B626.

3 It should also be added that in the *Beweisgrund* it is *'Dasein'* that is not a real predicate (Kant, *The One Possible Basis for a Demonstration of the Existence of God*). In the first *Critique*, it is *Sein*; *Dasein* there being reserved for the name of one of the modal categories deduced and listed as a fundamental concept of the understanding. To use this category in saying that something exists or does not exist, is to say that it is actualised or non-actualised, that it is or is not actual. So used, as a real predicate, it is synthesised with an intuition. The truths it is employed to express are contingent. Their negations are not contradictions. 'God is actual' can never be an analytical proposition. Some things are actual, some things are not: some things are possible, some things are not. But the 'are' here does not predicate actuality or possibility of non-actual things or impossible states of affairs. It belongs rather to the non- (or extra-)categorial *Sein*. To say that God's actuality (God's actually existing) is possible is simply to say that an analysis of the concept of God in terms of being (*Sein*), i.e., in terms of positing 'There is God', does not result in a contradiction. The attentiveness to a difference reflected in this technical distinguishing between *'Sein'* and *'Dasein'* demonstrates one of the important effects of Kant's step into critical philosophy. The critical Kant has a far subtler way of explaining why the thesis about being can theoretically support neither theism nor atheism. The critical thesis, at least in its negative phase, does seem to suggest either a sense of the copula that cannot be captured in traditional subject/predicate logic or a sense of being that cannot be conflated with being extant, with *Vorhandensein*.

4 Friedrich Nietzsche, *Daybreak*, trans. R. J. Hollingdale (Cambridge, Cambridge University Press, 1982), sec. 92, p. 54.

5 Ibid., sec. 95, p. 54.

6 Friedrich Nietzsche, *The Anti-Christ*, trans. R. J. Hollingdale (Har-

mondsworth: Penguin, 1968), p. 197.

7   Nietzsche, *The Gay Science*, sec. 193, pp. 205–6.

8   Kant, *CPR*, Bxxxii.

9   Kant, *CPR*, Ax.

10 Nietzsche, *The Gay Science*, sec. 335, p. 264, t.m.

11 See Kant, *Op.p.*, p. 211; *Ak*.XXII: 51–2.

12 Friedrich Nietzsche 'On Truth and Lies in a Nonmoral Sense', in *Philosophy and Truth – Selections from Nietzsche's Notebooks*, ed. D. Breazeale (Atlantic Highlands, NJ: Humanities Press, 1990).

13 Kant, *EG*, p. 239.

14 As an aside, note that, once released from the monotheistic ontology, Nietzsche is willing to use or mention the word 'god'. In *The Gay Science*, the one who propounds the doctrine of eternal return, the demon who comes to 'your loneliest loneliness', is described – by 'you' – as 'a god' (sec. 341, pp. 273–4). The point though is that it is the thought (of eternal return) that strikes the hearer as divine. Contrast this with the dull inertia of the god named 'God' whose most important feature, philosophically, is said to be his having to exist.

15 Ibid., sec. 374, pp. 336–7.

16 Nietzsche, *Daybreak*, sec. 95, p. 54, emphases added.

17 Kant, *CPR*, A602/B630.

8

Exposing Community: Towards a Dynamics of commercium

Kath Renark Jones

A subjectivity hears itself from far off and intimately at the same time, in this frail and singular unison, the subjectivity is being born, but it will never be born as such. Once born, the subject is only the *Ich denke*.[1]

But there would be no power relations, nor would there be such a specific unleashing of power (there would merely be a mechanics of force), if the political were not the place of community – in other words, the place of a specific existence, the existence of being-in-common, which gives rise to the existence of being-self.[2]

Contemporary political and philosophical theory tends to derive its understanding of the meaning of community from the work of Hegel. Hegel distinguished between *Moralität* (morality understood as relating to the abstract and universal subject) and *Sittlichkeit* (morality understood as relative to a certain kind of being). This distinction informs mainstream analytic understandings of community as being based either upon the model of an abstract 'unencumbered' self (Rawls and liberal individualism) or upon the socially, culturally and historically contextualised self (Sandell and communitarianism). The problem with both of these accounts is that they begin with an uncritical assumption that there exists a clearly understood distinction between the subject and community and that community is founded upon a complete and accurate extrapolation of the nature of this subject (on the basis of a principle of the just or the good). Political thinkers falling into a broadly continental tradition tend not to take for granted any specific model of the subject, indeed, many are critical of the very basis from which formulations of the subject are derived. It remains the case, however, that on the whole their conceptions of community emerge from out of their critique, deconstruction or performative models of this problematised subject.

The presupposition of a separation between subject and community – the (Hegelian) 'I' and 'we' – connected through the moral law and the further uncritical assumption that community can be explained by, or is derived from, an accurate depiction of the nature of the subject should not, however, be taken for granted. The use of 'community' in a philosophical context long pre-dates Hegel, playing an important role in the works of Aristotle, Cicero, Augustine, Aquinas, Burke and Rousseau, to name but a few. It is, however, only in post-Kantian philosophy that community takes on the form which dominates current discourse on the subject, namely, the specific subject-community definitional relation circumscribed by morality. It is therefore to the works of Kant that this paper directs its attention for, it will be argued, it is in Kant's critical philosophy that the division between the subject and community is first articulated in the way which informs today's critical (and less than critical) debates. This paper attempts to locate the emergence of the modern conception of community in Kant's critical philosophy and, more importantly, argues that this conception is based upon a particular interpretation of certain elements of the critical project. The aim of the paper is to suggest how it is possible to read these elements in a different light (one already explored to some extent in the works of Foucault and Lyotard) and to derive therefrom an alternative productive and dynamic conception of community.

Kant formulates a number of hierarchically conceived yet interdependent theories of community between the texts of the first and third *Critiques*. The most important of these, for our purposes, will be the epistemological community (concerning conceptual knowledge) and the aesthetic community (based upon judgements of taste concerning the beautiful and the sublime). In exploring and comparing these, we will immediately be drawn to a distinction Kant ambiguously draws between ways in which community can be realised, namely, in the forms of *commercium* and *communio*. *Communio* is the name of community operating on a principle of unity. *Commercium* is community conceived as interactive multiplicity ungoverned by any organising or binding principle. Community is given in the *Critique of Pure Reason* as the third division of the logical moment of relation in the table of categories. These categories, we are told, are to be discovered by means of 'an exhaustive statement of the functions of unity in judgement';[3] they are functions which 'specify the understanding completely, and yield an exhaustive inventory of its powers.'[4] As a pure concept of the understanding, community is derived from the disjunctive form of judgement, the third form of judgement under the heading of relation (the other two being the categorical and the hypothetical forms, of which it is a combination).

Judgements: Relation	Categories: Relation
– Categorical	– Of Inherence in Substance
	(*substantia et accidens*)
– Hypothetical	– Of Causality and Dependence
	(cause and effect)
– Disjunctive	– Of Community
	(reciprocity between agent and patient)

As a concept, 'community is the causality of substances reciprocally determining one another'.[5] As disjunctive judgement, it is the relation between two or more concepts or propositions, a relation which is not that of logical sequence but of logical opposition. Thus, 'if one member of the division is posited, all the rest are excluded, and conversely.'[6] The category of community is then a pure synthetic concept contained *a priori* in the understanding which holds together the conceptual elements that constitute the territory of that which can come to be known on the basis of a principle of exclusive disjunction. This concept of community is that which makes possible the transcendental object (the object $= x$), that is, the object of knowledge, by determining the space (the intellectual terrain) into which it must arrive if it is to be known at all. '[T]his unity must be regarded as necessary *a priori* – otherwise knowledge would be without an object'.[7] The relation between epistemological community and the field of what can be known will be shown to presuppose an epistemological subject whose separation (from others) and unity (as a subject) relies upon the more originary community of the transcendental unity of apperception.

The nature and status of the aesthetic community is not so straightforward. This form of community, it will be shown, is a necessary prerequisite for the formulation of subjectivity, which both ethical and epistemological community require for their articulation. In consequence, it will be argued, aesthetic community must be understood as both pre-conceptual and pre-schematic, ontologically preceding the formulation of the subject and occurring prior to, or in conjunction with, the community designated as a *communio*. Having established that the aesthetic community is a *commercium* rather than a *communio*, however, we will be faced with the problem of deciding to which kind of aesthetic experience it properly belongs, the beautiful or the sublime. Given the association of community with the idea of the *sensus communis*, which Kant deems the subjective principle determining the judgement of the beautiful, this issue may seem unproblematic. The fact that judgements of taste (regarding the beautiful) rely upon community does not, however, entail that community is discovered only in this relation, nor indeed that the relation between community (qua *sensus communis*) and aesthetic judgement (regarding the beautiful) is primordial. What is crucial here is Kant's analysis of the sublime and especially his analysis of enthusiasm, as an extreme form of sublime experience, for it is through this feeling – often misunderstood because of its association with forms of political action – that the sublime can be understood to open on to a being-in-common that is immediate and invokes an ethos for the subject that emerges out of it. The subjective principle necessary for the judgement of taste in the beautiful depends upon the more originary relation between sublime experience and community as being-in-common, for it is only in relation to being-in-common that subjective experience is possible. The ethos here invoked is thus to be understood as the mode of existence appropriate to the coming-into-being of the (Kantian) subject.

This means that the mode of existence and appropriation of a 'self' (which is not necessarily, nor exclusively, an individual) is the mode of an exposition in common and to the in-common, and this exposition exposes the self even in its 'in itself', in its 'ipseity', and in its own distinctiveness, in its isolation or in its solitude. Only a being-in-common can make possible a being-separated.[8]

What is being argued here is that the fundamental seat of aesthetic community, understood as a *commercium*, grounding humanity's sense of community (which is not a consensus but a *sensus communis*), is exposed in the experience of the sublime. The sense of community glimpsed in the sublime experience requires the invocation of an ethos of being-in-common prior to any specific being of community. This ethos is the force of animation, breathing life into the 'we' of humanity, for it is that which marks out human being by putting into play the full range of its faculties.

Citing the sublime experience as an opening on to all other forms of community has far-reaching consequences, most importantly, the fact that it establishes a basis for interaction, association and exchange (qua *commercium*) prior to Kant's wedding of community (as *sensus communis*) to the ethical domain governed by practical reason. It is community in this latter sense that forms the basis of the humanist identification of the 'we' with an 'us', that is, of the undetermined multiplicity with a unifying principle, quantifying and qualifying being-in-common. The judgement of taste in the beautiful, despite its origination in the free-flow of purposivelessness and the non-determinative play of the faculties, is nonetheless equated with the force of the moral law in its claim to universality based on a hierarchy. That is, insofar as the judgement of taste in the beautiful privileges specific cultural and historical traditions,[9] it always determines the 'we' (being-in-common) as a specific 'us'. In this way, the potential for association, interaction and transformation present in the *commercium* of human being is limited by the determination of an 'us', a *communio* where all forms of interaction are prescribed for in advance by the governing system.

It is a fundamental proposition of this paper that aesthetic community, that form of *commercium* exposed in the experience of the sublime, be thought of as ontologically prior to both epistemological and ethical (moral) community, in that it is out of this former that both the knowing subject (required for the formulation of epistemological community) and the reasoning-moral subject (necessary for the formulation of ethical community) emerge. The possibility of there being a subject who makes a judgement upon the beautiful is thus also dependent upon this former insofar as the subjective principle upon which their judgement depends, namely, the sharing out of a sense in-common (which affords the judgement the status of universality), first requires the possibility of a feeling of being-in-common. Furthermore, it will become clear from this that being-in-common is only erroneously equated with consensus.

Both forms of aesthetic community (that is, *sensus communis* in the beautiful, and aesthetic *commercium* in the sublime) are pre-conceptual, operating independently of concepts, interest and purposiveness. The community of the faculties experienced in the judgement of the beautiful involves a harmonic process, a process driven by the productive imagination. This faculty, however, is only designated and determined in its nature and limitations in and through the experience of the sublime. It is thus out of the sublime experience of being-in-common that mutually exclusive faculties emerge as belonging together in exclusive disjunction. It is the *felt* community of this exclusive disjunction – the feeling of harmonisation – that the judgement of taste in the beautiful supplies, a harmony which is attuned by the imposition of a principle of *communio*. Attunement here is ultimately dictated, as we will see, by the law of morality, in whose hand is grasped the baton for organising and ordering the time of appearance (of what will be heard, when, and in what arrangement it will be heard).

> For this attunement is the subjective condition of [the process of] cogni-
> tion, and without it cognition [in the sense of] the effect [of this process]
> could not arise. ... the only way this attunement can be determined is by
> feeling (rather than by concepts).[10]

The possibility of engaging with the originary aesthetic sense of community, exposed in the moment of the sublime (as the birth of the subject), must be differentiated from that work of the imagination
underlying the function of intuition in the Transcendental Aesthetic of
CPR. For whilst this earlier engagement suggests the possibility of confronting an originary *sensus* of the 'we', of the in-common, the productive force of the imagination in this text is vanquished by the demands
of knowledge (of human nature understood specifically as knowing subjectivity) and reduced to a mere chaos of sensation.[11] The role of
schematisation is central to this enslavement and delimitation of the
power and role of the productive imagination, where the transcendental
schema (as both intellectual and sensible) is the product of the imagination in its role as negotiator between the faculties. In the diplomatic
service of the subject, of a knowing 'I' which already presupposes the
'us' of knowing subjectivity and is, as such, a determination of the 'we'
of being-in-common, the relation to the matter of sensation (of *sensus*-
in-common) is already domesticated. The forms in which it can arrive,
that is, the potential for human association, exchange, interaction and
transformation are already prescribed. As Jean-François Lyotard
remarks, in the process of schematisation: 'The question of *there is*,
momentarily evoked on the occasion of the sensible given, is quickly forgotten for the question of *what there is*.'[12]

The matter of sensation is that which cannot be calculated, that which
disconcerts us and seizes us. Only as in-formation (i.e., as 'what there
is'), in its formation, can it be calculated conceptually. Two forms of pure
imaginative receptivity are discernible within the critical project. The
first, as already remarked, arises in the Transcendental Aesthetic of *CPR*
but is transformed and domesticated by virtue of the authority accorded
to schematisation and in the synthetic processes leading to knowledge.[13]
The second is given in the *Critique of Judgement* in the contemplation of
the form of the beautiful object and in the experience of the sublime. In
the latter experiences, the production of a feeling arises upon the occasion of a perception unbounded by the constraints of cognition. There
is no determinate schematisation in this experience but rather an affective relation, a harmonisation that does not require the mediation of a

transcendental schema. In the aesthetic experience of judgements of taste in the beautiful there is no presupposed unity, unity is rather brought about in and through harmonisation. There is, however, an underlying *sensus* in the form of feeling, which is understood by Kant as the bringing-into-attunement not merely of the faculties as such, but of the nature of communication in general. 'Moreover, this attunement itself, and hence also the feeling of it …, must be universally communicable, while the universal communicability of a feeling presupposes a common sense.'[14] This common sense must thus be understood as that which is attuned, that is, as the feeling of being-in-common, a *commercium* brought into attunement (designated as a unity through imposition of *communio*) by virtue of the principle of universal communicability. There will then be for Man (as the individuated and totalised product of community as unity) only one voice, the universal, common voice, *die allgemeine Stimme*.

No sense of community accessed through the aesthetic can be bound by concepts, nor can it be subject to schematisation. At least, it is possible to appreciate that it must be pre-schematic, where this pre- is itself compromised by the immediate and synchronic nature of aesthetic experience. How then, if it is neither conceptually determined nor informed, is this sense of community experienced? We can read Kant as allowing for two possibilities: it may be experienced either as Idea, transcending the conceptual (and its limitations), or as feeling, for which no concept or idea is properly appropriate. If the former (Idea), it will reside ultimately in the domain of freedom and will fall under the legislative authority of reason, if the latter (feeling), it will be hard-pressed to escape condemnation (by the combined forces of the faculties of reason and understanding) as, at best, unrepresentable and, at worst, pathological. For community to fall under reason's remit requires that it be formulated as a *communio*, that is, as a community of unity in oneness: the unconditioned totality of identity and difference that is the supersensible destination of the species thought as a whole (the moral community). This entrapment of the sense of community is achieved in the Dialectic of Aesthetic Judgement in *CJ*, through the resolution of the antinomy of taste. The disjunctive judgement determines, through opposition, the delimitation of community as the product of sense in its relation to the supersensible substrate of humanity. This is the community of feeling, the *sensus communis* attuned as an 'us', which it is then possible to share in (or parcel out) in the form of universal communicability. This, all too often, is the fate of the modern sense of community reduced to a belief in some mystical and unrepresentable source of attunement (unification in the one common voice), or governed by a dogmatic and authoritarian principle of abstract justice in which the 'us' of dominant discourse holds the baton.

In what follows it will be suggested that it is possible to think of the ontologically prior community exposed in the sublime rather than the beautiful (which, for Kant at least, is always subservient to attunement) in a way that frees it from the necessity of association with either mysticism or authoritarianism. A community which, rather than falling into chaos and meaninglessness (as did the productive imagination in *CPR*), preserves the possibility of anticipating an ethos – a being-in-common – peculiar to beings-in-becoming. Such a *commercium* does not determine in advance what there is or may be (i.e., what may come into community and the nature of the relations in which it will figure), on the grounds of prescriptive (exclusive) determinations of interaction, association and transformation. In order to realise this possibility, however, the feeling of community (its *sensus*) will have to be shown to be separable from the idea (and demands) of morality. Such a move will have to contend with Kant's claim that, 'the beautiful is the symbol of the morally good' and furthermore, 'only because we refer ... the beautiful to the morally good ... does our liking for it include a claim to everyone else's assent'.[15] What will be required, then, will be a dissociation of the aesthetic claim to universality from its symbolic link with the moral which avoids simply reducing aesthetic community to the conceptual *commercium* which can be seen to be implicit in *CPR*,[16] that is, to community articulable through concepts governed by the principle of non-contradiction (exclusive disjunction) and preserving a primary relation to being-in-common.

In order to understand better the unsatisfactory limitation that this reduction would involve, it is necessary to look more closely at epistemological community (the community of possible knowledge) in *CPR*. Kant accords a high status to the pure concept of community, insofar as it is that 'without which even local community (*communio spatii*) could never be empirically known.'[17] *Communio spatii* is conceptually unified community whose binding force is derived from its being directed towards a specific end, or from its sharing some founding principle of identity. Specific domains of knowledge (or, to use a Lyotardian frame of reference, genres of discourse) collectively belong to the more general epistemological community, that is, the community of possible knowledge, yet their relation to one another is disjunctive. We can see this to be the case in Kant's explanation of the relation between propo-

sitions in a judgement, where we extend such disjunctive epistemological community to cover the relationship between genres of discourse:

> Finally, the disjunctive judgement contains a relation of two or more propo-
> sitions to each other, a relation, not, however, of logical sequence, but of
> logical opposition, in so far as the sphere of the one excludes the sphere of
> the other, and yet at the same time of community, in so far as the proposi-
> tions taken together occupy the whole sphere of the knowledge in ques-
> tion. The disjunctive judgement expresses, therefore, a relation of the parts
> of the sphere of such knowledge, since the sphere of each part is a com-
> plement of the sphere of the others, yielding together the sum-total of
> divided knowledge. … There is, therefore, in a disjunctive judgement a cer-
> tain community of the known constituents, such that they mutually exclude
> each other, and yet thereby determine *in their totality* the true knowledge.
> For, when taken together, they constitute the whole content of one given
> knowledge.[18]

On the basis of the logic of the principle of the excluded middle, epistemological community determines all possible domains of know-
ledge/genres of discourse which are included (disjunctively) within the
community of what can be known.[19] The rule of the infinitation of the
negative operates here to ensure that any element, relation or exchange
between elements not determined in accordance with the principle of
identity will be located in the non-place of the 'other', that is, of the negatively defined, indeterminate and unrepresentable (within which no
differentiation is possible, there being no internal boundaries).[20] The
unity of epistemological community is thus based on a logic of identity
and exclusive disjunction. Aesthetic community in the judgement of
taste on the beautiful, on the other hand, whilst also being a *commercium*
of disjunctive elements, is of a non-conceptual nature and its disjunction
is presented as a harmony of heterogeneous elements. Each of these
modes of *commercium* is governed by an underlying principle of community as *communio* and it is in this that they are fundamentally differentiated from the *commercium* exposed in the experience of the
sublime. In this latter, difference is inclusive as non-determinative disjunction respecting no principle of identity or law of the excluded
middle.

This underlying feature grounding the principle of identity for epistemological community is a *communio* that does not admit of multiplicity:

> In our mind, all appearances, since they are contained in a possible experi-
> ence, must stand in community (*communio*) of apperception, and in so far

as the objects are to be represented as coexisting in connection with each other, they must mutually determine their position in *one* time, and thereby constitute a whole.[21]

This *communio* of the transcendental unity of apperception instantiates the 'I' that determines the 'we' of multiplicity as an 'us' (a unified in-common) through the transcendental determination of time (transcendental schematisation). Its control, disciplining and organising (through synchronisation) and unifying (with the baton of attunement), is analogous to the function of the moral law in its relation to the aesthetic community of taste in the beautiful (although in the former the time signature establishes time reference whereas, in the latter, there is merely the promise of a supersensible destination). The transcendental unity of apperception, as *communio*, is the condition for the possibility of knowledge, that is, of epistemological *commercium* on the basis of which empirical knowledge is possible. Any *communio spatii* (a specific field of knowledge or genre of discourse) is reliant upon the community of possible knowledge that is epistemological *commercium*, which we now see is in turn dependent (in order to be constituted as knowledge for the subject) upon the community that is a *communio* of apperception using transcendental schematisation, the time signature for its attunement. 'Real' community, the 'real community (*commercium*) of substances',[22] is accessible only under the binding force of the *communio* that determines it as possible knowledge of and for a subject. It cannot be accessed in any way other than through the schematic processes that belong to the transcendental unity of apperception, that is, not 'real' but ideal community, community as *communio*. The crucial point to establish here, however, is that this very *communio* that is the subject (transcendental unity of apperception) is itself the product of a more fundamental *commercium*, which, it will be shown, is that community of being-in-common exposed in the sublime. Moreover, through examining the work of the productive imagination in the sublime experience, we can re-access the relation of sense and nature (the matter of sensation) begun in the Transcendental Aesthetic of *CPR*, which was so quickly abandoned and lost to sense in the face of the demands made by the pursuit of the conceptual schema.

The move to recuperate this loss, made possible by the re-working of the productive imagination in *CJ*, is performed by way of a transformation of the attempt at expressing the matter of sensation. In order to guard against the risk of falling into transcendental illusion, the productive imagination in *CPR* is domesticated and any affective relation to the matter of sensation is sacrificed to silence, a silence that is the sign of that which cannot be expressed, of the non-sense of affectivity.

The subject emerges out of its own activity insofar as it conjoins those heterogeneous elements which themselves emerge as independent and contesting faculties only through this bridging in a harmonious relation that is designated as the work of Man. In order to succeed in this work, however, it must reach out beyond itself to being-in-common, for it is only from out of this in-common that it can come to itself, come into its own being. The 'I' of individuation is forever conjoined to, and yet at odds with, the 'we' of its multiplicity (totalised as an 'us'). The 'we' that is *commercium* is an undifferentiated multiplicity that is unified as a *communio* under the ascription of an 'us'. A domain of *communio* realisable through the logic of exclusive disjunction is thus consolidated for the newly emerging subject able to name and identify itself at any moment in its own being, its own community.

In the feeling of the sublime, the presentation lacks those free forms brought into harmony and accord in the feeling of the beautiful. The imagination suffers a failure here and must make an appeal to the Ideas of reason, specifically to the Idea of freedom, in order to accommodate and be accommodated within the domain of experience. But to speak of a failure of the pure productive imagination is not quite accurate, for the experience of the sublime precisely exceeds any presentation in a form. What fails is, rather, on the one hand, the transcendental determination of time which would make possible the installation of a schema in preparation for cognition, and, on the other hand, the attempt by the imagination to re-present its own activity in the movement of the free-floating forms which bring about a harmonisation of the faculties. The sublime enacts both a closing-down of the subject upon its own limitations – a binding or bonding – yet at the same time, an opening, a horizon on to that which goes beyond it. It is an experiment in ego-annihilation, where the singular and collective are not separate, that is, where being-in-common has not yet spawned a unified 'I'. There are no impermeable boundaries here, no criteria (no laws of logic, no skin) for the separation and determination of identities. There is no self–Other relation, that is, in Kantian terms, the transcendental object 'x' is not yet distinct from the transcendental subject of apperception. Becoming moves through dynamic relations where there is no subject of becoming as such.

To describe this as an activity would be potentially misleading. Per-

haps we should rather, as Lyotard suggests, think of it in terms of pleasure and pain, as passibility:

> Passibility as the possibility of experiencing (*pathos*) presupposes a dona-
> tion. If we are in a state of passibility, it's that something is happening to us,
> and when this passibility has a fundamental status, the donation itself is
> something fundamental, originary. What happens to us is not at all some-
> thing we have first controlled, programmed, grasped by a concept.[23]

Does not such a move blur Kant's distinction between the beautiful and
the sublime? For it is the passibility that enlivens us in the experience of
the beautiful which, according to Kant, directs us beyond the subject,
towards our supersensible destiny (enabling us to become subjects
proper and thus beings of humanity, of the morally constitutive community: 'us'). But this is precisely the point, the sublime experience is an
experiment in non-humanist (or even anti-humanist) ego-disruption,
whereas the beautiful enacts a consecration of the ego coming-into-
being by way of its universality (its link to the morally good). The sublime directs the imagination and feeling away from the consolidation of
an ideal of human destiny (a supersensible 'us') by preventing the formulation of an ego. No subject can be born in this experience for there
can be no appeal to a moral community, to a 'we' made 'us' in relation
to which the 'I', as subject (bound by its law), will emerge and identify
itself. The appeal to moral community comes only after the fact, as a
legitimation of the experience, once the imagination has been forced
back to the stand in the tribunal court of reason and called upon to
explain itself. In the determination that explanation demands, the experience is immobilised in accordance with the laws of logic and the polar
relations of a fixed dynamics of power.

The aesthetic (beautiful) and cognitive communities are mediated,
subject *a priori* to the progression implicit in the Ideas of reason (progression toward the infinite, the unconditioned): impelled by maximisa-
tion, and polarised by the principle of a supersensible substrate. What
then prevents the communal force, exposed in the experience of the
sublime, from being similarly motivated? Indeed, does not reason
demand that the imagination show more respect for uniforms (instead
of playing games with them), that it recognise the ultimate authority
transcending any particular scene? The sublime in its extreme form, in
enthusiasm, is blind to such an injunction for here the relation between
reason and the imagination is not governed by a concept, its presentations of the law are parodic. The sublime enacts the performance of law

in a relation whose poles of regulator and regulated, legislator and governed, are indeterminate and reversible, a space of vibration and oscillation, 'a rapid alternation of repulsion from, and attraction to[ward]'.[24]
The relation between the oscillating force of attraction and repulsion in the sublime and the harmonisation (the play of the faculties) that occurs in the aesthetic of the judgement of taste in the beautiful resides in the difference between experimental and safe play. Both effect an enlivening, but whereas the beautiful claims universality immediately because of its symbolic relation to the morally good, the universality of the sublime is suspended (it remains in suspense), as singularity that is already a collective in play. The sublime cannot be subsumed under the power of the ethical (its universality for the individual), for its relation to the Law is parodic and its constitution remains unwritten. This is a crucial point, not only for acknowledging the role the sublime may play in reformulating, in principle, the possibility of thinking *commercium* independent of the moral law, but for recognising and avoiding a return to the erroneous equation of enthusiasm as exemplary feeling of the sublime, with enthusiasm politicised in relation to an ideal. It is this latter move that limits the experience of the sublime to a feeling of respect by wilfully misinterpreting the sense of awe it engenders. As Lyotard remarks, in the context of the French revolution:

> They [revolutions] result from a confusion (which is *the* political illusion) between the direct presentation of the phenomenon of the *gemeine Wesen* [common being] and the analogical presentation of the Idea of a republican social contract.[25]

What occurs in political appeals to community to legitimate action on an individualising and totalising basis, is a coercive attempt to conceptually fix the feeling of the *sensus communis* in order to capture its capacity for binding together disparate elements into an apparent unity, so that the active 'we' becomes the reactive 'us'. In attempting to preserve the non-determinative character of the unifying power of the *sensus*, the 'we' of being-in-common, yet delivering it of an ethical universality, an analogical relation is effected and the appeal goes out to a mystical idea of *communio* for 'us', binding each 'I' to a self-identical 'us'. This appeal is directed either towards that which is deemed forgotten or lost in an immemorial past, or towards some progressive ideal of humanity (the supersensible destiny for the species) which ensures that the 'we' that is being appealed to in the formulation of an 'us' remains hidden. The call is made to the subject, to the individual 'I', whose identity is presumed to be consolidated in its relation to the common (to the mystical, unrepresentable 'we'), a 'we' always already transformed into an 'us'. The principle of difference at the heart of community (qua *commercium*), instead of being a bulwark against the formation of an ego-subject and the top-down imposition of identity, in this transformation of the 'we' to an 'us' becomes a mechanism of exclusion and conformity en route to cultural, racial, sexual and other forms of ghettoisation.

It might be objected here that such a critique (of politicised appeals to community, where difference is turned into a mechanism of disjunction), is inapplicable to modern political philosophy which tends towards the rejection of accounts of community based on the idea of *communio* (unity in oneness) as metaphysical, sentimental or otherwise threatening to individual liberty. In its place, and to satisfy the desire for communality, liberal humanism, in all its various guises, appeals to community understood on the basis of what appears at first to be a *commercium* unregulated by any abstract ideal. Upon closer examination, however, this *commercium* can be seen to be mediated by institutional structures mimicking the ideal function, functioning, that is, as placeholders for the identity of the subject as both 'I' and 'us'. Interaction and association is regulated by institutionalised forms of identity that offer, in palliation for the limitations thus placed upon the subject, a sense of belonging. Appeals to a mediated and politicised form of community nevertheless require universal communicability insofar as they claim there to be context-transcendent norms or values on the basis of which disputes (conflicts between individuals and genres of discourse) can be resolved.

In the case of liberal individualism, a bond of remunerative service affords the individual immunity from the perceived coercive relations implicit in overtly *communis*-based forms of exchangism. The individual is protected from the perceived threat to her/his privacy and the potential appropriation of her/his rights and power and is (at least in principle) free to choose whether or not to participate in the exchange of services available. Reciprocal *commercium* in individualism is thus based upon the joint ideas of immunity and remuneration and takes place primarily through the medium of social institutions (family, school, church, union, etc.) within the broader context of the municipality (the *munis*). The call to and reliance upon *communio* here is not so much extinguished as redirected and mediated through the *munis* in such a way that it is transformed; it is politicised and made safe from the potential threat to individuality feared in unqualified (fundamentalist and/or sentimentalist) calls to *communio*. The principle of universal communicability is thus maintained in and through the operations of institutional bodies in their ambiguous relations to the individuals they claim to represent.

In the case of right-wing and/or fundamentalist calls to *communio*, that is, (coercive) community in unity, the *sensus communis* is tied up inextricably with a conception of the morally good. These appeals, it should be noted, like those made by theories of individualism, are grounded in an abstract ideal of the subject. Moreover, their appeal to feeling is better understood as the demand for the recognition of and protection for a pure, fixed and sovereign identity usually grounded in a politically motivated ideal construction of nationalism or culture claiming the role and sovereignty of blood.[26]

In the cognitive community there is always mediation, this being necessary for the agreement, the consensus, upon rules for establishing truth. In the ethical community, mediation is effected by the ideal of practical reason, free will, itself mediated by the idea of the moral law containing, in circular manner, the principle of *communio*.[27] Insofar as cognitive and ethical communities are thus dependent upon mediation established through the mechanisms of the subject they are not in direct and immediate relation to the affective *sensus communis*, *commercium* in the sublime, that is, they cannot call upon it as such.[28] And yet, it is the *sensus* that *becomes*, after the fact, in experience (after the schematisation that establishes the time of the subject) the seat of all possible experience. For it is that, on the basis of which movement between domains of knowledge/genres of discourse is possible; the promise of universal communicability offered as a gift by the *sensus communis*. The status of this communicability, however, is unclear. Is it one voice or a chorus? One or many voices? The answer is, of course, that it is both, and neither. It is the voice that *is* a chorus; the voice that refuses to be delivered as a consensus. The *Einstimmung* is prior to the possibility of identity and thus is non-self-identical, at most it is a sketch or paradigm of and for the subject as individuated and totalised being. It is exemplary, but as a mere example it cannot turn itself into a determinate model except by capitulating to reason (becoming subservient to the moral law) or becoming crystallised in schematisation and conceptualisation. It is the aesthetic experience of the sublime which uniquely unlocks the *sensus communis* as affective *commercium*.

A subjectivity hears itself from far off and intimately at the same time, in this frail and singular unison, the subjectivity is being born, but it will never be born as such. Once born, the subject is only the *Ich denke*. And the aesthetic pleasure will always come along to disconcert it, to make it indeterminate, to make it be at a loss through its own concert, and its reflexive relation to itself.[29]

Notes

1   Jean-François Lyotard, '*Sensus communis*: the Subject in *statu nascendi*', in *Who Comes After the Subject?*, eds. Eduardo Cadava, Peter Connor and Jean-Luc Nancy (London: Routledge, 1991), p. 233.

2   Jean-Luc Nancy, *The Inoperative Community*, trans. Peter Connor and Lisa Garbus (Minneapolis: University of Minnesota Press, 1991), p. xxxvii.

3   Kant, *CPR*, A69/B94.

4   Kant, *CPR*, A79/B105.

5   Kant, *CPR*, B111.

6   Kant, *CPR*, B112.

7   Kant, *CPR*, A109.

8   Nancy, *The Inoperative Community*, p. xxxvii.

9   'Models of taste in the arts of speech must be composed in a language both dead and scholarly' (Kant, *CJ*, p. 79 n49; *Ak*.V: 232n).

10 Kant, *CJ*, p. 88; *Ak*.V: 238–9.

11 The demand for knowledge requires that representations have empirical reality (through the forms of space and time) and transcendental ideality. These representations, should the forms be withdrawn from them, are 'nothing at all' (Kant, *CPR*, A28/B44). There are, however, other representations (hearing, sight and touch) which, Kant tells us, have no such ideality, 'although they agree with the representation of space...they belong merely to the subjective constitution of our manner of sensibility' (Kant, *CPR*, B44). These 'mere sensations' (ibid.) are inseparable from the perceiving subject and, as such, presuppose the already differentiated 'I' of empirical subjectivity, which, in turn, presupposes the transcendental unity of apperception.

12 Jean-François Lyotard, *The Differend: Phrases in Dispute*, trans. Georges Van Den Abbeele (Minneapolis: University of Minnesota Press, 1988), p. 65.

13 The pure *a priori* imagination involved in schematisation is obviously associated with the pure productive imagination which underlies intuition in the Transcendental Aesthetic. Yet, for Kant, this relation necessarily remains hidden and mysterious: 'This schematism of our understanding, in its application to appearances and their mere form, is an art concealed in the depths of the human soul, whose real modes of activity nature is hardly likely ever to allow us to discover, and to have open to our gaze.' (Kant, *CPR*, A141/B180–1).

14 Kant, *CJ*, p. 88; *Ak*.V: 239.

15 Kant, *CJ*, p. 228; *Ak*.V: 353.

16 Conceptual *commercium* (epistemological community) is, in *CPR*, 'a reciprocal influence…of substances; without [which] the empirical relation of coexistence could not be met with in experience.' (Kant, *CPR*, A214–15/B261). This community is not, however, a primary *commercium* for it concerns relations already determined in experience (schematised and conceptualised) and is thus dependent upon the prior community (*communio*) of the transcendental unity of apperception.

17 Kant, *CPR*, A213/B260.

18 Kant, *CPR*, A73–4/B99.

19 See Kant, *CPR*, B112.

20 Thus, on the basis of the establishing of an identity, A, by means of the principle of identity, A = A (if anything is A then it is A), supported by the principle of non-contradiction, −(A&−A) (a thing cannot be both A and not A), it is established that the principle of the excluded middle, Av−A (a thing must be either A or not A), supports a binary exclusive disjunction where only one term is positively identified. Whatever is contiguous with the not-identified, with not A (B,C,D,E,…), is then necessarily not A itself.

21 Kant, *CPR*, A214/B261.

22 Kant, *CPR*, A214–15/B261.

23 Jean-François Lyotard, *The Inhuman: Reflections on Time*, trans. Geoffrey Bennington and Rachel Bowlby (Cambridge: Polity Press, 1991), pp. 110–11.

24 Kant, *CJ*, p. 115; *Ak*.V: 258.

25 Lyotard, *The Differend*, p. 167. 'If the enthusiasm of the spectators is a probative *Begebenheit* for the phrase which says that humanity is progressing toward the better, it is because enthusiasm, as a pure aesthetic feeling, requires a common sense, and calls upon a consensus which is nothing more than a *sensus* which is undetermined, but *de jure*; it is a sentimental anticipation of the republic.' (Lyotard, *The Differend*, p. 168).

26 As Hildyard remarks in the context of societal conceptions of community: 'There is a world of difference between…the yearning most people feel to be part of a community, and the New Right's systematic attempt to create communities peopled exclusively by one internally-homogeneous ethnic group – in effect, to make exclusion and conformity the organising principle of society.' (Nicholas Hildyard, 'Ethnic Conflict and the Authoritarian Right', Briefing Document (London: The Cornerhouse, January 1999), p. 11).

27 Here *communio* is more than the mere unity in Oneness that is promised in the supersensible destiny of Humanity, it is also the debt, the obligation which, on the basis of this promise, can never be paid.

28 It has already been established that the third possible mode of community,

sensus communis in the beautiful, is mediated in a relation to the moral law and is, as such, closed to the affective *commercium* operating in the sublime. It is accessible only in the form of a *communio*, a 'we' that is already modified as an 'us'.

29   Lyotard, '*Sensus communis*', p. 233.

9
Framing Infinities: Kantian Aesthetics After Derrida

Simon Malpas

The "sublime" is clearly part of the post-Kantian problem of the "absolute".
... As figures for an exceeding of boundaries, however, the sublime and the
absolute function as partially reversed mirror images of each other, and
generate two very different narratives about the contest of disciplines in
post-Enlightenment theory.[1]

How might one think the Kantian sublime as 'part of the post-Kantian
problem of the "absolute"', which finds its most powerful formulation in
G. W. F. Hegel's speculative dialectic, without eliding one with the
other? To mediate between the Kantian sublime and the Hegelian
absolute is to reduce the former to the logic of the latter, whereas to
posit the sublime as that which remains unpresentable in the Hegelian
thought of the absolute is immediately to privilege a non-speculative
account of speculation. As 'partially reversed mirror images of each
other', the two figures hold crucial positions within their respective
philosophical systems, and the 'different narratives' each generates
seem wholly at odds.

And yet this difference remains a fundamental problem for much
contemporary critical thought. The absolute and the sublime have
become key tropes in recent writing about modernity and the postmodern: Hegel and Kant are set at odds as representative thinkers of these
two discourses, and, for some postmodernists at least, the latter's analytic of the sublime has become the figure which provides the means to
move beyond the truth-laden metaphysics of modernity. Following Jean-
François Lyotard's descriptions of the sublime as 'wage[ing] a war
against totality' by 'present[ing] the fact that the unpresentable exists'
and postmodernism as a sublime moment that 'puts forward the unpresentable in presentation itself', literary and cultural theorists have very
frequently posited the postmodern sublime as a universal panacea for

the totalising, and supposedly totalitarian, tendencies of scientific or speculative rationality.[2] Rather than remaining elusive, this unpresentable seems never to have been presented so frequently or in so many different guises as it has in the fractured and fragmented narratives of our purportedly postmodern culture.

But where does this leave the absolute and, more precisely, Hegel's critique of Kantian finitude? According to Rodolphe Gasché,

> The question is crucial. For even if one may no longer find convincing Hegel's speculative solution of the problem of the full totalisation of what according to its concept must lend itself to such an operation – the Concept itself, or Reason – Hegel's arguments against spurious infinity remain perfectly valid. They remain relevant because the relegation of spurious infinity to the empirical discredits it as a tool of philosophical analysis.[3]

Sublime presentation is inextricably tied up with the infinite, and, as Gasché's argument makes clear, rather than precipitately presenting the postmodern sublime as a break with the cognitive structures of a dialectical modernity, it seems necessary to interrogate their relationship if one is to avoid falling foul of Hegel's stricture about the naive empiricism of spurious infinity.

A related difficulty with Lyotard's formulation of the sublime is identified by Philippe Lacoue-Labarthe:

> Bluntly put, this formula has two flaws: it separates out the unpresentable (positing its existence somewhere beyond presentation) and in doing so, it substantializes or hypostatizes it. By definition, only the presentable is presented. Therefore, the unpresentable, if such a thing exists, cannot present itself. Or if it does, it is like the Jewish God in the Hegelian analysis of sublimity, breaking through presentation itself, annihilating it for its greater (dialectical) glory.[4]

Separating out the presentable and the unpresentable, and thereby substantialising the latter to create two realms locked in opposition will, as Lacoue-Labarthe suggests, immediately fall prey to speculative sublation. And this is an accusation frequently levelled at postmodernity: the postmodern sublime, in the gesture of breaking with dialectical modernity by presenting the fact of the unpresentable's existence, is caught up in the very speculation that it seeks to evade.

My contention here will be that in order to think the sublime in relation to speculation (and, by extension, the postmodern in relation to modernity) one must take Hegel's critique of Kantian infinity seriously. I will argue that one basis for this might be the argument that Jacques

Derrida puts forward in his reading of the *Critique of Judgment* in *The Truth in Painting*. Derrida reads the third *Critique* in the light of Hegel's *Aesthetics* and Martin Heidegger's 'The Origin of the Work of Art', arguing that both of the later thinkers, despite their different aims and procedures, have 'a common interest, that they exclude – [that] which then comes to form, close and bound them from inside and outside alike', what Derrida calls the *parergon* or frame.[5] On the basis of this notion of the frame, I will argue that the Kantian sublime can be read, not as a break with the speculative absolute, but as a disjunction occurring in relation to the possibility of its presentation. The first task, however, is to discuss the ways in which Hegel's rejection of spurious infinity relates to the Kantian sublime.

Hegel, Kant and the infinite sublime

[S]pirit cognizes the Idea as its *absolute truth*, as the truth that is in and for itself; the infinite Idea in which cognition and action are equalized, and which is the *absolute knowledge of itself*.[6]

Hegel's speculative dialectics rests on a crucial distinction between good infinity and bad, or spurious, infinity. The most sustained discussion of this distinction occurs in the chapter on 'Determinate Being' in the *Science of Logic*. Briefly, the analysis of infinity emerges out of the progressive definition of being as becoming that takes place in the opening section of the *Logic*. Here, Hegel presents two problems with the commonplace notion of infinity: first, following both Aristotle and Spinoza, that an infinite regress or progress is the intellectual equivalent of a vicious circle; and, second, that an infinite that is posited as distinct from the finite is itself limited by its opposition to finitude and cannot, therefore, be truly infinite. Accordingly, the 'infinite as thus posited over against the finite, in a relation wherein they are qualitatively distinct others, is to be called the *spurious infinite*, the infinite of understanding'.[7] Left at this point, understanding deals only with conceptual counters whose relation remains inexplicit: the finite and spurious infinite, entirely distinct from one another, are locked in a binary opposition. However, as a determination of the understanding, the infinite is opposed to the finite in such a way that the limit between them both separates and holds them in relation: 'since the otherness is determined as *limit* … the otherness immanent in the something is posited as the connection of the two sides'.[8] Speculative reason, by working through the logic of this limit, draws out what holds the terms in relation in order to move from the fixed opposition to a point at which true infinity emerges from the limit itself by 'embrac[ing] both itself and finitude – and is therefore the infinite in a different sense from that in which the finite is regarded as separated and set apart from the infinite'.[9] Thus, the spurious infinite of the understanding is a necessary, but necessarily incomplete, moment in the speculative movement to the true infinite of reason.

Rather than being posited as an indeterminate and unattainable beyond, the true infinite embraces both itself and the finite other in a circular movement of dialectical becoming which 'as the consummated return into self' is '*determinate* being for it contains negation in general and hence determinateness. It *is* and *is there*, present before us'.[10] Thus, as Gasché comments, for Hegel, 'the true infinite, an infinite which is no longer transcendent, but which is only *through* the finite, or *immanent* in the different forms of the finite, is *the* fundamental concept of philosophy': the absolute idea of reason.[11] As such, it is the dialectical sublation (*Aufhebung*) of the finite and spurious infinity, a necessary step in the self-movement of the concept towards the absolute idea.

For Hegel, the sublime – particularly in its Kantian formulation – is tied up with spurious infinity. In a later passage of the *Science of Logic*, he sets out a critique of the place of the infinite in Kantian ethics in a way that alludes directly to the spurious infinity of what Kant in the third *Critique* will describe as the mathematical sublime:

> The spurious infinite, especially in the form of the quantitative progress to infinity which continually surmounts the limit it is powerless to remove, and perpetually falls back into it, is commonly held to be something sublime and a kind of divine worship, while in philosophy it has been regarded as something ultimate. … As a matter of fact, however, this *modern* sublimity does not magnify the *object* – rather does this take flight – but only the *subject* which assimilates such vast quantities. The hollowness of this exaltation, which in scaling the ladder of the quantitative still remains subjective, finds expression in its own admission of the futility of its efforts to get nearer the infinite goal, the attainment of which must, indeed, be achieved by a quite different method.[12]

Many attributes of the Kantian sublime seem to be here: the progress of imagination towards infinity, the experience of the limit, the lack of a determinate object, and the stress on subjective experience.[13] As such, I want to use this account to frame a reading of Kant's analysis of the sublime in the *Critique of Judgment*.

According to Kant, a sublime experience occurs when something is perceived that is more than can be taken in and represented for cognition: in those 'appearances whose intuition carries with it the idea of their infinity'.[14] This apperception causes what Kant describes as a 'mental *agitation* connected with our judging of the object ... this agitation is to be judged subjectively purposive, and so the imagination will refer this agitation to the *cognitive power* or the *power of desire*. ... The first kind of agitation is a *mathematical*, the second a *dynamical*, attunement of the mind'.[15]

In the mathematical sublime, Kant distinguishes two discrete moments in the aesthetic apperception of an object by imagination: 'In order for the imagination to take in a quantum intuitively, so that we can then use it as a measure or unity in estimating magnitude by numbers, the imagination must perform two acts: *apprehension* ... and *comprehension*'.[16] The first, apprehension, is the recognition of each discrete unit of measurement, whereas comprehension is the combination of these units to form a whole. Apprehension is the imaginative processing of the discrete 'manifold representations', and comprehension the reproduction of past representations 'while advancing to those that follow': the former delimits each unit while the latter combines them within an encompassing whole.[17] While this process of reproduction occurs unproblematically in everyday apperception, when confronted with the 'absolutely large' of the mathematical sublime something breaks down:

> [C]omprehension becomes more and more difficult the farther apprehension progresses, and it soon reaches a maximum. ... the partial presentations of sensible intuition ... are already beginning to be extinguished in the imagination, as it proceeds to apprehend further ones, the imagination then loses as much on the one side as it gains on the other; and so there is a maximum in comprehension that it cannot exceed.[18]

In other words, the imagination can no longer unify the manifold of representation which it receives in order to allow it to be brought under a concept by the understanding. Inadequate to this task of synthesising the manifold, imagination becomes agitated and this arouses a feeling of displeasure at its inferiority in the face of the magnitude. According to Kant, this inadequacy opens the possibility of another relation to the magnitude: the subject's imaginative 'inability uncovers in him the consciousness of an unlimited ability which is also his, and that the mind can judge this ability aesthetically only by that inability.'[19] Instead of the magnitude being referred to a concept of the understanding, imagination's striving gives rise to the feeling of reason's supersensible moral vocation:

> For it is a law (of reason) for us, and part of our vocation, to estimate any sense object in nature that is large for us as being small when compared with ideas of reason; and whatever arouses in us the feeling of this super-sensible vocation is in harmony with that law. ... If a [thing] is excessive for the imagination (and the imagination is driven to [such excess] as it appre-hends [the thing] in intuition), then [the thing] is, as it were, an abyss in which the imagination is afraid to lose itself. Yet, at the same time, for reason's idea of the supersensible [this same thing] is not excessive but conforms to reason's law to give rise to such striving by the imagination. Hence [the thing] is now attractive to the same degree to which [formerly] it was repulsive to mere sensibility.[20]

The displeasure experienced in the face of an excessive sensible magni-tude is thus imbricated with the sense of a supersensible vocation that holds out the possibility of an 'intellectual comprehension [compared] to which all aesthetic comprehension is small'.[21] Recognition of the supersensible vocation supplements the unpleasurable inferiority with pleasure in the face of a magnitude that now appears 'small when com-pared with ideas of reason'.[22]

Sublime experience thus arises from a conflict between the faculties in which imagination's inability to comprehend a magnitude gives rise to an 'idea of the absolute whole. ... [that] is precisely what makes the aes-thetic judgement itself subjectively purposive for reason'.[23] What I want to draw attention to in this conflict is the excessiveness of Kant's for-mulation: an idea of reason is evoked by the sublime as that which is beyond the power of presentation and incommensurable with imagina-tive comprehension. The sublime is thus an experience of the limit that takes place at the limits of the presentable. It holds out the possibility of moving beyond the limits of experience, and yet this transgression never occurs as such: the absolute never appears to comprehension and thus cannot be grasped as a concept.

It is in this way that the Kantian sublime is differentiated from the Hegelian dialectic: for Kant, the faculty of representation cannot pass the limits of experience but is rather caught up on them, receiving inti-mations of an absolute it can never attain. And yet, as I hope my dis-cussion of the Hegelian infinite has made apparent, this is an almost exact analogy with spurious infinity: a disjunction occurs at the limit between finite phenomenal presentation and the infinite realm of the ideas of reason which remain aesthetically unpresentable. On this reading, then, the Kantian sublime seems to be little more than an incomplete moment in the movement of Hegelian speculation.

There is a temptation here to simply dismiss this critique: Hegel is discussing logic and Kant aesthetic experience, and what has art to do with knowledge or the sublime with speculation? To succumb to this is to concur with those readers of Lyotard who posit a differend between epistemology and aesthetics, construing the latter as a different language game whose rules remain incommensurable to the genre of speculative discourse.[24] However, instead of this, I want to follow Derrida by arguing that a productive way to think the Kantian sublime is precisely through its proximity to Hegelian speculation, to run the risk of bad infinity in order to work through its relation with aesthetic speculation.

This, therefore, returns to the problem that I identified at the beginning: how can one think the relation between the sublime and the absolute without reducing one to the logic of the other or abandoning logic altogether? What becomes necessary, then, is an analysis of the limit.

Speculation and the sublime: a problem of presentation

Towards the beginning of his essay, *'Parergon'*, Derrida explicitly raises the question of the relationship between, on the one hand, Hegel's account of aesthetics as 'a circle in a circle of circles' that makes up the 'totality of philosophy',[25] and, on the other, Kant's analysis of reflective judgement in the third *Critique*:

> What holds of speculative dialectic in general is made rigorously clear in the *Lectures* [Hegel's *Aesthetics*]: an affinity with the *Critique*, the only book – third book – which it can reflect and reappropriate almost at once. The first two critiques of pure (speculative and practical) reason had opened an apparently infinite gulf. The third could, should, should have, could have thought it: that is, filled it, fulfilled it in infinite reconciliation. … But it still suffered, according to Hegel, from a lacuna, a "lack" (*Mangel*), it remained a theory of subjectivity and of judgement. … The reconciliation is only announced, represented in the third *Critique* in the form of a duty, a *Sollen* projected to infinity. And so it indeed appears.[26]

Thus, the basis of Derrida's reading is that, for Hegel, the third *Critique* is that which stands closest to speculative philosophy, which only fails to be speculative because it remains a theory of subjective judgement. And

it is this very proximity, caught up as it is with the problem of the infinite, that allows the possibility of thinking a relation between sublimity
and the absolute.

Derrida's approach to the third *Critique* is to follow closely the development of Kant's text, teasing out the implications of the examples Kant
uses to present his argument. Thus, rather than setting out a theory of
the unpresentable, Derrida's reading of the sublime focuses very closely
on the disruption of presentation by that which is disproportionate to
presentation itself. Beginning from the finite side of the limit, that of
phenomenal presentation, he finds this disruption in the primary example Kant gives of the sublime, which is described as the 'colossal'. For
Kant, the colossal is,

> what we call the mere exhibition of a concept if that concept is almost too
> large for any exhibition (i.e., if it borders on the relatively monstrous); for
> the purpose of exhibiting a concept is hampered if the intuition of the
> object is almost too large for our power of apprehension.[27]

Neither a determinate object nor a determinate concept but rather the
'exhibition' of a concept that is 'almost too large' for exhibition, the
colossal presentation is what gives rise to the inadequation between
apprehension and comprehension by the imagination, and by extension
phenomena and the ideas of reason, in the Analytic of the Sublime.

Although barely mentioned in the third *Critique*, this colossal exhibition that 'qualifies the presentation' of the concept is central to Derrida's reading because it allows him to move away from any simple
opposition between the presentable and the unpresentable: it is not
'simply unpresentable', but rather *almost unpresentable*. And by reason
of its size: it is "almost too large". This concept is announced and then
eludes presentation on the stage'.[28] It is by focusing on the 'almost too
large' of the colossal that Derrida draws out a crucial difference (which
is also a relation) between the sublime of the third *Critique* and Hegelian
speculation.

The relation between being announced and eluding presentation in
the 'almost too large' of the colossal opens up the problem of a relationship between the finite and infinity in the sublime. For Derrida, 'if
the sublime is not contained in the finite natural or artificial object, no
more is it the infinite idea itself. It inadequately presents the infinite in
the finite and delimits it violently therein'.[29] Thus Derrida's reading
comes back to the problem of the limit: the colossal rears up at the limit
between the finite and infinite that forms the crux of the distinction

between Kantian sublimity and the Hegelian dialectic. According to Derrida, it is at this limit that the problem of presentation appears:

> The feeling of the colossal, effect of a subjective projection, is the experience of an inadequation of presentation to itself, or rather, since every presentation is adequate to itself, of an inadequation of the presenter to the presented of presentation. An inadequate presentation of the infinite presents its own inadequation, an inadequation is presented as such in its own yawning gap, it is determined in its contour, it cises and incises itself as incommensurable with the without-cise.[30]

As the inadequation in a presentation of a 'concept [that] is almost too large for any exhibition',[31] the colossal cannot be captured by any formal system of measurement (and is therefore not the infinite progression that Hegel dismisses as spurious), but rather appears at the limit between apprehension and comprehension. In other words, for Derrida, this is not a 'dimension in the quantitative sense',[32] but rather the disruption of quantitative development, of the mathematical progression towards infinity as it runs up against 'the nonphenomenal infinity of the idea [that] must always be presented in intuition'.[33] What happens at the limit is thus a conflict of spurious infinities: the infinite progress of apperception clashes with a 'nonphenomenal infinity' that remains entirely distinct from the finite. The moment of sublime inadequation in Kant shares, almost precisely, the structure of Hegel's supreme adequating moment, the *Aufhebung*, with the crucial difference that the result is not Hegelian speculation but an inadequation in presentation.

Thus, Derrida's stress on the inadequation of presentation is also, crucially, a description of an inadequation between Kant and Hegel that distinguishes the sublime from speculation. For Hegel, it is through the insistence on subjective presentation – the 'premised reduction of all categories to something subjective, to the powers of mind, imagination, reason, etc.'[34] – that Kant's sublime fails to reach the good infinite. Instead, speculative thought must approach the limit from the other side, the side of reason and the infinite, 'grasp[ing] it as grounded in the one absolute substance *qua* the content which is to be represented'.[35] On the other hand, the Kantian response to speculation would be that in order to think the limit of the infinite, it has to be presented: in Derrida's words, 'it has to be presented, even if it is presented without presenting itself adequately, even if it is merely announced, and precisely in the *Aufhebung*'.[36] The inadequation of sublime presentation, the announced that eludes presentation, thus takes place 'precisely' in the place of the *Aufhebung* itself. In other words, Kant and Hegel – each as the 'partially reversed mirror image' of the other – are left face to face at the limit between the finite and infinite, the sublime and sublation (*Aufhebung*), staring at each other across the cut:

> the question opens of *knowing*, or rather *thinking* whether one must first *think* (as Hegel thinks) sublimity, set out from the thought of sub-limity, or on the contrary (as Kant figures) from presentation, inadequate to this thought, of the sublime, etc. Kant and Hegel nevertheless reflect the line of cut or rather the *pas* crossing this line between finite and infinite as the proper place of the sublime and the interruption of symbolic beauty.[37]

This seems to return immediately to the incommensurability between finitude and infinity, the sublime and the absolute, with which I began. However, things have changed somewhat: crucially, the limit between finitude and infinity, the Kantian sublime and Hegelian speculation, has been refigured as a 'cut', a 'cise', and a '*pas*' (at the same time a 'not', a 'passage' and a 'step') that mark what is at once a crossing and an inter-ruption of that limit. In other words, the problem of sublime presenta-tion takes place 'between the presentable and the unpresentable, the passage from one to the other as much as the irreducibility of one to the other. Cise, edging, cut edges, that which passes and happens, without passing, from one to the other'.[38] And it is at this point that the opposi-tion between the presentable and unpresentable, while not reducing one to the other, is opened to a passage. The question is, what is this passage that 'passes and happens, without passing, from one to the other'? What is the passage that appears at the limit?

Framing presentation: the sublime abyss of speculation

The circle and the abyss, that would be the title.[39]

Derrida opens '*Parergon*' by positing the aesthetic as that which opens an abyss in the circle of philosophical thought, most particularly the ulti-mately systematic thought of the speculative absolute. The key figure for presenting this abyss is the sublime.

In order for Hegel to approach the limit from the side of reason, to think rather than figure sublimity, his discussions of beauty and the sub-lime in the *Aesthetics* have to occupy a particular place in the fully devel-oped philosophical system. According to Derrida, for Hegel,

[A]rt figures one of those productions of mind thanks to which the latter returns to itself, comes back to consciousness and cognizance and comes to its proper place by *returning* to it, in a circle. ... But art forms only one of the circles in the great circle of the *Geist* or the revenant (the visitor can be called *Gast*, or *ghost, guest* or *Gespenst*). The end of art, and its truth, is religion, that other circle of which the end, the truth, will have been philosophy. ... The fact remains that here art is studied from the point of view of its end. Its pastness is its truth. The philosophy of art is thus a circle in a circle of circles: a "ring" says Hegel, in the totality of philosophy. It turns upon itself and annulling itself it links onto other rings.[40]

In other words, art is always already comprehended and 'annulled' in the system of reason: it is a part, a stage, a circle in the totality of the absolute. It is this preconceived notion of the aesthetic that allows Hegel to approach the limit of the sublime from the side of thought rather than figuration. The question Derrida raises in response to this is, '*Is there* any abyss in the Hegelian circulation?'[41] This is not a question of simply presenting the abyss as a separate structure, an alternative logic that takes a step outside of speculative metaphysics: one cannot 'break the circle violently (it would avenge itself)'.[42] Neither is it another version of that poststructuralist favourite, the *mise en abyme* as, for Derrida, the '*operation* of the *mise en abyme* always occupies itself ... with somewhere filling up, full of abyss, filling up the abyss'.[43] Rather, it becomes a question of figuring the abyss as part of the circulatory movement of the system, the part that the system cannot think. The impetus of Derrida's analysis is, therefore, to

economize on the abyss: not only to save oneself from falling into the bottomless depths by weaving and folding back the cloth to infinity, textual art of the reprise, multiplication of patches within patches, but also establish the laws of reappropriation, formalize the rules which constrain the logic of the abyss and which shuttle between the economic *and* the aneconomic, the raising (*la relève* [*Aufhebung*]) and the fall, the abyssal operation which can only work toward the *relève and* that in which it regularly reproduces collapse[44]

It is this movement of infinite multiplication, of raising and falling, a moment that closely recalls what appeared at the limit between sublimity and speculation, that Derrida discovers in the notion of the frame, the *parergon*.

Kant introduces the *parergon* in §14 of the Analytic of the Beautiful, called 'Elucidation by Examples':

> Even what we call *ornaments* (*parerga*), i.e., what does not belong to the
> whole presentation of the object as an intrinsic constituent, but [is] only an
> extrinsic addition, does indeed increase our taste's liking, and yet it does so
> only by its form, as in the case of picture frames, or drapery on statues, or
> colonnades around magnificent buildings.[45]

What Derrida finds in this passage is a disruption of any simple opposition between aesthetic judgement and the non-aesthetic: the *parergon* is
not an 'intrinsic constituent' of beauty but, as an 'addition', it enhances
our liking for it, making the beautiful more beautiful. This follows a logic
of supplementarity: added to the 'whole' presentation, it comes to indicate a lack in that whole by augmenting its beauty. In other words, what
constitutes *parerga* is 'not simply their exteriority as a surplus, it is the
internal structural link which rivets them to the lack in the interior of the
ergon. And this lack is constitutive of the very unity of the *ergon*'.[46] If it
were not lacking, the *ergon* would need no *parergon*, but the *parergon* as
such can occur only as an 'extrinsic addition', albeit a necessary one.
There is thus a movement, a passage, between the inside and the outside of the aesthetic object 'whose transcendent exteriority comes to
play, abut onto, brush against, rub, press against the limit itself and intervene in the inside only to the extent that the inside is lacking'.[47] But the
parergon is not simply an empirical phenomenon associated with art: in
his reading of the third *Critique*, Derrida posits it as an essential structure of the relation between thought and presentation. Kant's text on
aesthetics is itself framed by the analytic of concepts in the *Critique of
Pure Reason*; the analytic of the beautiful frames that of the sublime; and
the very notion of the *parergon* is framed by Kant's discussion of it in
Religion within the Limits of Reason Alone where it designates grace, mys-
teries and miracles that supplement reason's inability to satisfy society's
moral needs.[48] As such, the *parergon* attains the 'status of a philosophical
quasi-concept, designate[s] a formal and general predicative structure'.[49] And, not only does it operate in Kant's philosophy, it also occurs
in Hegel's framing of the Kantian sublime.

Although Derrida is insistent that, in itself, the 'colossal excludes the
parergon ... because the infinite is presented in it and the infinite cannot
be bordered',[50] his whole discussion of the sublime rests on the problem
of presentation and, therefore, of framing. In fact, the very passage from
presentation to the unpresentable that marks their irreducibility to each
other, the passage that happens without passing from one to the other and
presents the inadequation of presentation, *is* the passage of their *parergon*.

And it is this passage that Hegelian speculation refuses to think. By positing art as that which is already surpassed, annulled and comprehended by thought, Hegel is unable to countenance the problem of framing. For Derrida, the reduction of the frame is the quintessential gesture of philosophy, and one that deconstruction sets its sights against:

> Philosophy wants to arraign [the *parergon*] and can't manage. But what has produced and manipulated the frame puts everything to work in order to efface the frame effect, most often by naturalizing it to infinity. ... Deconstruction must neither reframe nor dream of the pure and simple absence of the frame. These two apparently contradictory gestures are the very ones – and they are systematically indissociable – of *what* is here deconstructed.[51]

The task of deconstruction, the aim of Derrida's reading of Kantian aesthetics, is thus to work through the logic of the frame: to read the limit between sublimity and the speculative *Aufhebung* as a *parergon* through which inside and outside, good and bad infinity, are continually drawn together and opened to the economy of the circle and the abyss.

The sublime is thus figured as an abyssal moment within the circular movement of the *Aufhebung*, a moment of inadequation in presenting the movement of speculation which opens its restricted economy to the possibility of 'loss'.[52] As close as possible to sublation, the sublime frames its presentation as an infinite shuttling back and forth between spurious and true infinity which disrupts any simple or straightforward opposition between the two.[53] The relation between the sublime and speculation, of the sublime in speculation, is thus a 'Colossal *Fort: Da*' that 'erect[s] itself in the excessive movement of its own disappearance, of its unpresentable presentation. The obscenity of the abyss. ... Neither originary nor derived, like the trace of each trait.'[54]

Notes

1 Tilottama Rajan and David L. Clark, 'Speculations: Idealism and its Rem(a)inders', in *Intersections: Nineteenth-Century Philosophy and Contemporary Theory*, eds. Rajan and Clark (Albany: SUNY Press, 1995), pp. 29–30.

2 Jean-François Lyotard, *The Postmodern Condition: A Report on Knowledge*, trans. Geoff Bennington and Brian Massumi (Manchester: Manchester University Press, 1984), pp. 82, 78 and 81. In this text, Lyotard sets up science and speculation as the two grand narratives of modernity which the postmodern sublime opens up to disruption.

3 Rodolphe Gasché, *Inventions of Difference: On Jacques Derrida* (Cambridge, MA and London: Harvard University Press, 1994), p. 130.

4 Philippe Lacoue-Labarthe, *Poetry as Experience*, trans. Andrea Tarnowski (Stanford: Stanford University Press, 1999), p. 90.

5 Jacques Derrida, *The Truth in Painting*, trans. Geoff Bennington and Ian McLeod (Chicago and London: University of Chicago Press, 1987), p. 23. Hereafter *TP*. I shall refer to the following versions of the other texts mentioned in this sentence: G. W. F. Hegel, *Aesthetics: Lectures on Fine Art*, vol. 1, trans. T. M. Knox (Oxford: Clarendon Press, 1975); Martin Heidegger, 'The Origin of the Work of Art', in *Poetry, Language, Thought*, trans. Albert Hofstadter (New York and London: Harper and Row, 1975), pp. 15–87.

6 G. W. F. Hegel, *Science of Logic*, trans. A. V. Miller (Atlantic Highlands, NJ: Humanities Press, 1989), p. 760. Hereafter *SL*.

7 Hegel, *SL*, p. 139.

8 Hegel, *SL*, p. 131.

9 Hegel, *SL*, p. 144.

10 Hegel, *SL*, pp. 148–9.

11 Gasché, *Inventions of Difference*, p. 133.

12 Hegel, *SL*, pp. 228–9.

13 Hegel reiterates this point in the *Aesthetics*. He argues that the 'first decisive purification of the absolute and its express separation from the sensuous present, i.e. from the empirical individuality of external things, is to be sought in the *sublime*', and that the 'sublime in general is the attempt to express the infinite, without finding in the sphere of phenomena an object which proves adequate for this representation. Precisely because the infinite is set apart from the entire complex of objectivity as explicitly an invisible meaning devoid of shape and is made inner, it remains, in accordance with its infinity, unutterable and sublime above any expression through the finite' (Hegel, *Aesthetics*, vol. 1, pp. 362–3).

14 Kant, *CJ*, p. 112; *Ak*.V: 255.

15 Kant, *CJ*, p. 101; *Ak*.V: 247. While the differences between the mathematical and dynamic sublime should be noted, this argument will focus on the former because of its relation to infinite quantity.

16 Kant, *CJ*, p. 108; *Ak*.V: 251.

17 Kant, *CPR*, A102.

18 Kant, *CJ*, p. 108; *Ak*.V: 252.

19 Kant, *CJ*, p. 116; *Ak*.V: 259.

20 Kant, *CJ*, p. 115; *Ak*.V: 257–8.

21 Kant, *CJ*, p. 117; *Ak*.V: 260.

22 Kant, *CJ*, p. 115; *Ak*.V: 257.

23 Kant, *CJ*, p. 117; *Ak*.V: 260.

24 The basis of this type of move is laid out in Jean-François Lyotard, 'Analysing Speculative Discourse as Language-Game', in *The Lyotard*

Reader, ed. Andrew Benjamin (Oxford: Blackwell, 1989), pp. 265–74.

25   Derrida, *TP*, p. 26.

26   Derrida, *TP*, p. 35.

27   Kant, *CJ*, p. 109; *Ak*.V: 253.

28   Derrida, *TP*, p. 125. The passage continues, 'One would say, by reason of its almost excessive size, that it was obscene' (ibid). The possibility of obscenity as that which breaks the economy of philosophical reappropriation (particularly through the speculative dialectic) in a similar way to the figure that I am discussing here is examined in more detail by Derrida in 'Economimesis', trans. Richard Klein, *Diacritics* 11.2 (1981) 3–25.

29   Derrida, *TP*, p. 131.

30   Derrida, *TP*, p. 132. Derrida's employment of the word 'cise' (in French, '*taille*') suggests both size and a cut, and comes to indicate the moment at which, when faced with the colossal, the disjunction between imaginative apprehension and comprehension that gives rise to a feeling of the sublime occurs.

31   Kant, *CJ*, p. 109; *Ak*.V: 253.

32   Derrida, *TP*, p. 135.

33   Derrida, *TP*, p. 137.

34   Hegel, *Aesthetics*, vol. 1, p. 362.

35   Hegel, *Aesthetics*, vol. 1, p. 363.

36   Derrida, *TP*, p. 133.

37   Derrida, *TP*, p. 134.

38   Derrida, *TP*, p. 143.

39   Derrida, *TP*, p. 24.

40   Derrida, *TP*, p. 26.

41   Derrida, *TP*, p. 27.

42   Derrida, *TP*, p. 33.

43   Derrida, *TP*, p. 34. According to Gasché, Derrida rejects the *mise en abyme* because it 'inevitably produces a continuity…between the chasm [abyss] and what the *mise en abyme* pretends to ruin by infinitely reflecting it. When such a continuity is achieved, the radical difference between both is missed, in all senses of this word. Such continuity is revelatory of the empirical essence of the operation of the *mise en abyme* because it is oblivious of philosophical difference in general, *of the difference philosophy makes*' (Gasché, *Inventions of Difference*, p. 145).

44   Derrida, *TP*, p. 37.

45   Kant, *CJ*, p. 72; *Ak*.V: 226.

46   Derrida, *TP*, p. 59.

47   Derrida, *TP*, p. 56.

48   See Kant, *Religion within the Limits of Reason Alone*; *Ak*.VI.

49   Derrida, *TP*, p. 55.

50   Derrida, *TP*, p. 128.

51 Derrida, *TP*, p. 73.
52 Georges Bataille's opening of the speculative dialectic to the possibility of loss is set out by Derrida in 'From Restricted to General Economy: A Hegelianism without Reserve', in *Writing and Difference*, trans. Alan Bass (London: Routledge, 1978), pp. 251–77.
53 This 'infinite shuttling' between the sublime and speculation is similar to Gasché's description of the structural infinity of dissemination in *Inventions of Difference* (see especially pp. 129–49).
54 Derrida, *TP*, p. 145.

10
Disjunctive Reading: Kant, Heidegger, Irigaray

Joanna Hodge

Disjunctive reading

The ontological and the psychoanalytical rewritings of Kant's theory of the imagination, proposed by Heidegger and by Lacan respectively, come together in Irigaray's diagnosis, in *Speculum of the Other Woman* and in other writings,[1] of an originary materiality. This she supposes to be repressed in the emergence of philosophical thinking both at its inception among the Greeks, as rehearsed in Plato's description of the emergence from the cave in *The Republic*,[2] and at each occasion of its renewal, as in its reinscription in Freud's psychoanalytical theory.[3] For Heidegger, Kant's theory of the imagination as set out in the *Critique of Pure Reason*, conceals an originary finitude of time, to be understood through the elaboration of a fundamental ontology as the meaning of determinate being.[4] For Lacan, the imagination is to be rewritten as the imaginary,[5] the term reinvented by him to capture the unformed libidinal identifications and misrecognitions underlying and repressed on entry into the symbolic order.[6] This essay will lay out the argument that a choice between these two undoubtedly incompatible rewritings of Kant's imagination closes down the challenge of Kant's analyses, whereas Irigaray's move of keeping the two possibilities open reveals a receptiveness to the radicality of the Kantian initiative,[7] at odds with any diagnosis that she proposes to reject and supersede Kantian critique. Irigaray thereby initiates a debate concerned not with the respective claims of empirical realism and transcendental idealism to capture the character of Kant's analyses, but much more with a reinvention of materialism, signalled but not affirmed by Kant.[8]

This essay, then, does not propose an analysis of Irigaray's readings of Kant, as an affirmation of a materialist Kant, still less does it propose to give a detailed account of either Heidegger's or Lacan's complex responses to Kant. It proposes instead an analysis of these two apparently incompatible rewritings of Kant's theorising of the imagination, under the title 'disjunctive reading', by rehearsing aspects of Kant's account of the logic of illusion, set out in book two of the Transcendental Dialectic, the Dialectical Inferences of Pure Reason, in his *Critique of Pure Reason*. The essay starts with an account of the Irigarayan originary materiality and of Irigaray's disjunctive mode of reading, in which the question of the truthfulness of reading recedes in favour of its capacity to generate effects. It moves on to a consideration of Kant's account of three kinds of fallacious reasoning, paralogism, antinomy and the ideal of pure reason. This provides the basis for explicating the paradoxical implications of Irigaray affirming both the Lacanian and the Heideggerian readings of Kant. A brief indication of the contentiousness of these two readings can be given in terms of Kant's distinctions between these different kinds of fallacious reasoning. In *Being and Time*,[9] Heidegger assigns to Kant's philosophy an importance second only to that assigned to the investigations of Husserl. However, in the contemporaneous lectures and in his highly contentious book *Kant and the Problem of Metaphysics*,[10] he proposes to relocate Kant's account of the imagination and of the transcendental unity of apperception back in the ontological terms from which Kant sought to detach them, while at the same time reconstructing ontology as the site for a retrieval of the question of the forgetting of being. Thus Heidegger's reading might be thought systematically to ignore the distinction between concepts of the understanding and concepts of reflection, as laid out in the Amphiboly of Concepts of Reflection,[11] and thus to dispute Kant's distinction between the empirical and the transcendental deployments of the understanding.

Lacan's rewriting of the imagination as the imaginary threatens to reimpose a substantivist account of the soul, of psyche, which the Paralogisms of Pure Reason, in their two versions,[12] are exactly designed to disrupt.[13] Indeed, Lacan's responses to Kant do not work at the level of a reading of texts but rather interrupt any immunisation of an order of understanding and reason from its psychic disruption and displacement. For Lacan, the institution of an order of understanding, as in the *Critique of Pure Reason*, presupposes the suspension of the demand for instant gratification and thus simultaneously constitutes an order of resistance to and potential disruption of that order, in a series of imaginary identifications and idealisations. Thus for a lacanian reading of

Kant, the paradoxes of pure reason explored in the Transcendental Dialectic must conceal an inarticulable dynamic also at work in meaning and understanding which threatens to disrupt its order at any moment. The departure of lacanian psychoanalysis from the horizon of philosophical enquiry happens then precisely on the ground that any insistence on consequential deduction will in all likelihood mask at best repression and at worst psychosis. Such cavalier responses to the requirements of reason, needless to say, generate rather more difficulties concerning meaning and understanding than they can resolve. It is, however, crucial to Irigaray's intervention in philosophy that any overhasty closing down of such deviations from the requirements of reason may rather conceal the mechanisms of repression and exclusion, whereby any organisation and institution of reason sets out a non-assimilable remainder, rather than permitting their articulation. The re-entry of psychoanalysis into the philosophical horizon takes place when a certain homology between the analyses of psychoanalytical theory and those of philosophical enquiry concerning personal identity, slippages of meaning and a disruption of an account of time as unilinear sequence comes to the fore.[14]

I shall suggest, minimally, that Irigaray, by affirming the readings of both Lacan and Heidegger, prevents either from succumbing to the kantian charge of infringing the requirements of reason.[15] Kant's notion of a disjunctive judgement plays a crucial role here:

> There is, therefore, in a disjunctive judgement a certain community of the known constituents, such that they mutually exclude each other, and yet thereby determine in their totality the true knowledge. For, when taken together, they constitute the whole content of one given knowledge'.[16]

Here Kant marks up a distinction between exclusive disjunction, when judgements are read in terms of truth conditions, and inclusive disjunction, when judgements are read transcendentally. The lacanian response to Kant, criticising the will to truth as a will to reduce and repress ambiguity, and the readings proposed by Heidegger and by Irigaray occur in distinct registers. Keeping these registers open requires an openness of reading, as performed by Irigaray. Irigaray reads Lacan's and Heidegger's responses to Kant disjunctively, and this essay proposes to show how reading Irigaray, Lacan and Heidegger disjunctively opens out a new dimension for philosophical thinking.

Reinventing the other: originary materiality

One of the gestures characteristic of Irigaray's mode of reading is to adopt and adapt a line of thinking from the text of the other, in this case Lacan, Heidegger and Kant, and to transform it by relocating it within her own more open horizon of enquiry. From Heidegger she borrows, and transforms, the notion of an originary occurrence, through which temporal order is constituted; from Lacan the notion of the imaginary; from Kant that of a transcendental delimitation of experience. The Heideggerian notion of originary occurrence, thematised extensively in terms of the *Ereignis*, the event, as *Er-eignis*, emergence of propriety, and as *Ent-eignis*, non-propriety, forecloses the possibility of a self-appropriation of thinking and sets up an initial instability of a thought out of synchrony with itself.[17] The emergence of propriety does not belong to the order of propriety set up. Irigaray recasts the notion of originary occurrence as originary materiality, while maintaining an allegiance to the opening of thought made available by Kant. The notion of originary materiality is grounded in a relation of rewriting which holds between Irigaray's thinking and that of Martin Heidegger.

By contrast to the notion of an origin which might be supposed to be temporally prior to that which arises out of that origin, the term 'originary' is deployed by Heidegger to suspend such notions of temporal sequence, leaving open the possibility that the emergence and the origin are simultaneously constituted, or constituted with a time-lag of deferral, which similarly occurs neither before nor after but in conjunction with the emergence or appearance of the phenomenon in question. This distinction between an origin thought of as prior in time and an originary constitution of temporal order permits a suspension of any basic assumption about an ordered sequence of time as unilinear succession. It is a rewriting of Kant's insistence in the Transcendental Aesthetic that there is a form of time given in inner sense in advance of the constitution in the Analogies of Experience of temporal succession. For Heidegger, originary occurrence is important since he thinks of time as successive only by derivation from a more basic givenness of time as finite and transformational.[18] In the Heideggerian thought that the primary form of time is finitude there is then a commitment to the view that in that finitude a form of materiality is immediately given in advance, in such a way as to be irrecuperable in language and theory, which arrive after the event. The error would then be to fail to attend to this inarticulability of a lapse between materiality and the thinking to which it gives rise on the mistaken grounds that the inexpressible is insignificant. Heidegger's, and indeed Irigaray's, view would be that the manner in which a relation to this inexpressibility is constructed is all-important for an understanding of what can be expressed.

Human beings, for Heidegger as Dasein and for Irigaray as sexual difference, are the site at which a lack of fit between conception and that which is conceived can be both registered and then become obscured by the conviction that conception matches what there is. This conviction is put in question both by Kant's distinction between categories of the understanding and concepts of reflection, as discussed in the Amphiboly of Concepts of Reflection,[19] and by Heidegger's insistence on the withdrawal from inspection of a part of the process through which the given is given. This lack of fit and hypothesising of distinct orders of reflection, one open to rational delimitation and one continuously threatening to disrupt that rational order in an irrecuperable remainder, is also thematised by Freud in his account of the unconscious registration of affect and its temporal deployment in an after-effect where the work of a non-representational memory constitutes an event in the past for the first time. The human then is the site of a non-transparency in that presentation, which is definitely not a re-presentation of a previous presentation and which is conditional on a partial and sometimes undetectable absenting. The human thus becomes a locus for tracing out a movement between what is present and what absents itself, as a condition for presentation. Taking a hint from the impact of psychoanalysis on philosophy, it is possible to retrieve a concept of the soul, or *psyché*, in order to articulate this movement, as a lack of fit in human beings, between the movements of spirit or intellect and those of materiality or corporeality, thus providing a site for thinking this originary materiality.

The writings of Luce Irigaray are read here as playing a major role both in opening out this thought of a work of repression in relation to materiality and in identifying in kantian critique an articulation of this work of repression. In the analysis of the disjunctive syllogism, Kant develops the thought of a condition of transcendental critique which can be thought but not known. This then has the structure parallel to that of a thinking of the unconscious affect. A connection could be made here to Heidegger's diagnoses of an inevitable self-deflection at work in the emanations of being, although the linkage between these two arises from Heidegger's recasting of transcendental conditions as an abyssal ontological ground. Here, the difficulty would be to set out the distinc-

tion between the recasting of transcendental conditions proposed
in terms of the affirmation of fundamental ontology still at work in
Kant and the Problem of Metaphysics, and a recasting proposed in terms
of the suspension of this affirmation in the turn from an analysis of
Dasein to the charting of the fateful turns, withdrawals and forgettings
of being, which for Heidegger constitute the vicissitudes of the history
of philosophy.[20]

Heidegger and Irigaray reading Kant

There are in Heidegger's readings of Kant two potentially incompatible
movements. Heidegger's ontological reading of the imagination given in
Kant and the Problem of Metaphysics reimposes an Aristotelian closure on
the relation between thought and matter, which Kantian critique precisely opened up. As already suggested, what is here in dispute is Kant's
distinction between the empirical and the transcendental employment
of the understanding and deployment of concepts. Heidegger's insistence on the primacy of fundamental ontology as a site at which empirical existence and transcendental ground come together and turn out to
be inseparable unsettles the distinction and introduces a third kind of
concept of the understanding, which he calls existentials. These are both
empirical and transcendental in deployment. Heidegger introduces his
notion of existentials in *Being and Time*, contrasting them to both Kantian and Aristotelian categories: 'Because Dasein's characters of Being
are defined in terms of existentiality, we call them *"existentialia"*. These
are to be sharply distinguished from what we call *"categories"* – characteristics of Being for entities whose character is not that of Dasein. Here
we are taking the expression "category" in its primary ontological signi-
fication, and abiding by it'.[21] For Heidegger, category deployment consists in 'making a public accusation, taking someone to task for
something in the presence of everyone.'[22] Thus a system of categories for
Heidegger presupposes a shared public domain and its existential
grounding in Dasein, which *Being and Time* proceeds to analyse.[23] Given
Heidegger's repeated insistence on the emergence of philosophy from
Parmenides' gnomic utterance: 'thinking and being are the same',[24] it
might be thought that, for Heidegger, the virtue of his own thinking, by
contrast to that of Kant, is precisely that such a distinction between the
empirical and transcendental is rendered illegitimate. Such a logic of
misidentification, or indeed misrecognition, might be thought, in Kant's
terms, to be systematic in Heidegger's thinking.

Heidegger's insistence on recasting the articulations of temporality in the *Critique of Pure Reason* as fundamental ontology is a conservative move. It reinstalls ontological certainties, where the Kantian break with ontology is made precisely to introduce the possibility of variant conjugations of faculties, inaugurating distinct orders of experience, and, incipiently, variant, indeed multiple, schematisations of the categories, depending on how the intuitions of space and time are understood. These distinct conjugations of the faculties anticipate Irigaray's suggestion that there might be more than one configuration of the imaginary. However, Heidegger also insists on Kant's disruption of the formal status of space and time with respect to the workings of temporality in the transcendental unity of apperception, and suggests that the further determinations of time in the Schematism, as well as in the discussion of the Principles, might have similar significance. Thus, Heidegger appears on the one hand to be reinstalling an Aristotelian dogmatism with respect to ontology and on the other to be catapulting the kantian thinking of time and temporality into the discontinuities of time as theorised in twentieth-century physics. Instead of reading the Heideggerian account of Kant as one, or other, but not both of these, the Irigarayan appropriation permits both to stand open, in a manner which suggests the structure of Kant's Antinomies. While reinscribing Kant's critical philosophy within an Aristotelian concern with ontology, Heidegger releases Kant's accounts of space, time and the soul for further thinking. Irigaray, by inscribing a reading of Kant within a lacanian frame, reveals the logical structure of such reading and inscription.

Thus Irigaray's own reading of Kant, in the first essay of *An Ethics of Sexual Difference*, reveals her view that the formal structures of Kant's Transcendental Aesthetic are put in question by the rethinking of space and time prompted by raising the question of gender as a system of sexual difference.[25] In the brief section entitled 'Paradox A Priori', in the central part of the earlier *Speculum of the Other Woman*, Irigaray suggests that this system of sexual difference, and indeed the possibility of recognising it at work, are repressed in the production of the accounts of time and space as the forms of inner and outer sense, respectively.[26] The implication here is that in the Transcendental Aesthetic Kant makes constitutive use of the third set of concepts of reflection, inner and outer, correlating to the categories of relation which, as he subsequently makes clear in the Amphiboly of Concepts of Reflection, can apply only to the workings of the faculties and not to the component parts of intuition. Again, such a diagnosis would not indicate the need for a correction of Kant's argument, in order to permit it to resist such criticism. Rather, the mode of reading here is one which reveals the constitutive role of paradox and antinomy in the articulation of human thinking. Irigaray's readings have the structure of showing how Kant himself can provide the best criticism of his own attempt to demarcate and delimit the workings of reason.

Irigaray deploys the lacanian notion of the imaginary to capture what she understands to go missing in the workings of a transcendental unity of apperception. In *Speculum* she puts it like this: 'This is the first instance of the passage from sensation to understanding whereby – not unmysteriously – a schematism arises that will never do justice to the sensible world. For the most sophisticated faculty of the senses, the imaginary, will remain the slave of the understanding'.[27] In the course of the next few pages, dedicated to a discussion of what she calls Kant's paradox *a priori*, she traces out an account of the suffering, indeed masochism, involved in this move of cutting off from materiality, from embodiment, from 'this most sophisticated faculty of the senses',[28] and from human connectedness, invoking Lacan's identification of a proximity between the thinking of Kant and that of de Sade. The rigorous attachment to law-like relations in Kant's writings and the insistence on the sovereignty of reason above the negotiations of contractual association reveal a privilege assigned in the kantian text to an ascetic renunciation of the pleasures of the flesh, which can also work to release the flesh from the order of moral imperatives, into that of physiological experimentation.

In a characteristic double move Irigaray also challenges the Lacanian account of the imaginary. Famously, she was expelled from the lacanian school of psychoanalysis, on publication of *Speculum*, for challenging Lacanian orthodoxy. She had, however, already insisted on the unthought-through impact of the role and function of gender in the formation of the psychoanalytical techniques of free association, dream interpretation and regression to the time of trauma. Granted her views on the different modes of inhabiting speech and language exhibited by women and by men,[29] it is hardly surprising that she should arrive at a point where the psychoanalytical insistence on the talking cure should turn out to have different implications for women and for men. The articulation of trauma in a speech colonised by the habits of self-depreciation merely reinscribes the trauma of having no right to a view about what happens and no role in determining how it is interpreted and what happens next. Whereas the articulation of trauma in a medium in which the speaker supposes themselves to be a speaking rather than a spoken subject may perhaps prove in some cases to work the required emancipation from an acquired habituation of self-subversion; it may also merely confirm a predilection to psychosis.

For Irigaray, the symbolic order, as constituted, presupposes the subordination, indeed invisibility, of women and of sexual difference, sexual difference understood now not as a metaphysical principle concerning different essences, but as the principle naming the condition of there being different kinds of embodiment which result in a self-transforming generativity of the human species.[30] This then presents the hypothesis that alternative symbolic orders would position women and sexual difference with greater and lesser degrees of invisibility and significance, and with greater and lesser degrees of suffering for those positioned as either entirely visible and saturated with significance, as men, or as entirely invisible and insignificant, as women. Irigaray hypothesises the possibility both of more than one symbolic order and of more than one imaginary. This then poses the possibility that there might be more than one Transcendental Aesthetic, the one hypothesised by Kant, which permits a thinking of a continuity between reason in general and the rationality of human beings, and another, in which the question of the specificity, and indeed singularity, of the human might come to the fore. The suggested position of the Irigarayan conception of the imaginary in the place of the kantian Transcendental Aesthetic, if thought through, might have just this effect. For each entry into a symbolic order constitutes distinct imaginary configurations of which an ordering of space and time is one significant aspect. A multiplication of possible spatio-temporal orderings, of topologies, brings with it a multiplication of theorisings of necessity, possibility and actuality. Thus one ground for resisting such multiplication is the fear of a disruption of established notions of modality. Whereas one ground for pursuing such a multiplication is to demonstrate how such a disruption of established notions of modality might be thought through. Since the imaginary, precisely by contrast to the notions of reality established in a symbolic order, permits a positing of that which is not and an analysis of potential which is neither given nor even susceptible of being given, there is an important connection to be traced out between the constitution of the imaginary, as transcendental aesthetic, and a rethinking of modality. This move entails that where for Kant the disjunctive syllogism, read transcendentally, leads to the postulation of the God of the Christians, for Irigaray, it leads to the postulation of divinities, in the plural.[31]

Irigaray's challenge to Lacan's account of the imaginary disputes the status of necessity Lacan ascribes to its current configuration. She identifies the lacanian imaginary as the abjected ground out of which a system is organised whereby the existence of men as embodied is overlooked and the existence of women as women is denied. This abjected ground she identifies as the denied maternal body, the connection to which, both physical and emotional, must be broken in order for the child to become an independent human being, but which as a consequence of not being recognised cannot be broken except in the form of obsessive repetition or neurotic denial. The relation between the imaginary and the symbolic order, like sexual difference, turns out to be not single and unified, but at best singular and certainly multiple, making possible the inauguration of innumerable compossible symbolic orders, all of course embodying normativities and grounds for normativity but without any necessary content or indeed any necessary form, each one presupposing different imaginary orders. The suggestion that there might be a multiplicity of imaginaries as conditions for alternate symbolic orders poses a challenge to Lacan's and to Freud's retrievals of the Greek notion of necessity, *ananke*,[32] which would then take the form, not of a generalisable law, either Oedipus complex or categorical imperative, but of singular necessity.

Illusions of reason: paralogism, antinomy, ideal

In the Transcendental Dialectic, Kant distinguishes between three kinds of fallacious reasoning on the basis of the kinds of formal syllogism, invoked in the third group, of relation, in the table of judgements: the categorical, the hypothetical and the disjunctive.[33] These are discussed in the Paralogisms of Pure Reason, the Antinomies of Pure Reason and the Ideal of Pure Reason. By contrast, the fallacies discussed in the Amphiboly of Concepts of Reflection, before the Dialectic, are not grounded in syllogism but in a misrecognition of the status of concepts. The manner in which the discussion of fallacious reasoning straddles the division of Kant's *Critique of Pure Reason* into Transcendental Analytic and Transcendental Dialectic is indicative of the central role of these diagnoses to Kant's conception of critique. In the History of Pure Reason, in the closing pages of the *Critique of Pure Reason*, Kant sets out an opposition between Plato and Aristotle with respect to the origin of knowledge, opining that in this Locke follows Aristotle and Leibniz follows Plato, appending the intriguing qualification: 'However we may regard Epicurus, he was at least much more consistent in this sensual system than Aristotle and Locke, inasmuch as he never sought to pass by inference beyond the limits of experience.'[34] This picks up on the remark in the Amphiboly of Concepts of Reflection, where Locke and Leibniz are diagnosed as committing the two versions of the fallacy of amphiboly, as are, by implication, readings of Plato which seek out a theory of the empirical world; and readings of Aristotle which seek out a systematic rationalism.

There is an important disanalogy between the three kinds of fallacy. The conclusions of the first, of paralogism, are simply designated by Kant as false; those of the second, antinomy, are designated by Kant as contradicting one another; and those of the third as both false, if thought of as constitutive of knowledge, and true, and indeed necessarily so, if thought of as regulative ideas necessary for the deployment of reason. This disanalogy between the three is a consequence of the distinct notions of relation at work in each kind of syllogism, from the misdeployment of which the fallacy arises: categorical, hypothetical and disjunctive. In a categorical judgement, the relation is between subject and predicate; in a hypothetical judgement, the relation is between two judgements; and in a disjunctive judgement, the relation is between 'several judgements in their relation to each other.'[35] The form of paralogism concerns the 'unconditioned unity of the subjective conditions of all representations in general (of the subject or soul), in correspondence with the *categorical* syllogisms, the major premiss of which is a principle asserting the relation of a predicate to a subject.'[36] Paralogism, the first kind of dialectical syllogism, based on a false categorical judgement, is distinguished by Kant into two kinds:

> A logical paralogism is a syllogism which is fallacious in form, be its content what it may. A transcendental paralogism is one in which there is a transcendental ground constraining us to draw a formally invalid conclusion. Such a fallacy is therefore grounded in the nature of human reason, and gives rise to an illusion which cannot be avoided although it may, indeed, be rendered harmless.[37]

'Harmless' is Kemp Smith's inaccurate but suggestive translation of '*nicht unauflöslich*', 'not insoluble'. It is for Kant in the nature of such illusions that although the arguments on which they are based can be definitively refuted, they arise over and over again. Illusions cannot be refuted once and for all.

It is furthermore the nature of such illusions to be instructive about the workings of human reason. Rendering them 'harmless' suggests a view of reason in which reason can be sanitised of this tendency to err in a way which then closes down any openness to and understanding of the recurrence of such error. The proximity of Kant and Freud on this topic is precisely their willingness to hold their accounts of human reason open to a diagnosis of its tendency to err, in short, to its pathology, as inseparable from its legitimated functioning. The dynamics of repression and disavowal set in with the gesture of supposing that either such illusion does not happen at all or that it can once and for all be firmly separated off from reason's legitimate functioning. In the twentieth-century readings of Kant, associated with the names Deleuze, Lyotard, Irigaray, Derrida, and Nancy, there is a collective intent to prevent paralogisms being rendered 'harmless' in this way.[38] In this spirit, Lacan can be read as cheerfully affirming the incidence of such fallacious reasoning which must, according to Kant, arise from any substantivist theorising of the soul.[39]

The second form of fallacious reasoning, antinomy, is introduced by Kant in the following terms: 'The second type of dialectical argument follows the analogy of the hypothetical syllogisms. It has as its content the unconditioned unity of the objective conditions in the field of appearance.'[40] Kant sets out the distinction between this fallacy of antinomy and that of paralogism in the following terms:

> We have here presented to us a new phenomenon of human reason – an entirely natural antithetic, in which there is no need of making subtle enquiries or of laying snares for the unwary, but into which reason of itself quite unavoidably falls. It certainly guards reason from the slumber of fictitious conviction such as is generated by a purely one-sided illusion, but at the same time subjects itself to the temptation either of abandoning itself to sceptical despair, or of assuming an obstinate attitude, dogmatically committing itself to certain assertions, and refusing to grant a fair hearing to the arguments for the counter position. Either attitude is the death of sound philosophy, although the former might perhaps be entitled the euthanasia of pure reason.[41]

Both options of sceptical despair and dogmatic assertion are described as the death 'of sound philosophy' but only the former is called a mercy killing of pure reason, put out of its misery for failing to come into its own. According to Kant, it is better to be baffled by the validity of both arguments than to endorse one against the equal validity of the other, but better still, of course, to understand that: 'The ideas are such that no object congruent with them can ever be given in any possible experience, and that even in thought, reason is unable to bring them into harmony with the most universal laws of nature.'[42]

As is well known, the four ideas discussed in the Antinomies are those of world, substance, causality and beginning, corresponding to the Axioms of Intuition, the Anticipations of Perception, the Analogies of Experience and the Postulates of Empirical Thought, in the System of All Principles of Pure Understanding, in the Transcendental Analytic. These principles are for Kant definitively not grounded in or derivable from any such series of concepts. Kant opens up a gap where Aristotle's account of concept and matter must, according to the Aristotelian notion of schema, map on to each other.[43] The phrase from *De Anima* runs as follows: 'If then we must say something in general about all types of soul, it would be the first actuality of a natural body with organs. We should not then enquire whether the soul and body are one thing, any more than whether the wax and its imprint (schema) are, or in general whether the matter of each thing is one with that of which it is the matter. For although unity and being are spoken of in a number of ways, it is of the actuality that they are most properly said.'[44] Less well established is the thought, pursued by Irigaray, and indeed by Derrida, that there is always a gap between a concept and what is given in experience.[45] This systematic deviation of a concept from intuition and of contents from thought is precisely what Kant sets out to refute in the famous phrase from the opening pages of the Transcendental Logic: 'Thoughts without content are empty, intuitions without concepts are blind.'[46]

The thought then that Irigaray is still within the spirit of the critical enterprise requires an argument to demonstrate that the illusions of reason cannot be contained in the fashion that Kant proposes. That argument, shaking the status of the distinction between concepts of the understanding and concepts of reason, proceeds in three steps: first, by pointing out the differences between the three kinds of dialectical illusion; then by showing that, at least for one of the illusions of reason, the third, the status of these illusions is set out by Kant as divided between erroneous constitutive use, deploying concepts of the understanding and genuine regulative use, deploying concepts of reason; and the third step raises the question about the status of a constitutive use for categories of the understanding within 'the limits of experience'. If the notion of the limits of experience cannot be sustained then the distinction between concepts of the understanding and concepts of reason is in jeopardy. For some readings of Kant this would constitute a refutation of the kantian project of critique. For those who read philosophical texts not for their truth content and for an internal consistency, but for their inevitable internal inconsistency, this has no such consequence. Indeed, Lacan and lacanians confronted with the diagnosis of committing the fallacy of paralogism could claim to constitute a still more radical kantian heterodoxy, by challenging the distinction between a categorical judgement and a categorical imperative, and insisting on the priority of the injunction: read my desire.

Notes

1   See Luce Irigaray, *Speculum of the Other Woman*, trans. Gillian C. Gill (Ithaca, NY: Cornell University Press, 1985), and Luce Irigaray, *This Sex Which is Not One*, trans. Catherine Porter (Ithaca, NY: Cornell University Press, 1985).

2   See Luce Irigaray, *Speculum*, pp. 243–364.

3   See *Speculum*, pp. 13–129.

4   See Martin Heidegger, *Kant and the Problem of Metaphysics*, 5th enlarged edn, trans. Richard Taft (Bloomington and Indianapolis: Indiana University Press, 1997).

5   The connection between Lacan and Kant on ethics is well known. See Jacques Lacan, 'Kant with Sade', trans. James Swenson, in *October* 51 (1989). For a commentary on Lacan's relation to Kant's ethics, see Elisabeth Roudinesco, *Jacques Lacan* (Cambridge: Polity Press, 1997), p. 313: '[H]e maintained that the ethics of psychoanalysis remains Spinozan when it proposes a truth of being that is based on the manifestations of desire – "Don't give up on your desire" – but becomes Kantian when it deals with the psychoanalytic experience through which the individual is subjected to the symbolic order.' The relations between Lacan and Kant on imagination, mediated as they are through Sartre's distinction between empirical imagination and a transcendental imaginary, remain to be discussed.

6   For a discussion of Irigaray's differences with Lacan concerning the symbolic order, see Margaret Whitford, *Luce Irigaray: Philosophy in the Feminine* (London: Routledge, 1991), ch. 4, pp. 89–97. While the term 'the imaginary' is in play in Lacan's thinking and writings from the 1930s, Lacan introduced the notion of the symbolic in the so-called Rome Report of 1953, 'Speech and Language in Psychoanalysis', published in Lacan, *Ecrits, A Selection*, trans. Alan Sheridan (London: Tavistock, 1977), and with an extended commentary separately in English as *Speech and Language in Psychoanalysis*, trans. Anthony Wilden (Baltimore and London: Johns Hopkins University Press, 1968).

7   The small case in 'kantian' indicates a difference between attributing the

thought to Kant, as in 'Kantian', and associating the thought with a structure to be found in Kant's text, with which Kant himself may not be in
agreement, or indeed must strongly contest. Thus 'Kantian' implies
'according to Kant', whereas 'kantian' implies 'in the manner of Kant's
thinking'. Lacan's move of aligning the Kantian system with de Sade's
explorations of the limits of pleasure and pain, and of moral and amoral
classifications, is then kantian not Kantian. Thus Heidegger's readings of
Kant are kantian, not Kantian, since they impose an existential and an
ontological concern with which Kant cannot agree.

8 For a recent defence of the view that Kant must be thought of as an idealist in a manner not incompatible with attributing to him a version of materialism, and for a contestation of Guyer's reconstruction of, amongst other
things, Kant's arguments in the so-called Refutation of Idealism, see Rae
Langton, *Kantian Humility: Our Ignorance of Things in Themselves* (Oxford:
Clarendon Press, 1998).

9 See Martin Heidegger, *Sein und Zeit*, 16th edn (Tübingen: Max Niemeyer
Verlag, 1986). Martin Heidegger, *Being and Time*, trans. Macquarrie and
Robinson (Oxford: Blackwell, 1962). See especially the discussions in sections 6 and 7a, in the Introduction, on forms of intuition and on the status
of the Kantian phenomenon; see section 23 for a discussion of Kant on
incongruent counterparts; see section 32 for the recasting of the Kantian *a
priori* as the fore-structure of understanding and the 'as-structure' of interpretation; see section 43a on the Refutation of Idealism, and section 64 on
the Paralogisms of Pure Reason.

10 I would suggest that this book is contentious in three quite distinct
respects. Firstly, it provided the basis for the famous discussion and disagreement with Cassirer concerning Kant, in Davos, in 1929. Secondly,
Heidegger himself subsequently expressed regret about having published
his critique of Kant in this form. Thirdly, the text appears to fail to follow
through its own line of argumentation, since it does not explore all of the
complexities of Kant's continuing re-specification of time and of temporality, from the initial definition of time as the form of inner sense, through the
Schematism and the Analytic of Principles, in the course of the *Critique of
Pure Reason*. Perhaps for reasons of expository unity Heidegger concen-
trates on the determination of time as self-affection in the transcendental
unity of apperception. It would be the work of an extended essay to draw
out the implications of this last point of contention.

11 Kant, *CPR*, A261–92/B316–49.

12 Kant, *CPR*, A341–405/B399–432.

13 It is not possible to discuss here the differences between the two versions
of Kant's arguments, nor yet the implications of moving the Refutation of
Idealism from the Dialectic, at A369–80, in the First Edition, to the discussion of the Postulates of Empirical Thought at B275–9, in the Second

Edition. The discussion of this by Paul Guyer in his book, *Kant and the Claims of Knowledge* (Cambridge: Cambridge University Press, 1987), is instructive. He distinguishes between an epistemological and an ontological independence of mental functioning and material order. He has the following helpful elucidation to offer: 'The majority position on the interpretation of the refutation has indeed been that it is intended to be entirely consistent with the ontological reduction of external objects to groups of representations advocated by the fourth paralogism of 1781. This is what has been argued by a long line of distinguished Kantians such as Hans Vaihinger, Edward Caird, Robert Adamson, H. J. Paton and Gerhard Lehmann. Only a scorned minority party of such figures as Benno Erdmann, Henry Sidgwick, Arthur Balfour and H. A. Prichard have clearly defended the view that the argument of 1787, whether so intended or not, requires a radical departure from the position of 1781. When the alternative to the reductionism of 1781 is understood to be that in knowing things in space we know things as they are in themselves, the reason for this scorn is obvious. The assumption on which this traditional debate about the refutation of idealism revolves is that Kant must either advocate the reduction of external objects to subjective states of mind or permit knowledge of things as they are in themselves. What will be argued here, however, is that this assumption conflates ontological and epistemological conceptions of independence – as indeed did Kant himself in 1781 – and thus misses the force of Kant's position in 1787....The Kant of 1787 advocates epistemological subjectivism but ontological realism.' (*Kant and the Claims of Knowledge*, pp. 281–2). See also Guyer's exemplary footnotes at pp. 452–3.

14   This re-entry might be thought to take place under the combined aegis of Jacques Derrida and Jean-François Lyotard in a number of writings spanning the previous thirty years. For Derrida on the interplay between psychoanalysis and philosophy, see 'Freud and the Scene of Writing', in *Writing and Difference*, trans. Alan Bass (London: Routledge, 1978); 'Beyond the Pleasure Principle', in *The Post Card: From Socrates to Freud and Beyond*, trans. Alan Bass (Chicago: The University of Chicago Press, 1987); *Archive Fever: A Freudian Impression*, trans. Eric Prenowitz (Chicago: University of Chicago Press, 1996); and *Resistances of Psychoanalysis* (Stanford: Stanford University Press, 1998). 'Despite appearances, the deconstruction of logocentrism is not a psychoanalysis of philosophy' (Derrida, *Writing and Difference*, p. 196); and concerning Freud's concepts: 'all these concepts, without exception, belong to the history of metaphysics, that is, to the system of logocentric repression which was organized in order to exclude or to lower (to put outside or below), the body of the written trace as a didactic and technical metaphor, as servile matter or excrement.' (Derrida, *Writing and Difference*, p. 197).

15   It will not be possible here to explore at any length the parallels and reso-

nances between Lacanian theory and kantian critique. However, Jean-François Lyotard, in *Heidegger and 'the jews'*, points them up in the following terms: 'In order to establish clearly the difference between a representational, reversible forgetting and a forgetting that thwarts all representation, it would be useful to read side by side, though scrupulously preserving their immense differences, the Kantian text on aesthetics and the Freudian text on metapsychology, i.e., the work that, all in all, Jacques Lacan has begun. More precisely, to dare to propose that secondary repression is to primary repression as the beautiful is to the sublime – and this with respect to the matter or quality of what for Kant is the given, for Freud the notion of excitation, with respect to the capacity to synthesise in Kant and to associate in Freud, with respect to the spatio-temporal form in the former or to the formation of unconscious-preconscious in the latter, and finally, with respect to the way in which neither the Kantian sublime nor the Freudian *Nachträglichkeit* lets itself be inscribed in "memory", even an unconscious one.' (*Heidegger and 'the jews'*, trans. Andreas Michel and Mark Roberts (Minneapolis: University of Minnesota Press, 1990), p. 5). This relation between a form of forgetting which can be recuperated in the constructions of memory and a kind of forgetting which cannot is the theme in common between Lacan's redeployment of Freudian theory and Heidegger's redeployment of the Kantian account of the imagination.

16   Kant, *CPR*, A74/B99.

17   For discussions of *Ereignis*, see essays in Martin Heidegger, *Early Greek Thinking: The Dawn of Western Philosophy*, trans. David Farrell Krell (New York: Harper and Row, 1975) and also Martin Heidegger, *Vom Ereignis: Beiträge zur Philosophie, GA 65* (Frankfurt am Main: Klostermann, 1989).

18   For the clearest accounts of this, see Martin Heidegger, *The Concept of Time*, ed. and trans. Will McNeill (Oxford: Blackwell, 1992), and Martin Heidegger, *The History of the Concept of Time*, ed. and trans. Theodore Kisiel (Bloomington and Indianapolis: Indiana University Press, 1985).

19   Kant, *CPR*, A260–92/B316–49.

20   These complications make the task of setting out a discussion between Lacan, Freud, Heidegger and Kant all the more daunting. It is, however, these relations which form the context of differentiation in which the writings of Irigaray, and indeed of Derrida and Lyotard, on Lacan, Freud and Kant, would have to be set out. These complications must here be put to one side. The complications in setting out the relation between Heidegger and Kant result from this shift of perspective in his writings from the time of composing *Kant and the Problem of Metaphysics* to the greater impact of the thinking of the self-deflections of being in the analyses of Heidegger's second book on Kant, *Die Frage nach dem Ding* (Tübingen: Max Niemeyer Verlag, 1962). This text was presented as lectures in the winter semester of 1935–6, under the title *Grundfragen der Metaphysik*. It was translated by

W. B. Barton jnr. and Vera Deutsch as *What is a Thing?* (Chicago: Henry Regnery, 1967), and is also in the *Gesamtausgabe* as volume 41 (Frankfurt am Main: Klostermann, 1984).

21 Heidegger, *Sein und Zeit*, p. 44; *Being and Time*, p. 70.

22 Ibid.

23 Derrida's analyses in *Of Grammatology* would similarly unsettle the distinction, but would rather show the necessary contamination of the empirical use by a transcendental ground, and of transcendental grounding by empirical commitments. See *Of Grammatology*, trans. G. C. Spivak (Baltimore and London: Johns Hopkins University Press, 1976).

24 Parmenides: 'For the same thing can be thought and can be' [B 3], in *Early Greek Thinking*, ed. Jonathan Barnes (Harmondsworth: Penguin, 1987), p. 132, t.m.

25 See Joanna Hodge, 'Sexual difference as transcendental aesthetic: Irigaray reading Kant', in *Reading Ethics of Sexual Difference*, eds. Bergoffen and Silverman (Evanston: Northwestern University Press, 2001).

26 I am especially grateful to Rachel Jones for insisting on the importance to Irigaray of the kantian notion of schemata; and to Roxana Baiasu for opening out the question of Heidegger's rewriting of Kant's Schematism, in part two of *Being and Time*.

27 Irigaray, *Speculum*, p. 204.

28 Ibid.

29 See Luce Irigaray, *Le langage des dements* (The Hague: Mouton, 1973).

30 For the significance of distinguishing between sexual difference as metaphysical principle and sexual difference as process of transformation, see Joanna Hodge, 'Forays of a Philosophical Feminist: Sexual Difference, Genealogy, Teleology', in *Feminists Transforming the Political*, eds. Ahmed, Lury, McNeil, Kilby and Skeggs (London: Routledge, 2001).

31 See Grace Jantzen, *Becoming Divine* (Manchester: Manchester University Press, 1999).

32 In 'The Economic Problem of Masochism', Freud invokes necessity in the following way: 'The last figure in the series that began with the parents is the dark power of destiny which only the fewest of us are able to look upon as impersonal. There is little to be said against…Multatuli when he replaces the Μοῖρα [Destiny] of the Greeks by the divine pair Λόγος καὶ Ἀνάγκη [Reason and Necessity]; but all who transfer the guidance of the world to Providence, to God, or to God and Nature, arouse a suspicion that they still look upon these ultimate and remotest powers as a parental couple, in a mythological sense, and believe themselves linked to them by libidinal ties. In *The Ego and the Id* I made an attempt to derive mankind's realistic fear of death, too, from the same parental view of fate. It seems very hard to free oneself from it.' (In *On Metapsychology: The Theory of Psychoanalysis*, trans. James Strachey (Harmondsworth: Penguin, Penguin Freud

Library, vol. 11, 1991), p. 423). This reveals a work of naturalisation in the relation between child and parent which is then carried over into some set of assumptions about a rigid order of things, held up by a reinscription of sexual difference, in the metaphysical form of the pair, reason and necessity.

33   Kant, *CPR*, A70/B95.

34   Kant, *CPR*, A854/B882.

35   Kant, *CPR*, A73/B98.

36   Kant, *CPR*, A406/B432–3.

37   Kant, *CPR*, A341/B399.

38   Lyotard explicitly endorses the operations of paralogism in section fourteen, entitled 'Legitimation by Paralogy', the last section of *The Postmodern Condition: A Report on Knowledge*; and the transition from the thinking of *The Postmodern Condition* to that of *The Differend: Phrases in Dispute* can be understood as one from a restricted to a general deployment of paralogism. See *The Postmodern Condition: A Report on Knowledge*, trans. Geoff Bennington and Brian Massumi (Manchester: Manchester University Press, 1984); and *The Differend: Phrases in Dispute*, trans. Georges Van Den Abbeele (Minneapolis: University of Minnesota Press, 1988). Fredric Jameson, in his introduction to *The Postmodern Condition*, helpfully marks up the significance for Lyotard of paralogy, in his location of a proximity between Lyotard's thinking and a schizophrenic ethic: 'Lyotard's celebration of a related ethic emerges most dramatically in the context of th[e] repudiation of Habermas' consensus community…, in which the dissolution of the self into a host of networks and relations, of contradictory codes and interfering messages is prophetically valorised. This view not surprisingly will then determine Lyotard's ultimate vision of science and knowledge as a search, not for consensus, but very precisely for "instabilities" as a practice of paralogism, in which the point is not to reach agreement but to undermine from within the very framework in which the previous "normal science" has been conducted.' (*The Postmodern Condition*, p. xix).

39   Gilles Deleuze and Félix Guattari, in part two, 'Psychoanalysis and Familialism – The Holy Family', of their *Anti-Oedipus: Capitalism and Schizophrenia* (trans. Robert Hurley, Mark Seem and Helen R. Lane (New York: The Viking Press, 1977)) rewrite Kant's paralogisms as paralogisms of psychoanalysis. They name their first four paralogisms those of extrapolation, the Oedipal double bind, Oedipus as bi-univocal application and displacement or the disfiguration of the repressed. They add a fifth paralogism, that of the afterward, concerned with the passing of time and the structure of the immemorial retrieval of trauma. With this reinscription they can be understood to take up and see off this Lacanian cheerfulness on the topic of paralogism. It will not be possible here to discuss the respective claims of Lacan and of Deleuze an Guattari as readers of Kant, nor to pursue their

various receptions of the Freudian theme of *Nachträglichkeit*, for which see the entry on 'deferred action', in Laplanche and Pontalis, *The Vocabulary of Psychoanalysis*, in *The French Freud*, ed. Jeffrey Mehlman, Special Issue of *Yale French Studies* 48 (1972).

40 Kant, *CPR*, A406/B433.

41 Kant, *CPR*, A407/B434.

42 Kant, *CPR*, A462/B491.

43 For a defence of Aristotle against this move, indeed for a response to Kant's reception of Aristotle and for a contestation of the usefulness of translating *energeia* and *dunamis* as actuality and potentiality, see Martin Heidegger, *Aristotle's Metaphysics Theta 1–3*, trans. Walter Brogan and Peter Warnek (Bloomington and Indianapolis: Indiana University Press, 1995). For a disputation of Aristotle's privilege to the actual over the potential, and to the privilege to *energeia* as a setting to work, as ready to hand, as opposed to the distinctive modalities of Dasein, in its relation to being, see Martin Heidegger, *Being and Time*.

44 Aristotle, *De Anima*, trans. Hugh Lawson-Tancred (Harmondsworth: Penguin, 1986), 412 b 7. Judith Butler in her discussion of Aristotle and Irigaray in 'Bodies that Matter' points out the significance of the word 'schema' in this remark. See Butler, 'Bodies that Matter', in *Engaging with Irigaray*, ed. Carolyn Burke, Naomi Schor and Margaret Whitford (New York: University of Columbia Press, 1994), pp. 141–73, p. 146.

45 For a discussion of this relation between Derrida and Kant see Irene Harvey, 'Derrida, Kant and the Performance of Parergonality', in *Derrida and Deconstruction*, ed. Hugh Silverman (London: Routledge, 1989), pp. 59–76, and Irene Harvey, *Derrida and the Economy of Differance* (Bloomington and Indianapolis: Indiana University Press, 1986). See also Rodolphe Gasché: 'God, for example', ch. 6 of his *Inventions of Difference: On Jacques Derrida* (Cambridge, MA, and London: Harvard University Press, 1994), pp. 150–70; and his *The Tain of the Mirror: Derrida and the Philosophy of Reflection* (Cambridge, MA, and London: Harvard University Press, 1986).

46 Kant, *CPR*, A51/B75.

11

Relations and Reversals: Deleuze, Hume and Kant

Martin Bell

The question of relations is one of the most important that arise in philosophy, as most other issues turn on it: monism and pluralism; the question whether anything is true except the whole truth, or wholly real except the whole of reality; idealism and realism, in some of their forms; perhaps the whole existence of philosophy as a subject distinct from science and possessing a method of its own.[1]

This paper is concerned with some aspects of Kant's thought about relations, particularly the role played by the concepts of 'internal' and 'external'. Beyond this issue, the above quotation from Russell makes a large claim about the significance of 'the question of relations' in general. My exploration is located within some of the larger territory Russell invokes.

Reading Deleuze alongside Kant, what is surprising is the insistence of the former that empiricism can be characterised by a thesis of the externality of all relations. A thesis of the externality of relations can be found in Kant's critical philosophy, particularly with regard to matter and phenomenal substances. Is this therefore a mark of empiricism in Kant? Deleuze's earliest engagement with the question of relations comes in his book on Hume, whom Deleuze credits with making a thesis of the externality of relations central to empiricism. Here there is, I think, a kind of reversal in play. While Kant can indeed be read as responding at times to a certain reading of Hume, Deleuze's Hume makes Hume respond to Kant. This makes the Deleuze-Hume thesis of the externality of relations into a critique of Kant. It also at the same time makes Hume into a kind of transcendental philosopher. In section I the focus is on Deleuze's reading of Hume. The argument of the section is that the thesis of the externality of relations which Deleuze extracts from Hume is neither logical nor epistemological. To investigate further what its status is, I hypothesise that Deleuze thinks it in a Kantian context.

Section II explores this hypothesis. Two possibilities are considered for understanding the Kantian context. One reading interprets Kant as propounding a metaphysics of relations in the sense of an ontological thesis. The other reading stresses transcendental reflection. I give some explanation of these terms in the section. My conclusion is that Kant's account of relations is best seen in the context of his transcendental idealism. My hypothesis about Deleuze's approach then becomes the hypothesis that his thesis of the externality of relations is part of his rethinking the transcendental. The final section explores this thought further. It suggests that what can be seen in Deleuze's response to Kant, which is already in play in his reading of Hume, is the attempt to transpose the thought of the externality of relations from the domain where Kant locates its work, the empirical, into the transcendental domain. The thesis of the externality of relations becomes the thought of relations between the faculties, and of these relations as external. As should become clear from this whole discussion, when Deleuze speaks of relations as external to their terms, what he is primarily exploring is the thought that something other than the terms brings them into relation. Taking this thought into the transcendental, then, is seeking that which relates the faculties, insofar as they ever are related, when the 'harmony' of the faculties which Kant sees as necessary for experience is no longer assumed. This 'transcendental empiricism' is, for Deleuze, an opening up of a space in which the relations of the faculties of the mind (its capacities for sensation, memory, imagination, conceptualisation, and systematisation) are to be thought first of all not in terms of harmony but in their differences.

I

In his reading of Hume,[2] Deleuze displaces more orthodox interpretations in favour of one which sees Hume as a transcendental philosopher exploring the conditions for the possibility of the constitution of a subject:

> Hume's project entails the *substitution of a psychology of the mind by a psychology of the mind's affections*.[3]

The substitution Deleuze here finds in Hume is a means to make Hume confront Kant's transcendental investigation of the subject of experience. Deleuze's Hume does not assume an already constituted unified subject but explores the forces which affect the mind and produce the subject. Deleuze is proposing to understand such terms as 'mind' and 'imagination' in Hume in two ways. On the one hand, these terms designate simply collections of perceptions; at this level the mind in general and the imagination in particular are not to be thought of as having as yet a character or a nature. Mental events happen *in* the mind, they are not actions performed *by* the mind. On the other hand, the various ways in which the mind (in this first sense) is affected produce a mind (in the second sense), one which does have a character (powers, dispositions and tendencies). Here, for Deleuze, Humean associationism is 'the *substitution of a psychology of the mind by a psychology of the mind's affections*'.

Deleuze first finds the thesis of the externality of relations in Hume's doctrine of the association of ideas. He says that Hume does not explain association as a product of the nature of the terms, the qualities of the ideas themselves, but as the effect of the principles of human nature. It is the principles which relate ideas. Relations between perceptions that are effects of the principles of human nature constitute what Hume calls 'natural relations'.[4] Here the essence of relation consists in an association of perceptions which gives a character to the imagination. In the case of Humean natural relations it is clear why Deleuze should say that relations are external to their terms, because what brings two or more perceptions into relation is always the operation of some principle of association, and Hume regards the question of what associative principles there are in human nature as something to be discovered by the experimental method.

But in the *Treatise* there is another sense of 'relation' in which it designates 'that particular circumstance, in which, even upon the arbitrary union of two ideas in the fancy, we may think proper to compare them,'[5] A relation in this second sense Hume calls 'philosophical', and he identifies seven general kinds. Furthermore, within these kinds he distinguishes a class of four kinds (relations of resemblance, of proportions in quantity or number, of degrees in a quality, and of contrariety) which are 'such as depend entirely on the ideas, which we compare together', and a class of three kinds (relations of identity, of time and place, and of causation) which are 'such as may be chang'd without any change in the ideas'.[6] Hume also describes the difference between the two classes by saying that relations in the first class depend 'solely upon ideas',[7] while those in the second class 'depend not upon the idea'.[8]

At least since Kant,[9] many philosophers have taken this division of relations into two classes to be based on a distinction between analytic judgements on the one hand and synthetic judgements on the other hand. Deleuze, however, understands Hume's division differently. Certainly relations which depend 'solely upon ideas' are knowable *a priori*. But when Hume speaks of how such *a priori* knowledge is acquired (for example, how 'from the idea of a triangle, ... we discover the relation of equality, which its three angles bear to two right ones')[10] he speaks of an act of 'comparison', a bringing together of ideas, rather than an act of analysis, a separation of a complex idea into its components. The latter is what Hume usually means by 'definition',[11] and he is explicit in rejecting the notion that mathematical truths are true by definition:

> 'Tis true, mathematicians pretend they give an exact definition of a right line, when they say, *it is the shortest way betwixt two points.* But in the first place I observe, that this is more properly the discovery of one of the properties of a right line, than a just definition of it. For I ask any one, if upon mention of a right line he thinks not immediately on such a particular appearance, and if 'tis not by accident only that he considers this property? A right line can be comprehended alone; but this definition is unintelligible without a comparison with other lines, which we conceive to be more extended. In common life 'tis establish'd as a maxim, that the streightest way is also the shortest; which wou'd be as absurd as to say, the shortest way is always the shortest, if our idea of a right line was not different from that of the shortest way betwixt two points.[12]

That the shortest way is always the shortest is analytically true. Hume evidently means to contrast geometrical truths, and mathematical truths in general, with merely analytic judgements.[13] Humean relations which depend 'solely upon the ideas' are relations discoverable *a priori*, by comparison rather than analysis. Deleuze claims that the relation depends upon the comparison, citing the passage in which Hume, referring to the definition of equality of geometrical figures by their congruity, says, 'In order to judge of this definition let us consider, that since equality is a relation, it is not, strictly speaking, a property in the figures themselves, but arises merely from the comparison, which the mind makes betwixt them'.[14] He argues that, for Hume, all relations are 'external' because all depend on something other than the terms themselves.

Relations are all discovered by comparison, and the difference between the two classes depends on the scope of the comparison. In the case of *a priori* relations, the comparison is restricted to the ideas in question 'consider'd as such',[15] whereas in the case of relations discoverable *a posteriori* the scope of the comparison is wider. The relations of causation, identity, and time and place emerge only from comparison of ideas considered, as Deleuze puts it, 'collectively ... distributively ... in the determinable collection where their own modes of appearance place them'.[16] *What other ideas enter the comparison* is then a matter of taking ideas not merely 'as such' but as ideas of objects in space and time. But what other ideas of objects in space and time must be compared cannot be known *a priori*. As Hume says, for instance 'the place [of an object in space] depends on a hundred different accidents, which cannot be foreseen by the mind'.[17]

Two points have emerged in this brief account of Deleuze's reading of Hume. Firstly, Deleuze thinks that Hume asserts a thesis of the externality of relations which is not based on a contrast between analytic and synthetic judgements, nor on a contrast between *a priori* and *a posteriori* knowledge. The discovery of relations is said to depend on comparison, an act of the mind which becomes possible when something affects the mind in such a way that ideas are conjoined. Secondly, in Deleuze-Hume (and, as we shall see, not in Kant) active cognitive powers, such as comparison, are themselves effects of that which affects the mind, producing unity and constancy. This is important for Deleuze's thought of a transcendental empiricism,[18] to which I shall return in section III.

II

The activity of comparison and its connection to relations is prominent in Kant's *Critique of Pure Reason*. Comparison is mentioned at the very beginning of the B edition.[19] Of course, Kant's point here is to introduce his main concern, namely what is contributed *a priori* to the constitution of experience (knowledge of objects) as he immediately goes on to say. But it is a mistake to think that for Kant comparison does not already involve an *a priori* condition. This emerges very clearly from an important recent study of Kant's theory of judgement by Béatrice Longuenesse.[20] This presents the act of judgement and the capacity for such acts as having a pivotal place in Kant's philosophy, and Longuenesse is able to connect many of Kant's most important discoveries to one another and to clarify many difficulties by the assignment of this place to judgement. In particular, her reading provides the possibility for a particular interpretation of Kant's account of relations (of objects, of intuitions and of concepts) which puts most weight on transcendental reflection. This interpretation will shortly be considered, and contrasted with another approach to Kant's account of relations which puts the emphasis on claims which it sees as metaphysical or ontological theses.

What is it that Kant is concerned with in his thought about relations?

The answer that may well first come to mind would invoke Kant's use of the term 'relation' in the table of logical forms of judgement (categorical, hypothetical, disjunctive)[21] and then in the corresponding categories of relation (substance, causality, community).[22] Then there is Kant's reference to 'the relations in which concepts in a state of mind can stand to one another'.[23] Further, there are frequent references to the relations between faculties, and between representations (sensations, intuitions, concepts, ideas) and faculties. In such passages the term 'relation' is being employed by Kant in the context of his transcendental investigation into the powers and processes which must be given *a priori* in the mind as conditions for the possibility of knowledge. Here I use the term 'transcendental' in accordance with Kant's initial explanation:

> I entitle *transcendental* all knowledge which is occupied not so much with objects as with the mode of our knowledge of objects in so far as this mode of knowledge is to be possible *a priori*.[24]

There are, however, many passages in which Kant appears to be using the term 'relation' not transcendentally (as just described) but rather in relation to the objects of which we may or may not have knowledge. For example:

> everything in our knowledge which belongs to intuition … contains nothing but mere relations.[25]

> a thing in itself cannot be known through mere relations.[26]

> In an object of the pure understanding that only is inward which has no relation whatsoever (so far as its existence is concerned) to anything different from itself. It is quite otherwise with a *substantia phaenomenon* in space; its inner determinations are nothing but relations, and it itself is entirely made up of mere relations.[27]

> According to mere concepts the inner is the substratum of all relational or outer determinations.[28]

In these passages Kant seems to be speaking of relations as possible objects of knowledge, as entities. He speaks of 'mere' relations, suggesting perhaps an ontological distinction between relations and some other kinds of entities. Furthermore, relations are 'outer determinations' and as such seem to stand in contrast to what is 'inner', suggesting that the 'inner' is not relational, although the third passage quoted above prevents this simple equation by making 'inner' itself relative to the type of object being considered. These passages are drawn either

from the Transcendental Aesthetic or from the Appendix to the Transcendental Analytic, The Amphiboly of Concepts of Reflection. In both
these parts Kant refers to and criticises Leibniz's metaphysics as involving a confusion between appearances and things in themselves. According to Kant,

> Leibniz took the appearances for things-in-themselves, and so for intelligi-
> bilia, i.e. objects of the pure understanding (although, on account of the
> confused character of our representations of them, he still gave them the
> name of phenomena).[29]

In terms of Kantian principles, Leibniz is criticised for *reducing* knowledge of phenomena, which is possible only through the combined contribution of concepts and sensible intuition, to knowledge of
intelligibilia, noumena, which is allegedly knowledge of things in themselves through concepts alone. I emphasise here the suggestion that
Kant is criticising Leibniz for carrying out an illegitimate reduction.

This brings me to one way of understanding Kant's treatment of relations in the second kind of passage I have referred to. This is a reading
of Kant proposed by Rae Langton.[30] The essence of this reading is that
Kant's distinction between phenomena and things in themselves is a
metaphysical distinction not between things but between the properties
of things.[31] One and the same thing is both phenomenal and noumenal.
Langton does not mean that Kant is saying merely that we can *consider*
a thing phenomenally (under the conditions of sensibility) or *consider*
that same thing in itself (abstracting from these conditions). She means
that the idea of a phenomenon is the idea of a thing which possesses
properties of one kind, and the idea of a noumenon is the idea of a thing
which possesses properties of another kind. Therefore the distinction is,
she says, metaphysical, because it is between two different kinds of entities. The point is that the entities are properties, not things possessing
these properties. The properties whose possession makes a thing a phenomenon are relational or extrinsic, which is how she understands
Kant's references to 'outer determinations' or 'mere relations'. The
properties whose possession makes a thing a thing in itself are intrinsic
or, in Kant's terms, 'inner'.

As Langton understands it, the intrinsic or inner properties of a thing
are those the possession of which depends in no way on the existence of
any other thing whatever. Extrinsic or relational properties are those,
possession of which depends on the existence of some other thing.
Kant's denial of the possibility of knowledge of things in themselves is

therefore the denial of the possibility of knowledge of the intrinsic or inner properties of things. All that we can know are relational properties, that is, phenomena. The relational properties of a thing include their appearances, for an appearance of a thing is a relational property. To say that a property F is an appearance of some thing x is to say that there is some y to which x appears F.

In terms of this reading, Langton then argues that Kant's rejection of Leibniz's metaphysics turns upon the question of the ontology of relations and relational properties. She suggests that Kant understands Leibniz as arguing that relations between things and the relational properties they possess are ontologically dependent upon the things as things in themselves, which is to say that relational properties, as extrinsic, are reducible to intrinsic properties. Reducibility here is best understood, she suggests, in terms of a concept of supervenience. A thing's extrinsic properties cannot alter without an alteration in its intrinsic properties, because extrinsic (outer, external) properties, which are always relational, supervene on intrinsic properties. If so, the way is at least open for Leibniz to argue that knowledge of phenomena is itself a form of knowledge of things in themselves, since, to use a Leibnizian term, one can see external relations as 'expressions' of intrinsic states. Kant's rejection of Leibniz now becomes a rejection of the key thesis of the reducibility of external relations to internal or intrinsic properties, and Langton devotes a good deal of her book to the elucidation of what she sees as Kant's argument against reducibility. In sum, Langton ascribes to Kant this thesis about relations: relations are external in that they cannot be reduced to intrinsic properties.

Langton's interpretation is independent of Kant's transcendental idealism, as she points out. She stresses that, on her reading, Kant's statement that things in themselves cannot be objects of knowledge is not an epistemological consequence of a transcendental, but of what she calls a metaphysical, argument. Despite its ingenuity, insight, and textual support, this independence from the transcendental seems to me a weakness in this reading and not a strength. I now want to show that Longuenesse's reading of Kant, which makes central his transcendental investigation of the capacity for judgement, unifies his concern with relations between representations and faculties and his concern with relations between objects of experience in a way which illuminates both, and also illuminates Kant's rejection of Leibniz's metaphysics of relations. This will allow for another interpretation of Kant's commitment to the externality of relations. Of the two readings it is this one, I believe,

which best allows us to bring into a clearer light Deleuze's thought of
relations and the response to Kant of which it forms a part.

Longuenesse argues that the logical forms of judgement have a role,
for Kant, in the generation of concepts to be combined in judgements.
The Kantian notion of logical form is not the same as that used in contemporary formal logic. It refers not to the constants and formation
rules of a calculus but to what Longuenesse calls 'the universal rules of
discursive thought'.[32] She shows how Kant presents forms of judgement
as specifications of the capacity to judge which he identifies with the
understanding:

> Now we can reduce all acts of the understanding to judgements, and the
> *understanding* may therefore be represented as a *faculty of judgement*.[33]

The central place in Kant's thought, which Longuenesse gives to the
capacity or faculty of judgement, yields an illuminating perspective on
Kant's treatment of relations. In section III, below, it will be argued that
this perspective can then also be used to locate Deleuze's response to
Kant.

In the Appendix to the Transcendental Analytic, The Amphiboly of
Concepts of Reflection, Kant distinguishes between 'logical reflection'
and 'transcendental reflection'.[34] Let us remember that reflection is
linked with comparison, and comparison is, Kant says, necessary for
judgement: 'Before constructing any objective judgement we compare
the concepts'.[35] This comparison of concepts is guided by 'concepts of
reflection', which come in four pairs: identity/difference; agreement/
opposition;[36] inner/outer; and matter/form. These relate to judgements
because they correlate with the four headings of the logical forms of
judgement, namely, quantity, quality, relation and modality, respectively.
For example, as Longuenesse explains, if we compare concepts A and B
by means of identity/difference we can arrive at, say, a universal judgement (objects thought under A are identical with respect to concept B,
so all As are Bs), or again at a particular judgement (objects thought
under A differ with respect to concept B, so some As are Bs, and some
are not). Similarly, comparison by means of agreement/conflict corre-
lates with affirmative and negative judgements.[37]

Kant does not directly explain how the pairs of concepts of reflection
inner/outer and matter/form correlate to relation (categorical, hypothetical, disjunctive) and modality (assertoric, problematic and apodeictic).
Here we shall concentrate on inner/outer and relation in logical forms of
judgement. It may look, at first, as if any suggestion of a connection

between what Kant says here and the questions about the nature of relations raised above can generate nothing but confusion. What does the sense of 'relation' in which judgements are categorical, hypothetical or disjunctive have to do with relations in the sense discussed earlier? And what does 'inner/outer' in this context have to do with 'internal' and 'external' relations? Longuenesse shows how these questions can be answered.[38]

Although Kant does not spell out the correlation between inner/outer and the heading 'relation' in the table of logical forms, he does say:

> If we reflect in a merely logical fashion, we are only comparing our concepts with each other in the understanding, to find whether both have the same content, whether they are contradictory or not, whether something is contained within the concept or is an addition from outside, which of the two is given and which should serve only as a mode of thinking what is given.[39]

The reference here to 'merely logical fashion' might suggest that therefore all Kant has in mind by comparison in terms of inner/outer is the difference between analytic and synthetic judgement. But, as Longuenesse says,[40] that would mean that Kant is suddenly dropping the correlation previously asserted between concepts of reflection (comparison) and logical forms, because, for Kant, the difference between analytic and synthetic is not a matter of logical forms, that is, a categorical judgement may be either analytic or synthetic, for example. In fact, she argues, the pair inner/outer do correlate with categorical and hypothetical forms, because what Kant means by 'relation' in a judgement is explained in the *Jäsche Logic* as follows:

> All rules (judgements) contain objective unity of consciousness of the manifold of cognition, hence a condition under which one cognition belongs with another to one consciousness. Now only three conditions of this unity may be thought, however, namely: as subject of the inherence of marks, or as ground of the dependence of one cognition on another, or, finally, as combination of parts in a whole (logical division). Consequently there can only be just as many kinds of universal rules (*propositiones majores*), through which the *consequentia* of one judgement from another is mediated. And on this is grounded the division of all inferences of reason into *categorical*, *hypothetical*, and *disjunctive*.[41]

This explains the logical forms as potential major premises of syllogisms, but what matters here is Kant's use of the expression 'condition under which one cognition belongs with another to one consciousness'. This 'belonging together' is what Kant means by 'relation' in a judgement, and Longuenesse shows that a condition, in this context, is a concept under which something is thought insofar as some other concept is predicated of that same object[42] – the sameness of the object thought under the two concepts then being the unity of the cognitions in one consciousness. Thus in 'A is B' the object x thought under A is subsumed under the concept B, and in Kantian terminology this means that A expresses a condition under which B is predicated of x. Since in this case the condition of the predication is expressed by the subject concept itself, the condition of the assertion of the predicate is 'internal'. In the case of a hypothetical judgement, in contrast, say of the form 'if A is B then C is D', the condition for the assertion of the predicate D of the object thought under C is given by the antecedent 'A is B' which is thus 'external' to the concept under which the object x is thought, namely the concept C. Since the categorical and hypothetical forms can be forms of either analytic or synthetic judgements, the internal/external condition distinction is not the analytic/synthetic distinction. Thus when Kant implies that before we make categorical or hypothetical judgements we compare concepts with respect to the concepts of reflection inner/outer, what he means is that we consider whether the condition for the assertion of a predicate of an object x is expressed simply by the concept under which we think x as subject of the judgement, or whether it is to be expressed by a concept or combination of concepts as the antecedent of a hypothetical judgement.

At this point we must turn to Kant's distinction between logical reflection and transcendental reflection. The former is comparison of concepts irrespective of the status of the objects thought under them, whereas the latter requires reference to the cognitive faculties:

> The act by which I confront the comparison of representations with the cognitive faculty to which it belongs, and by means of which I distinguish whether it is as belonging to the pure understanding or to sensible intuition that they are to be compared with each other, I call *transcendental reflection*.[43]

This is the key to Kant's rejection of Leibniz's metaphysics. Leibniz assumed that concepts related to objects as they are in themselves, so that conceptual relations represented relations of objects. On that assumption, if we have two acts of thinking an object under concepts which do not differ in either quantity or quality, then we thereby think one and the same object. Hence comparison of objects is reducible to comparison of their concepts. Any judgement which through predicates ascribes to an object one of its properties, including of course relational properties, must therefore be reducible to a categorical judgement.[44] As we can see, Kant distinguishes categorical from hypothetical judgements by whether or not the condition for the assertion of a predicate (a 'determination') of an object has for its condition a concept expressed by the concept under which the object is thought, or by some concept or combination of concepts expressed by the antecedent of a hypothetical. Thus, to say that all judgement is reducible to categorical judgement is to say that all of an object's determinations are 'internal determinations'[45] and that includes all relational determinations. Hence, according to Kant, in a rationalist system in which the objects thought under concepts are noumena, objects of pure thought, *all relations are internal*.

Transcendental reflection relates representations to cognitive powers. As Kant states in the chapter on the Schematism, concepts have meaning only insofar as they are related to intuition:

> For we have seen that concepts are altogether impossible, and can have no meaning, if no object is given for them, or at least for the elements of which they are composed. They cannot, therefore, be viewed as applicable to things in themselves, independent of all question as to whether and how these may be given to us.[46]

Thus purely logical comparison of concepts does not tell us how the objects thought under concepts are related. For this we must consider our concepts, through transcendental reflection, in relation to 'how [things] may be given to us', namely under the conditions of sensibility. Thus, Kant says, in the case of comparison with respect to identity and difference objects given to us under sensible conditions may still differ in spatio-temporal location even though there is no conceptual difference. Similarly, he argues, in the case of relations, we have ultimately to think these under the conditions of sensibility. Even the so-called primary qualities such as impenetrability are 'inward only in a comparative sense',[47] that is, relative to a concept such as that of a body:

> The concept of body, in the perception of something outside us, necessitates the representation of extension, and therewith representations of impenetrability, shape, etc.[48]

But in terms of sensible conditions, impenetrability is predicable only under external conditions:

> We are acquainted with substance in space only through forces which are active in this or that space, either bringing other objects to it (attraction), or preventing them penetrating into it (repulsion and impenetrability).[49]

Even the concept of substance is applicable, hence meaningful, only under empirical conditions which are 'external', stated in hypothetical judgements:

> Causality leads to the concept of action, this in turn to the concept of force, and thereby to the concept of substance.[50]

> All that we know in matter is merely relations (what we call the inner determinations of it are inward only in a comparative sense), but among these relations some are self-subsistent and permanent, and through these we are given a determinate object. The fact that, if I abstract from these relations, there is nothing more left for me to think does not rule out the concept of a thing as appearance, nor indeed the concept of an object *in abstracto*. What it does remove is all possibility of an object determinable through mere concepts, that is, of a noumenon. It is certainly startling to hear that a thing is to be taken as consisting wholly of relations. Such a thing is, however, mere appearance, and cannot be thought through the pure categories; what it itself consists in is the mere relation of something in general to our senses.[51]

Objects given to us under conditions of sensibility are empirically real: they are thought under the categories applied to the conditions of sensibility, space and time. But they are transcendentally ideal: 'mere appearances' which 'so far as they are thought as objects according to the unity of the categories, are called *phaenomena*',[52] and to bring appearances to the status of phenomena, empirical objects, requires the constant searching for rules in the flux of appearances which can then be reflected under (empirical) concepts. This is why 'inner determinations' of objects are 'inward only in a comparative sense', and depend on external relations, expressed in hypothetical judgements.

In the light of this reading I think we can see an alternative to Langton's argument that Kant's rejection of Leibniz turns on a metaphysical thesis about reducibility or supervenience. For Kant, the notion of a determination of a thing as 'inner' or intrinsic is to be understood in terms of how a predicate relates to the condition of its predication, and this therefore concerns how the object is thought in the subject concept of the judgement. Since the thing in itself can be represented only by an idea but not by an objective concept, we cannot even make sense of the idea of the intrinsic determinations of a thing in itself. The thought of the thing in itself provides no concept of an object relative to which a determination might be either inner or outer. In fact, the thing in itself can itself be referred to only relatively, as 'the true correlate of sensibility'.[53] The mind cannot move beyond relational thought of the thing in itself and therefore no sense can be made of the 'intrinsic properties' to which extrinsic relations are to be reduced. The unknowability of the thing in itself renders the notion of reduction itself contentless.

III

Let us now return to Deleuze. Deleuze says that textbook definitions of empiricism as a theory according to which knowledge derives from experience are unhelpful. A better mark is the thesis that relations are external to their terms:

> empiricism will not be correctly defined except by means of a dualism. Such an empirical dualism exists between terms and relations ... Consequently, the criterion of empiricism becomes evident. We will call "nonempiricist" every theory according to which, *in one way or another*, relations are derived from the nature of things.[54]

In the introductory section of this chapter the question was raised whether Kant's treatment of matter and phenomenal substances is a mark of empiricism. More exactly, the question is whether Deleuze's criterion of empiricism, in the form just quoted, is applicable to Kant. Certainly we have seen that Kant's rejection of Leibniz can correctly be regarded as the rejection of a 'nonempiricist' theory of relations as 'derived from the nature of things'. However, if we follow Longuenesse's reading of the Amphiboly Appendix, we find that Kant's rejection of Leibniz rests on the differences between merely logical reflection and comparison on the one hand, and transcendental reflection and comparison on the other. For Kant, the illusion of rationalism arises from the failure to make this distinction, a failure which is, of course, no mere mistake but something which Kant makes fundamental to his Copernican revolution in philosophy. Transcendental reflection, like merely logical reflection, abstracts from the empirically given in experience, but unlike merely logical reflection it does not also abstract from the conditions which make possible experience of the empirically given. Transcendental reflection can then mount a guard against the illusion of rationalism by relating representations to cognitive powers, intuitions to sensibility, concepts to the capacity to think.

Nevertheless, this does not make Kant's account 'empiricist' in Deleuze's sense. In the previous section it was noted that making transcendental reflection central to Kant's response to rationalism is something Longuenesse can do because of her emphasis on the centrality in the Kantian philosophy of the capacity or faculty of judgement. Longuenesse's understanding of Kant's account of judgement in the *Critique of Pure Reason* emphasises the connection between judgement and reflection, and therefore she sees here more continuity with the *Critique of Judgement* than many other commentators.[55] On her reading, Kant regards empirical concepts as formed by a process of reflection on the sensible data which is aimed at the making of empirical judgements in which concepts are combined in accordance with the logical forms of judgement. In this reflective process an essential part is played by the synthesis of the imagination, both pure and empirical, and Kant stresses that the relation between functions of unity in judgement and functions of unity in synthesis in intuition is that of *identity*:

> The same function which gives unity to the various representations *in a judgement* also gives unity to the mere synthesis of various representations *in an intuition*; and this unity, in its most general expression, we entitle the pure concept of the understanding.[56]

Thus, while Kant rejects a rationalism in which (as explained above) all relations are internal, he does so, on Longuenesse's reading, through an account of the transcendental conditions of knowledge in which differences between the faculties – of sensibility, imagination and understanding – are represented as harmonised by the sameness of function to which he refers in the above quotation.

It is here, in the harmony of the Kantian faculties, and in the subsuming of differences under a higher unity, that Deleuze sees the non-empiricist nature of Kant's thought. At the empirical level Kant's account of relations is empiricist – all relations are external to their terms – but at the transcendental level, in the account of the relations of the faculties, relations are, in Deleuze's words, '*in one way or another* ... derived from the nature of things'.[57] Kant's account, as Deleuze puts it, makes all cognition *re-cognition*.[58] The action of discursive thought, by means of the uniting of concepts in one consciousness through the forms of judgement, *re-presents* the uniting of the manifold of appearance in intuition performed by the imagination under the original unity of apperception. Thus the *difference* between concept and intuition is itself comprised under a higher *identity* of the faculties themselves as modes of the action of one and the same self-consciousness.

In Kant's system, relations of phenomena are indeed always external. But the externality of relations is given by the fact that all knowledge requires intuition, and 'everything in our knowledge which belongs to intuition … contains nothing but mere relations',[59] because intuition is possible only under the forms of space and time. Relations depend on form, and form is given to experience, not abstracted from it. Space and time are not relations but forms that make relations possible. They also make possible, when united and harmonised with the spontaneous power of the understanding, the (empirically) real world. Thus the *a priori* nature of the mind is, in the end, what makes relations possible. '*In one way or another*', in Kant as read by Deleuze, 'relations are derived from the nature of things'. Kant's acceptance of the 'empiricist' thesis of the externality of relations is of course at the empirical level, not at the transcendental level. Deleuze sets out to think the externality of relations at the transcendental level, to develop a transcendental empiricism. A step on the way to that is Deleuze's reading of Kant's account of relations, inspired by a reading of Hume that is already a response to Kant. This Deleuzian reversal is the key to his reading of Hume and his response to Kant's treatment of relations.

Notes

1 Bertrand Russell, 'Logical Atomism', in *Logic and Knowledge*, ed. Robert Charles Marsh (London: Allen and Unwin, 1956), p. 333.

2 Gilles Deleuze, *Empiricism and Subjectivity. An Essay on Hume's Theory of Human Nature*, trans. Constantin V. Boundas (New York: Columbia University Press, 1991).

3 Deleuze, *Empiricism and Subjectivity*, p. 21.

4 David Hume, *A Treatise of Human Nature* (1739–40), ed. L. A. Selby-Bigge and P. H. Nidditch (Oxford: Clarendon Press, 1978), pp. 13, 94, 170. Hereafter *T*.

5 Hume, *T*, p. 13.

6 Hume, *T*, p. 69.

7 Hume, *T*, p. 70.

8 Hume, *T*, p. 73.

9 Kant, *Prolegomena*, pp. 15–16; *Ak*.IV: 272: 'what [Hume] said was equivalent to this: that pure mathematics contains only analytic, but metaphysics synthetic, *a priori* judgements. In this, however, he was greatly mistaken'.

10 Hume, *T*, p. 69.

11 The idea of cause can be defined because it is complex (Hume, *T*, p. 169), whereas the ideas of love and hatred cannot be defined because they arise from a simple impression (Hume, *T*, p. 329).

12 Hume, *T*, pp 49–50,
13 This point is made by Marina Frasca-Spada, *Space and Self in Hume's Trea-tise* (Cambridge: Cambridge University Press, 1998), p. 142. In this sec-tion, in which I am going beyond what Deleuze actually says in his discussion of Hume on the *a priori*, I am indebted to Frasca-Spada's study in general, and also to Donald W. Livingston, *Hume's Philosophy of Common Life* (Chicago: University of Chicago Press, 1984).
14 Hume, *T*, p. 46.
15 Hume, *T*, p. 448.
16 Deleuze, *Empiricism and Subjectivity*, p. 99. I take the phrase 'modes of appearance' to be a reference to Hume's doctrine that the ideas of space and time originate not in impressions of space and time (there are no such impressions – space and time are not objects) but in the 'manner of appear-ance' of impressions of objects. For a detailed discussion see Frasca-Spada, *Space and Self*. Frasca-Spada investigates the connections in Hume's thought between various 'manners' (manner of appearance, manner of conception) and the conception of the self. I think that Deleuze, too, would connect such 'manners' to the self, seeing in them the 'affection' of the mind which transforms a mere flux of perceptions into the mind of a subject.
17 Hume, *T*, p. 69.
18 See Gilles Deleuze, *Difference and Repetition*, trans. Paul Patton (London: Athlone, 1994), pp. 144, 147.
19 Kant, *CPR*, B1.
20 Béatrice Longuenesse, *Kant and the Capacity to Judge*, trans. Charles T. Wolfe (Princeton: Princeton University Press, 1998).
21 Kant, *CPR*, A70/B95.
22 Kant, *CPR*, A80/B106.
23 Kant, *CPR*, A261/B317.
24 Kant, *CPR*, A11–12/B25.
25 Kant, *CPR*, A49/B66.
26 Kant, *CPR*, A49/B67.
27 Kant, *CPR*, A265/B321.
28 Kant, *CPR*, A283/B339.
29 Kant, *CPR*, A264/B320.
30 Rae Langton, *Kantian Humility: Our Ignorance of Things in Themselves* (Oxford: Oxford University Press, 1998).
31 In my summary of Langton's proposed reading, I am following her uses of the terms 'thing in itself' and 'metaphysics', and their cognates. As I read her, firstly, Langton does not distinguish between Kant's use of 'thing in itself' and his use of 'noumenon', and, secondly, she does not seem to be using 'metaphysical' always in Kant's technical sense, but means by it, in some contexts, what I would express by the term 'ontological'. I note this

not as a criticism of Langton, but in order to forestall any possible misunderstanding.

32 Longuenesse, *Capacity*, p. 5.

33 Kant, *CPR*, A69/B94.

34 Kant, *CPR*, A262–3/B318–19. This is related to the distinction made earlier between general and transcendental logic. General logic 'abstracts from all content of knowledge, and considers only the logical form in the relation of any knowledge to other knowledge' (Kant, *CPR*, A55/B79), while transcendental logic abstracts only from all empirical content but is concerned with concepts of objects in so far as these concepts 'relate *a priori* to objects, not as pure or sensible intuitions, but solely as acts of pure thought' (Kant, *CPR*, A57/B81).

35 Kant, *CPR*, A262–3/B318–19.

36 'Opposition' is Kemp Smith's translation of *Widerstreit*. Longuenesse prefers to translate this as 'Conflict', and to use 'Opposition' to translate *Entgegensetzung*.

37 Obviously, comparisons by means of the first two pairs go together, and generate the classical 'square of opposition'.

38 I must emphasise that I am making use of Longuenesse's analyses in order to show how Deleuze's Hume-inspired thought about relations itself relates to Kant. Longuenesse herself does not make any explicit connection between her discussion and the issues about internal and external relations with which I began.

39 Kant, *CPR*, A279/B335.

40 Longuenesse, *Capacity*, p. 141.

41 Kant, *Lectures on Logic*, p. 616.

42 Longuenesse, *Capacity*, ch. 4.

43 Kant, *CPR*, A261/B317.

44 Such reduction would require the complete analysis of the concept of an object.

45 Kant, *CPR*, A272/B328.

46 Kant, *CPR*, A139/B178.

47 Kant, *CPR*, A285/B341.

48 Kant, *CPR*, A106.

49 Kant, *CPR*, A265/B321.

50 Kant, *CPR*, A204/B249.

51 Kant, *CPR*, A285/B341.

52 Kant, *CPR*, A249.

53 Kant, *CPR*, A30/B45.

54 Deleuze, *Empiricism and Subjectivity*, pp. 108–9.

55 See especially Longuenesse, *Capacity*, pp. 163–6.

56 Kant, *CPR*, A79/B105.

57 Deleuze, *Empiricism and Subjectivity*, pp. 108–9.

58 Deleuze's detailed discussion of this account of cognition as recognition is
    in Deleuze, *Difference and Repetition*, especially ch. 3, 'The Image of
    Thought'.
59 Kant, *CPR*, A49/B66.

12

Affinity, Judgement and Things in Themselves

Alistair Welchman

For most of the twentieth century, a psychological understanding of Kant has been almost universally regarded as an unpardonable philosophical naïveté. Indeed, one of the few points of unequivocal agreement between the main streams of both analytic and European philosophy has been that the psychological elements in Kant undermine the philosophical ones. Analytic philosophy was arguably initiated as a result of Frege's profound allergy to Kant's idea that logic is grounded in an (allegedly) psychological act of judgement. At about the same time, Husserl's phenomenology exhibited a similarly deep aversion to any attempted reduction of philosophical enquiry to the programme of a merely empirical psychological science.

These two general tendencies in twentieth-century thought are both developments – albeit in very different directions – of Kantianism. But their application to Kant's own work involves some historical ironies. The formalist conception of the synthetic *a priori* as the manifestation of an extra-logical choice of linguistic conventions is tied to new discoveries in logic and proof-theory which have no counter-part in Kant, since they were aimed precisely against Kant. Thus all that is left to characterise Kant's works is the austere apparatus of Fregean philosophy (conceptual analysis and the study of logical validity). The primary stream of analytic Kant interpretation follows Frege directly in associating psychologism with idealism, and rejecting the former because of the latter. As a result transcendental idealism all but disappears from the Kant literature, and is replaced by a common sense (transcendental) realism. The best icon of this interpretative strategy is to think of Kant as posing two problems[1]: a problem of conceptual analysis (what does the concept of experience actually involve?), and a problem of the logical validity of 'transcendental' arguments (where such arguments are understood to be simply of the form 'if experience then x').

There appears to be no such explicit consensus in European readings of Kant. But the variety of readings pursued, for instance, by Lyotard, Heidegger, Derrida, and Nancy, is undergirt by an implicit methodological consensus that Kant's works should be trawled for elaborations of the transcendental which reveal that it, as transcendental, can never be simply assimilated to something empirical. These readings do not simply ignore Kant's psychologism (Heidegger, for instance, was famously partial to the A Deduction),[2] but such psychological reference is never understood as merely empirical. It is instead a clue towards a more primordial – that is to say more transcendental – understanding of the subject (as Dasein etc.). Indeed, the whole structure of this kind of approach can be understood as a meditation on Kant's Paralogisms, extending the sense of Kant's critique of Descartes. The subject (understood in what Heidegger calls 'its broadest sense')[3] is paradigmatically transcendental because it is that which cannot be present to itself as it is in itself, as a subject, but only as what it is not (an object). Kant's analysis of the sublime in the third *Critique* stands as an icon of this kind of reading. The paradoxical problematic of this analysis is that of the presentation of the unpresentable, where the unpresentable is understood precisely as the condition of presentation.[4]

This geographical regionalisation is obviously inadequate. Within analytic philosophy, Henry Allison has defended a strong conception of transcendental idealism (although not a psychological one).[5] In the same tradition, Richard Aquila and John Zammito defend an essentially phenomenological understanding of Kant.[6] Even the doctrine of synthesis, which seems irremediably psychological, has occasionally become the object of a philosophical account.[7] Conversely, in Europe many recent German accounts of Kant operate within a more historically nuanced version of the ambit defined by analytic philosophy. And even the French – excluding the banality of the *nouveaux philosophes* – have one or two broadly analytic Kant interpreters, like Descombes.

What is more important than this cross-fertilisation, however, is that both traditions have been *internally* contested. The problems with each tradition – at the very least in terms of Kant interpretation – are clearly visible. The analytic approach has its own sense of the synthetic *a priori* as choice of axioms in a formal system. But this cannot be easily reapplied to an understanding of Kant himself. Consequently, this approach loses all sense of the novelty of Kant's arguments because it collapses the transcendental into general logic – albeit a new and modern form of general logic. On the other hand, the European tradition pays exceedingly close attention to the transcendental, but only to the conceptual problems of representing it (in its difference from the empirical, that is, from everything that could actually be present in experience).

In the anglophone world, the advent and increasing sophistication of cognitive science have begun to change things by gradually restoring philosophical respectability to the study of internal mental processes. For the most part, the historical backdrop of cognitive science has, however, been pre-critical: Chomsky refers his innatism about language to the rationalists; and the recently fashionable neural network models of mental processes have often been compared with Humean empiricism (indeed, some of them are called 'associationist engines'). But, within the last decade or so, several authors have begun to acknowledge the significance of Kant's work, understood as a kind of psychological constructivism, for cognitive science.[8] In broad outline, Kant's critiques of pre-critical rationalism and empiricism are sympathetically redirected on to rationalist and empiricist versions of cognitive science.

This new Kantian psychology faces an evident exegetical problem, related to the difficulty of understanding a project that is both transcendental *and* psychological. Kant is clearly committed to the necessity of certain mental processes (syntheses), and argues that they constitute transcendental conditions of the possibility of experience. He also has a place for psychology, as an empirical science of the succession of states of internal sense (although he does not hold out much prospect for its achievements).[9] But he is also committed to the view that transcendental syntheses are *not* accessible objects for a scientific inquiry.[10] They are mental processes of some sort, but can only be known through their effects, *viz.*, the constitution of experience. If they can be attributed to the subject at all, then it is not to the *empirical* subject, but to the subject as it is in itself. This is an unwelcome consequence (to say the least) for a Kantian cognitive science. A philosophical reconciliation with psychology is purchased at the inordinate price of consigning perhaps the most important part of psychology to the blankly unknowable.

The solution preferred by Kitcher and Brook is to side-step any problem of the transcendental by rejecting the tight connection Kant makes between his (interesting and illuminating) transcendental arguments for the conditions of the possibility of experience and his (incomprehensible and indefensible) metaphysical position of transcendental idealism. Constructivism is thereby divorced from idealism. Self-conscious experience of the world of objects is certainly not given at the sensory surfaces, and therefore has to be constructed. But the result of this construction of experience of objects from disorganised sensible traces is the construction of an experience of the world as it really is, in a transcendentally realist sense. In a nutshell, the psychology Kant provides is simply an empirical one: the psychological processes that construct experience are unproblematically empirical processes. This solution identifies the transcendental with abstraction at the level of cognitive task. Kant may well be right that such processes are not introspectively available as such because they are only known through their effects. But that does not in any way preclude their being the objects of an *external* empirical science (cognitive science, psychology, neurophysiology etc.).

In Europe, the work of Gilles Deleuze has developed a concept of the transcendental that differs from the empirical without being exhausted by the attempt to conceive a scarcely presentable condition of the presentation of the empirical. The transcendental for Deleuze is not the empirical but it is still material, involving a more capacious conception of material nature than that afforded by the empirical understood as everyday experience. Deleuze attends to and deepens the idea of the transcendental without making of it simply a kind of representational problem.

This essay is an attempt to engineer a cross-fertilisation between these deviations from orthodoxy. This will involve a critical interrogation of two Kantian distinctions: between things and things (regarded as they are) in themselves, and between constitutive and regulative principles. Taking a cue from Kitcher's re-worked psychologism, I shall argue that experience involves definite cognitive tasks, and that these tasks impose constraints on what kind of mental apparatus can perform them. However, I shall go beyond Kitcher's very weak conception of the transcendental (she understands it as just the abstraction of a task-based specification of mental process) by arguing that the mental apparatus cannot be simply identified with an everyday empirical object. What can be learned from Kant is that the processes required to construct experience of things (unified consciousness of objects in a mechanical-causal nexus) must, *in some respects*, not be themselves thing-like (unified, objective, mechanical-causal) processes. This insight leads to a deepened sense of the transcendental that is not simply the epistemological problematic of *the* transcendental, but, following Deleuze, an enhanced form of empiricism.[11]

1 Affinity

In the A Deduction Kant appears to confront the possibility that the data of intuition could in some sense go awry, that they might be inimical or even positively refractory to synthesis and, at the limit, incompatible with the constitution of cognitive experience. This problem later comes to form the systematic intent of the third *Critique*, and has led some commentators, especially Guyer and Tuschling, to regard the third *Critique* as having a priority over the first. This section will follow through this debate, and add to it a discussion, inspired by Kitcher's new transcendental psychological Kant reading, of the implications of this priority for the mechanisms of cognition.

1.1 The data

The A Deduction

Part of Kant's general strategy is to provide informal *reductio* arguments whose conclusions involve contemplating the possibility of some strange counter-factuals.[12] In the introduction to the Deductions (common to both editions), for instance, he writes:

> Appearances might very well be so constituted that the understanding would not find them to be in any kind of conformity with the conditions of its unity. Everything might be in such a confusion, that, for example, in the series of appearances, nothing would present itself that would yield a rule of synthesis and so correspond to the concept of cause and effect. In this case, the concept would be completely empty, null and meaningless. Nevertheless, appearances would still provide objects for our intuition, because intuition has no need at all of the functions of thought.[13]

Within the A version of the Deduction, Kant mentions several similar disquieting scenarios. In the Preliminary Explanation of the Possibility of the Categories (Section 4), for instance, he writes:

> For even though we should have the power of associating perceptions, it would remain entirely undetermined and accidental whether they would themselves be associable; and should they not be associable, there might exist a multitude of perceptions, and indeed an entire sensibility, in which much empirical consciousness would arise in my mind, but in a state of separation, and without belonging to a consciousness of myself. This, however, is impossible.[14]

The use of the term 'association' here, as well as the allusion to necessary connection at A90–1/B123, indicate that Kant is directing his comments towards Hume, and therefore that it is a Humean account of the mind whose falsity is being shown by the *reductio* argument.[15] A little after the above passage Kant presents his alternative:

> There must, therefore, be an objective ground (that is, one that can be comprehended *a priori*, antecedently to all empirical laws of the imagination) upon which rests the possibility, nay, the necessity, of a law that extends to all appearances – a ground, namely, which constrains us to regard all appearances as data of the senses that must be associable in themselves and subject to universal rules of a thoroughgoing connection in their reproduction. This objective ground of all as   appearances I entitle their *affinity*.[16]

The general structure of the argument appears fairly clear (even if its details are not). The empiricist conception of the mind does not provide any guarantee that experience will be constituted because it fails to provide an account of personal identity, that is, of the fact that the 'I think' must be able to accompany all experiences. On a logicist reading, this is the essence of the transcendental argument. On a psychological reading, what is important is what the unity of the 'I think' implies, namely, synthesis. But Kant seems clearly to add another condition that is of interest here, i.e., affinity.

Affinity appears on the face of it to be separate from – and prior to – the question of synthesis and synthetic unity. Without rehearsing Kant's argument for the requirement of synthetic unity in all its details, it nevertheless appears that affinity is Kant's name for the *capacity* of the manifold to undergo synthesis, and hence be unified in a single consciousness. This capacity – that appearances be *assoziabel* – is, however, not a function of any formal properties that might be introduced by the subject. It is not a result of synthesis, but rather a property of the *content* of the manifold, that which is the most direct consequence of the subject being affected by things as they are in themselves. Calling affinity the 'objective ground'[17] of association, or locating it 'in the object',[18] therefore seems to indicate a condition imposed on the content of experience, on things as they are in themselves. This is made most clear in a passage from the description of the Synthesis of Reproduction in Section 3 of the A Deduction, even though affinity is not mentioned by name:

> It is a merely empirical law, that representations which have often followed or accompanied one another finally become associated ... But this law of

reproduction presupposes that appearances are themselves actually subject to such a rule.[19]

That appearances are necessarily subject to the law of association cannot be a result merely of an *a priori* version of association (synthesis), but makes demands on the matter of experience as well as its form. The problems that such a doctrine would present for Kant are obvious: if the content of the manifold as well as its form are transcendentally conditioned, then the dualism of conceptual form and intuitive given, to which Kant clung tenaciously throughout the critical period, would be in serious jeopardy.

Regulation and reflection

Elsewhere, in the Dialectic of the first *Critique* and in the third *Critique*, Kant contemplates other slightly different, but still unwelcome, possibilities: that the manifold of intuition might be such as to prevent the formation of empirical concepts, or empirical laws, or, at the least extreme end, that a fully fledged system of empirical laws might not be possible. In each case he suggests a slightly different formulation of the affinity requirement, as a regulative idea of reason and then as the result of reflective judgement.

In the Dialectic of the first *Critique*, and then again, although implicitly, in the third *Critique*, Kant addresses a second conception of affinity – or perhaps delivers an increasingly sophisticated account of the first conception of affinity. In the Regulative Employment of Ideas section appended to the Dialectic of the first *Critique*,[20] Kant defends a set of scholastic maxims, reconceived as regulative ideas governing scientific research. These maxims express a transcendental but merely regulative presupposition that science converge upon an ordered tree of empirical concepts, laws and forms (as in the cladistic tree in evolutionary biology) which includes all knowledge in a universal encyclopaedia. Affinity is there defined as what guarantees the continuity of the tree, that is, that nothing is left in the gaps between concepts, and it corresponds to the maxim that nature makes no leaps.[21] Both the problem at issue here (that of the system of empirical laws etc.) and the mode of solution (merely regulative not constitutive) appear to indicate that this invocation of affinity is substantially different from the first.

In this section Kant follows a method similar to the *reductio* approach of the Deductions. Again, this involves him tabling a disquieting and strange counter-factual whose absurdity would show that the regulative presuppositions he defends are indeed necessary. What is interesting is just how radical this counter-factual actually is:

> If among the appearances which present themselves to us, there were so great a variety – I do not say in form, for in that respect the appearances might resemble one another; but in content, that is, in the manifoldness of the existing entities – that even the acutest human understanding could never by comparison of one with another detect the slightest similarity (a case which is quite conceivable), the logical law of genera would have no sort of standing; there would not even be the concept of a genus, or any other universal concept. Indeed, there would not even be understanding, since the understanding has to do only with such concepts.[22]

Although Kant is talking about the law of genera here, affinity clearly underwrites the possibility of genera (generic concepts generalise what the species that fall under them have in common, that is, their affinities). This counter-factual is just as devastating as those given in the A Deduction of the first *Critique*: without the regulative presupposition of affinity 'there would not even be understanding'. What becomes difficult to understand is how such a presupposition can be merely regulative. It seems as if Kant now acknowledges that affinity concerns the content of the manifold, and is therefore not a formal condition of experience. But he can only do so because he has avoided the issue of imposing a constitutive condition on things as they are in themselves by making affinity a regulative guideline.

The Introductions to the third *Critique* promise an architectonic revision that responds precisely to the problem of a system of empirical laws, concepts and forms. This leads Kant to invoke a third set of counter-factual possibilities. In the First Introduction to the third *Critique*, for instance, he writes that empirical laws might demonstrate

> so infinite a manifoldness, and so great a heterogeneity of natural forms ... that the concept of a system according to these (empirical) laws must be completely alien to the understanding. Neither the possibility, nor even less, however, the necessity of such a whole can be grasped.[23]

Similarly, he tables the possibility that:

> the manifoldness and heterogeneity of these [empirical] laws (as well as the natural forms that correspond to them) might be infinitely great, and present to us a raw chaotic aggregate without the slightest trace of a system.[24]

Kant does not explicitly determine whether experience itself would be impossible under these circumstances (although he is architectonically committed to thinking that it would *not* be impossible). But he is very clear about what a solution to the problem of empirical laws must look like. This solution involves drawing a new distinction between reflective and determinant judgements,[25] the latter being familiar from the *Critique of Pure Reason*,[26] and the former bearing a close (but not exact) resemblance to the regulative ideas of the first *Critique*. When Kant gives examples of the kinds of maxims involved in reflective judgement he uses the same set of scholastic tags that he had used as examples of ideas in the *Critique of Pure Reason*.[27] In the *Critique of Teleological Judgement* he explicitly associates regulative reason with reflective judgement.[28]

Reflective judgement is supposed to warrant the transcendental presupposition that we treat the world 'as if an understanding contained the ground of the unity of the manifold of its empirical laws'.[29] The argument of the *Critique of Judgement* as a whole is supposed to be a solution to the problem of the 'infinite manifoldness' of nature,[30] because we may assume (regulatively or reflectively) that nature has been produced in its content with a view to its 'fit' for our cognitive faculties.

1.2 Reception

The idea of affinity raises the following problem. If affinity imposes a constitutive transcendental condition on things in themselves, then Kant is faced with a dilemma that he never resolves. One the one hand, this condition would undercut the dualism that is crucial to Kant's whole project: things as they are in themselves would have, in their content and not only their form, to be subject to transcendental demands. The most historically obvious position that this entails would therefore be the absolute idealism of Fichte, Hegel, and the young Schelling. With the third *Critique* in mind, one way of summarising this is that reflective judgements must ultimately be taken as determinate. On the other hand, to deny that affinity is a constitutive condition, and instead to relegate it to a regulative ideal or an expectation of reflective judgement, is not to take Kant's own counter-factuals fully seriously. Since the expectations generated by regulation and reflection are compatible with their not being fulfilled, Kant would not have succeeded in proving what he set out to: that the counter-factuals are the conclusions of a *reductio ad absurdum*. Nature could indeed be as wild as he suggests, and if it were (or when it is), experience would be impossible.

Those immersed in the German Idealist tradition have, of course, welcomed the first prong of this dilemma, arguing that as Kant came increasingly to dwell upon the problem of the system of laws, he was entering into ever closer proximity with an idealist monism.[31] Most commentators, however, have been horrified by this possibility.[32] Some have therefore tried to read Kant's texts more exactly, and have disputed that he intends affinity to be a transcendental condition at all. Instead, it is – in the A Deduction – the *post hoc* phenomenal registration of the constitution of experience, of synthesis having taken place.[33] Then it is possible to make a clear distinction between this kind of affinity and that required for empirical laws. The latter may well have to do with the content of the manifold, but since it is not necessary for the constitution of experience, it can be sensibly understood as simply a regulative or reflective expectation. This move is probably true to Kant's own intentions, but does nothing to undermine the force of the counter-factuals. Even if Kant did not intend them to show this, the question they raise is: what could *possibly* stop nature from being refractory to synthesis?

Others have therefore found in the affinity problem a *reductio* of Kant's own project of transcendental idealism, and have used the insoluble nature of the problem – short of absolute idealism – to develop a transcendentally realist understanding of Kant. Guyer, for instance, sees affinity as the most extreme example of the 'metaphysical' (that is, transcendentally idealist) Kant, in which 'the mind can impose an "affinity" on all appearances'.[34] This leads Guyer – in ironic agreement with Tuschling – to suggest that the third *Critique* has priority over the first. For Guyer this means that even determinant judgements really have only the force of reflective ones;[35] for Tuschling it means more or less the reverse, that reflective judgements – that the manifold is produced so as to fit our faculties – must be thought determinately.

In a second irony, this in turn has led to a reappraisal of the idea of affinity[36] that makes it quite consistent with a transcendental realist reading of Kant like Guyer's.[37] The idea is that transcendental realism shows how Kant's transcendental arguments can be re-interpreted as logically conditional arguments, setting out the conditions required for experience, and not therefore attempting to demonstrate the unconditional modal necessity of experience. If this is so, then conditions can sensibly be imposed on the content of nature without lapsing into idealism. Such conditions merely (and convincingly) state that there would indeed be no experience if nature did not have some degree of regularity or affinity.

1.3 The priority of the third *Critique?*

Westphal maintains the regulative (or reflective)/determinant distinction and argues that some amount of affinity is a constitutive transcendental condition of experience (understood as meaning that if there is experience, then nature must have whatever regularity it takes to constitute experience). But how extensive a system of nature is possible is just an empirical matter, about which at best regulative or reflective expectations are possible.[38] Guyer and Tuschling, however, are right to suggest that this distinction is not as effective as Kant (and Westphal) want it to be.

The counter-factuals of the third *Critique* all present possibilities that Kant supposes to be compatible with the constitution of experience by the categories. Strong readings, however, are justified because what Kant succeeds in showing is how little is warranted by the Deductions; indeed, not enough is warranted to make experience possible. Take the example that taxes Kant so much in the Introductions to the third *Critique*, that of empirical law. The argument of the second Analogy shows that an objective or publicly accessible time-order of mental contents can only be achieved by positing a law-like necessary connection between objects,[39] that is, their subordination to causal law. Assuming the validity of the argument, the conclusion is nevertheless somewhat ambiguous. 'Causal law' could here refer either to some particular nomological generalisation (which, on Kant's argument, would therefore become a necessary law), or it could refer simply to the causal maxim that every individual event must (necessarily) have some individual cause.[40] What the sceptical possibilities raised by the Introductions to the third *Critique* show is that Kant comes to acknowledge that the arguments of the first *Critique* do not prove the necessity for *any* particular causal law. This acknowledgement has rather severe consequences. Every event could therefore be in principle deemed to have a cause, in fact necessarily to have the cause that it in fact has. But this is compatible with every actual instance of causation being the unique representative of its own law: there could be as many laws as there are events.

However, it is no longer clear that the argument of the second Analogy could be made out in the absence of particular empirical laws. If every event exhausts the law of which it is the unique instance, then the subjective time-order cannot be distinguished from the objective time-order. The subjective order in which mental contents enter consciousness is, in the absence of particular causal laws, compatible with saying that each unique mental event is necessarily connected with its predecessor. A putative objective time-sequence would not be qualitatively different from this subjective time-sequence. It would be *another* sequence in which each unique event would necessarily be preceded by the unique event that in fact precedes it.

If this were the case, then it is not even clear if *objects* would be constituted out of the aggregate of non-representative mental contents. It would follow from the absence of any particular causal law that, if there were objects, they could not share any causal properties. *A fortiori,* they could not share any of those properties that (empirically) cause registrations on human sensibility. But this implies that there could be no empirical *predicates* that could be applied to more than one object. Again, this situation is impossible to distinguish from the counter-factuals of the A Deduction: what criterion could there be for attributing predicates (which are no longer general terms) to objects? In the language of the A Deduction: there would be no synthesis of reproduction. This argument is parallel to that given above concerning the second Analogy. What the second Analogy shows is only the transcendental law that every individual event must have the cause that it in fact has; but what it needs is some empirical law which covers more than one cause-effect event pairing. Similarly, what the Deduction shows is only that mental contents must be ascribed to the transcendental object = x; what it needs to show is that there are particular empirical objects which *share* properties with one another.

It follows that Kant's arguments in the third *Critique* against the disquieting counter-factuals (in which no empirical laws appear at all) should be treated as indications of what must be the case for experience to be constituted. Correlatively, what Kant presents as merely regulative conditions (warranted only by reflective judgement) *can* be regarded as constitutive. Westphal's transcendental realism view of affinity permits this collapse of the third *Critique* into the first to avoid terminating in the absolute idealism of Tuschling's reading.

1.4 Mechanisms

The psychological interest of Kant's transcendental philosophy lies in the kinds of tasks that he shows need to be performed for experience to be constituted. Kitcher shows that these tasks are non-trivial even when Kant is interpreted as a transcendental realist. That there are in fact objects is only a necessary and not a sufficient condition of objective representation. Similarly, if the argument that empirical laws and forms are necessary for experience is correct, a further question may be raised. Assuming that nature is regular enough to permit the construction of such laws and forms, what mental *mechanisms* are required actually to perform such construction?

On a number of occasions, Kant suggests a structure for the autonomous (reflective) faculty of judgement that explains why it is specifically appropriate as a description of the mental processes required for the re-construction of empirical laws (and objects) from the data of sensation. In the First Introduction to the *Critique of Judgement*, Kant writes that judgement in general 'is merely an ability to subsume under concepts given from elsewhere.'[41] This is clearly true, but only applies to determinant judgement. The new thought being introduced is that of *reflective* judgement. Kant characterises it – by contrast with determinant judgement – as the capacity to subsume under concepts that are 'not given'.[42] Similarly, in §4, Kant makes the distinction between determinant and reflective judgement like this:

> For judgment is not just a capacity to subsume the particular under the universal (whose concept is given), but also the other way round, a capacity to find the universal for the particular.[43]

Clearly, 'find' here cannot be taken to mean looking around for something *already given*, for then the contrast would be vitiated, but must mean *made*. In the next section (§ 5), whose title is On Reflective Judgement, this becomes obvious. He writes, glossing the same contrast for a third time:

> Judgment can be regarded either as mere[ly] an ability to *reflect*, in terms of a certain principle, on a given presentation so as to [make] a concept possible, or as an ability to *determine* an underlying concept by means of a given empirical presentation.[44]

This certainly makes the case that the function of reflective judgement is consonant with the requirements of mental processes for re-constructing empirical laws and objects (processes also required for the constitution of experience of objects at all). But the description of the function is vague.

Kant does, however, say rather more than this about the structure of reflective judgement. In the *Critique of Aesthetic Judgement* in particular he attaches some importance to two slogans. He writes: 'Beauty is estimated on the ground of a mere formal finality, i.e., conformity to an end without an end [*eine Zweckmäßigkeit ohne Zweck*]'.[45] This first slogan, *Zweckmäßigkeit ohne Zweck*, pertains to judgement. The second pertains to the imagination. In the remark attached to § 22 of the *Critique of Aesthetic Judgement*, but intended to refer to all the previous text, Kant writes that in aesthetic experience the imagination manifests 'conformity to law without a law [*Gesetzmäßigkeit ohne Gesetz*]'.[46] Reference to the structure of a transcendental mental process is explicit: Kant writes that the imagination here must be taken in its *productive* and not its *reproductive* guise. The productive imagination he then defines as 'exerting an activity of its own (as originator of arbitrary forms of possible intuitions)'.[47]

These slogans of course have much to do with Kant's attempt to find a space within the critical architectonic for aesthetic valuations (in which specific ends and laws should not be reached, in order to preserve the autonomy of aesthetics). But they also play a crucial role in the systematic project of the third *Critique*. In this context, what Kant is saying is that the mental capacities required for the re-construction of empirical laws, forms and objects from sensory registrations (processes, it is argued here, that are also requisite for the re-construction of experience as such) are not oriented towards explicit ends, and not governed by explicit laws. These processes are autonomous in a sense analogous to the autonomy of aesthetics. They cannot be conceptually determined (that is, determined by explicit rules, laws or concepts) because they are *generative* of concepts. If they were so determined, they would presuppose the prior existence of what they are supposed to produce. It is, however, also important to observe that he does not thereby just assimilate them to random or completely chaotic processes (i.e., merely empirical, associationist or pathological ones). They exhibit, precisely, conformity to lawlikeness in general, but without being exhaustively governed by any specific law: *Gesetzmäßigkeit ohne Gesetz*.

The argument so far has been that reflective judgement is the mental process that permits the construction of representations of empirical laws and forms. These have turned out to be constitutive conditions of possibility of experience, and therefore Kant's description of reflective judgement must be regarded as the description of the mental processes required for experience. However, even in the first *Critique* Kant suggests an argument that implies that even *determinant* judgements cannot be rule-governed.[48] This argument is that the *application* of a rule cannot itself be rule-governed on pain of an infinite regress. Since determinant judgement *is* the capacity to apply rules, it cannot itself be rule-governed. Kant calls it instead a 'particular talent', 'gift of nature',[49] or 'mother-wit' which 'cannot be taught, but only practised'.[50] In brief, the discussion up to this point has demonstrated that the transcendental conditions for the possibility of experience (as a rule-governed unity) cannot themselves be (exhaustively) rule-governed processes.

2 Informal materialism

Affinity is a problem for Kant because the precise extent of regularity in nature cannot be legislated *a priori*. The 'counter-factuals' point repeatedly to the possibility that nature could always be wild. The wildness of nature is limited only by the fact that, if there is experience, at least some aspects of nature must be regular enough to permit its construction. But the affinity problem also suggests that this wildness is far from being the all-or-nothing matter that it is often taken to be. The limit case, in which affinity is at a minimum, is still compatible with the causal maxim that every event has a cause. Earlier this idea was used to raise the important doubt that experience of objects could be constituted at all under such circumstances. But it is also easy to imagine 'things' whose powers are not *entirely* rule-governed: affinity is a question of gradation rather than kind.

Indeed, the correlative of Kant's discussion of the structure of the processes of reflection, judgement and the productive imagination in the third *Critique* is that he also delineates two domains, those of art and biology, whose referents, works and organisms, are not strictly constituted experiential objects with definite cognisable properties according to the strictures of the first *Critique*. Works of art are both produced and judged without reference to explicit conceptual rules, and hence by the operation of a kind of causality, an 'inner causality',[51] that is neither mechanical nor teleological. Similarly, organisms are produced by a kind of causation that has no analogue in any conceptually determinate mode of production (mechanical causation or determination of the will by reason) and can only be recognised as organisms in the first place through a judgement of reflective teleology whose operation is irreducible to a conceptual determination.[52] Kant clearly contemplates the possibility that some object domains lack an exhaustive affinity (and are therefore not strictly speaking 'object' domains at all). What I have tried to show here is that even supposing that experience must have certain formal features (the pre-condition of Kant's transcendental arguments), the subject, the locus of the capacity to have such experiences, depends on a mode of production (synthesis) that cannot be completely formalised conceptually as a determinate experience. The subject is – must be – wild nature.

This view involves a slightly delicate operation on some of Kant's concepts, namely, distinguishing between the thing in itself and the noumenon. With the thought of the former, Kant introduces a material manifold of indefinite complexity (lack of affinity) at the base of experience. But by identifying this with the noumenon, a purely intellectual object, he assimilates an incipient thought of pre-empirical material complexity to the rational and obliterates its interest in the name of moral personality. But in the absence of such an identification, Kant's philosophy would point to the idea that the subject in itself (as a special case of a thing in itself) must possess a complexity refractory to experience as a transcendental condition of experience.

This sense of the transcendental pervades Deleuze's work. There is an occasional danger that when Deleuze insists that the transcendental not 'resemble' the empirical,[53] he may be understood to be invoking an antipsychologistic critique of Kant that runs parallel to the phenomenological critique of Kant.[54] But in fact his critique runs in the opposite direction. The notion of conditions of existence rather than possibility, conditions no bigger than what they condition,[55] opens up a transcendental field that is occupied by an informal materiality prior to the empirical of constituted experience, not a transcendental pre-occupied with prolonging, as Heidegger does, the spiritual sense of the Paralogism of Substantiality.

Deleuze regards this materialist sense of the transcendental, this transcendental empiricism, as the real upshot of critique.[56] In brief, an activity (a mode of production, a synthesis) is illegitimate or transcendent when its operation presupposes the prior application of a synthesis. The dominant mode of production in Kant's first *Critique* is conceptually determined, and invokes the familiar machinery of the transcendental unity of apperception, the table of categories etc. In this model, a numerically self-identical, purely formal, subject is regarded as the spontaneous operator of synthetic activity. What the third *Critique* shows is that the very capacity to unify experience into a formal whole requires a confrontation with the wild vagaries of empirical law, and therefore presupposes a synthetic activity that cannot be understood as formal or conceptual at all: law-likeness itself presupposes and is itself produced by law-likeness without a law. This constitutes a Deleuzian application of critique: the formal syntheses of Kant's earlier work are illegitimate (uncritical) because they presuppose the application of the informal syntheses of the later works.

The re-introduction of psychology into analytic Kant interpretation is significant, but ultimately of limited value. It enables an investigation of the processes of production (syntheses) that underlie the construction of experience, rather than collapsing the transcendental into a logical formalism. But it does so at the cost of assuming that the mechanisms of such constructive, synthetic psychological processes can be easily identified with the causal mechanisms of everyday empirical systems, a transcendental realism that associates things in themselves with constructed experience. Synthetic processes must confront a nature whose affinity is great enough to permit the construction of unified experience; but the synthetic processes themselves are a nature (the subject in itself) whose wildness is what allows it to be constructive at all. As Deleuze says (more or less): 'Things in themselves tend to appear as such in complex systems'.[57]

Notes

1 See Quassim Cassam, 'Transcendental Arguments, Transcendental Synthesis, Transcendental Idealism', *The Philosophical Quarterly* vol. 37 no. 149 (1987) 355–78.

2 See Martin Heidegger, *Kant and the Problem of Metaphysics*, trans. James S. Churchill (Bloomington and Indianapolis: Indiana University Press, 1962).

3 Martin Heidegger, *The Basic Problems of Phenomenology*, trans. Albert Hofstadter (Bloomington and Indianapolis: Indiana University Press, 1982), p. 73.

4 Jean-François Courtine et al, *Of the Sublime: Presence in Question*, trans. Jeffrey S. Librett (Albany: SUNY Press, 1993).

5 Henry Allison, 'Transcendental Affinity – Kant's Answer to Hume', in *Proceedings of the Third International Kant Congress*, ed. Lewis White Beck (Dordrecht, The Netherlands: D. Reidel Publishing Company, 1972), pp. 203–11.

6 See Richard Aquila, *Matter in Mind: A Study of Kant's Transcendental Deduction* (Bloomington and Indianapolis: Indiana University Press, 1989); and John H. Zammito, *The Genesis of Kant's* Critique of Judgment (Chicago and London: University of Chicago Press, 1992).

7 Robert Paul Wolff, *Kant's Theory of Mental Activity: A Commentary on the Transcendental Analytic of the* Critique of Pure Reason (Cambridge, MA: Harvard University Press, 1963).

8   See Patricia Kitcher, *Kant's Transcendental Psychology* (Oxford: Oxford University Press, 1990); and Andrew Brook, *Kant and the Mind* (Cambridge: Cambridge University Press, 1994).

9   See Kant, *Metaphysische Anfangsgründe der Naturwissenschaft, Ak*.IV: 471.

10   See, for instance, Kant, *CPR*, A78/B103.

11   Gilles Deleuze, *Bergsonism*, trans. Hugh Tomlinson and Barbara Habberjam (New York: Zone, 1991), p. 30.

12   They are strange because they suggest not another fact counter to one that is actually the case (i.e., a fact that is the case in some other possible world) but the presence to consciousness of the absence of facts at all (i.e., of any consciousness of objects).

13   Kant, *CPR*, A90–1/B123, t.m.

14   Kant, *CPR*, A121–2; see also A111.

15   Kant mentions Hume and affinity in a famous passage much later in the first *Critique* (A766–7/B794–5). Kitcher provides a detailed account of why Hume's account of personal identity is the object of Kant's critique in the Deductions, as well as why so many have not acknowledged this. Patricia Kitcher, *Kant's Transcendental Psychology* (Oxford: Oxford University Press, 1990), pp. 97ff.

16   Kant, *CPR*, A122; see also A113.

17   Kant, *CPR*, A122.

18   Kant, *CPR*, A113.

19   Kant, *CPR*, A100.

20   Kant, *CPR*, A642ff/B670ff.

21   Kant, *CPR*, A657/B686, A660/B688.

22   Kant, *CPR*, A653–4/B681–2, t.m.

23   Kant, *CJ*, First Introduction, sec. II, p. 392, t.m.; *Ak*.XX: 203.

24   Kant, *CJ*, First Introduction, sec. IV, p. 398, t.m.; *Ak*.XX: 209. Similar passages occur in the same section of the First Introduction (*CJ*, p. 398; *Ak*.XX: 210), in the next (*CJ*, p. 401; *Ak*.XX: 213) as well as, at somewhat less length, in the published Introduction (*CJ*, pp. 19, 22–3; *Ak*.V: 179, 183).

25   Kant, *CJ*, pp. 18–19; *Ak*.V: 179.

26   Kant, *CPR*, A132/B171.

27   Compare The Regulative Employment of the Ideas of Pure Reason (A641–2/B670–1, especially A652–3/B680–1 and A657–8/B685–6) with the *Critique of Judgement*, pp. 21–2, 24–5; *Ak*.V: 182, 185, and the First Introduction, sec. IV, p. 52; *Ak*. XX: 210.

28   Kant, *CJ*, pp. 254–5; *Ak*.V: 375.

29   Kant, *CJ*, p. 20, t.m.; *Ak*.V: 181.

30   Kant, *CJ*, First Introduction, sec. II, p. 392, t.m.; *Ak*.XX: 203.

31   Burkhard Tuschling, 'Apperception and Ether: On the Idea of a Transcendental Deduction of Matter in Kant's *Opus postumum*', in *Kant's Transcen-*

dental Deductions, ed. Eckart Förster (Stanford: Stanford University Press, 1989), pp. 193–216; Tuschling, 'Intuitiver Verstand, absolute Identität, Idee. Thesen zu Hegels früher Rezeption der „Kritik der Urteilskraft"', in *Hegel und die „Kritik der Urteilskraft"*, eds. Hans-Friedrich Fulda und Rolf-Peter Horstmann (Stuttgart: Ernst Klett Verlag, 1990), pp. 175–88; Tuschling, 'The System of Transcendental Idealism: Questions Raised and Left Open in the *Kritik der Urteilskraft*', *Southern Journal of Philosophy* 30 (1992, supplement) 109–27.

32   Kitcher, *Kant's Transcendental Psychology*, p. 247 n45; Lewis White Beck, 'Kant on the Uniformity of Nature', *Synthese* 47 (1981) 456.

33   Kitcher, *Kant's Transcendental Psychology*, pp. 78–9; Allison, 'Transcendental Affinity'; Beck, 'Kant on the Uniformity of Nature'; Aquila, *Matter in Mind*, ch. 4.

34   Paul Guyer, *Kant and the Claims of Knowledge* (Cambridge: Cambridge University Press, 1987), p. 132; see also Cassam, 'Transcendental Arguments, Transcendental Synthesis, Transcendental Idealism'.

35   Paul Guyer, 'Reason and Reflective Judgment: Kant on the Significance of Systematicity' *Noûs* vol. 24 no. 1 (March 1990) 19.

36   Kenneth Westphal, 'Affinity, Idealism and Naturalism: The Stability of Cinnabar and the Possibility of Experience', *Kant-Studien* 88 (1997) 139–89.

37   Guyer, *Kant and the Claims of Knowledge*; and 'Reason and Reflective Judgment'.

38   Westphal, 'Affinity, Idealism and Naturalism', pp. 159–60.

39   Following Wolff, the term 'mental content' refers to a representation or *Vorstellung* that is capable of constituting the content of a synthetic experience, but has not yet been fully synthesised.

40   See Beck, 'Kant on the Uniformity of Nature'.

41   Kant, *CJ*, First Introduction, sec. II, p. 392; *Ak*.XX: 202.

42   Ibid.

43   Kant, *CJ*, First Introduction, sec. IV, p. 398, t.m.; *Ak*.XX: 209–10.

44   Kant, *CJ*, First Introduction, sec. V, p. 399; *Ak*.XX: 211. The same terminology re-occurs in the passages of the First Introduction concerned with teleological (or objective) applications of reflective judgement: these 'make a concept possible' (Kant, *CJ*, First Introduction, sec. IX, p. 421; *Ak*.XX: 232). And the thought is preserved in both the Preface to the third *Critique*, where Kant writes that judgement 'has...itself to furnish a concept' (Kant, *CJ*, p. 6, t.m.; *Ak*.V: 169), as well as in sec. IV of the Second Introduction where reflective judgement has 'to find the universal' (Kant, *CJ*, p. 19; *Ak*.V: 179).

45   Kant, *CJ*, p. 73, t.m.; *Ak*.V: 226.

46   Kant, *CJ*, p. 92, t.m.; *Ak*.V: 241.

47   Kant, *CJ*, p. 91, t.m.; *Ak*.V: 240.

48 Kant, *CPR*, A133/B17? This argument is repeated almost word for word in setting up the problem of the *Critique of Judgement* (p. 6; *Ak*.V; 169). Its similarity – both textual and argumentative – to Wittgenstein's rule following considerations is very striking.

49 The same word (*Naturgabe*) with which Kant later describes genius in the third *Critique* (p. 174, t.m.; *Ak*.V: 307).

50 Kant, *CPR*, A133/B172, t.m.

51 Kant, *CJ*, p. 68; *Ak*.V: 222.

52 Kant, *CJ*, p. 248–55; *Ak*.V: 369–76.

53 Gilles Deleuze, *The Logic of Sense*, trans. Mark Lester with Charles Stivale, ed. Constantin Boundas (New York: Columbia University Press, 1990), p. 105.

54 Gilles Deleuze, *Difference and Repetition*, trans. Paul Patton (New York: Columbia University Press, 1994), p. 135.

55 Deleuze, *Difference and Repetition*, p. 285.

56 Gilles Deleuze, *Anti-Oedipus*, trans. Robert Hurley, Mark Seem and Helen R. Lane (London: Athlone, 1983), p. 75.

57 Deleuze, *Difference and Repetition*, p.156. Deleuze actually says 'noumena', but, given my distinction above, 'things in themselves' is a better term.

Select Bibliography

Agamben, Giorgio, *The Coming Community*, trans. Michael Hardt (Minneapolis: University of Minnesota Press, 1993).

Allison, Henry, 'Transcendental Affinity – Kant's Answer to Hume', in *Proceedings of the Third International Kant Congress*, ed. Lewis White Beck (Dordrecht, The Netherlands: D. Reidel Publishing Company, 1972) pp. 203–11.

Appel, Toby A., *The Cuvier-Geoffroy Debate: French Biology in the Decades Before Darwin* (Oxford: Oxford University Press, 1987).

Aquila, Richard, *Matter in Mind: A Study of Kant's Transcendental Deduction* (Bloomington and Indianapolis: Indiana University Press, 1989).

Aristotle, *Physics*, Books I–IV, trans. Philip H. Wicksteed and Francis M. Cornford (Cambridge, MA: Harvard University Press and London: William Heinemann, 1980).

——. *De Anima*, trans. Hugh Lawson-Tancred (Harmondsworth: Penguin, 1986).

Aviner, Shlomo and Avner de-Shalit, *Communitarianism and Individualism* (Oxford: Oxford University Press, 1992).

Ayrault, Raymond, *La Genèse du romantisme allemand*, 2 vols. (Paris: Montaigne, 1976).

Banham, Gary, *Kant and the Ends of Aesthetics* (London: Macmillan Press, 2000).

Bataille, Georges, *Visions of Excess: Selected Writings 1927–39*, ed. A. Stoekl (Minneapolis: University of Minnesota Press, 1985).

Baumgarten, A. G., *Reflections on Poetry: A. G. Baumgarten's Meditationes philosophicae de nonnullis ad poema pertinibus*, trans. Karl Aschenbrenner and W. B. Holther (Berkeley: University of California Press, 1954).

——. *Metaphysica*, in *Texte zur Grundlegung der Ästhetik*, ed. Hans Rudolf Schweizer (Hamburg: Felix Meiner Verlag, 1983).

——. *Aesthetica*, in *Ästhetik als Philosophie der sinnlichen Erkenntnis*, trans. Hans Rudolf Schweizer (Basel and Stuttgart: Schwabe & Co, 1973).

Baumgartner, Hans Michael, Wilhelm G. Jacobs and Hermann Krings, eds., *Friedrich Wilhelm Joseph Schelling, Historisch-kritische Ausgabe. Reihe 1,*

Ergänzungsband zu Werke Band 5 bis 9: Wissenschaftlicher Bericht zu Schellings naturphilosophischen Schriften 1797–1800 (Stuttgart: Frommann-Holzboog, 1994).

Beck, Lewis White, ed., *Proceedings of the Third International Kant Congress* (Dordrecht, The Netherlands: D. Reidel Publishing Company, 1972).

———. 'Kant on the Uniformity of Nature', *Synthese* 47 (1981) 449–64.

Bensaude-Vincent, Bernadette and Isabelle Stengers, *A History of Chemistry*, trans. Deborah van Dam (Cambridge, MA: Harvard University Press, 1996).

Bentham, Jeremy, *Introduction to the Principles of Morals and Legislation* (London: Hafner, 1948)

Berkeley, George, *An Essay Toward a New Theory of Vision* (London: Dent, 1954).

Brook, Andrew, *Kant and the Mind* (Cambridge: Cambridge University Press, 1994).

de Buffon, Georgs Louis, *Histoire de la nature*, vol. V (Paris: de l'Imprimerie Royale, 1756).

Burke, Carolyn, Naomi Schor and Margaret Whitford, eds., *Engaging with Irigaray* (New York: University of Columbia Press, 1994).

Butler, Judith, 'Bodies that Matter', in *Engaging with Irigaray*, eds. Carolyn Burke, Naomi Schor and Margaret Whitford (New York: University of Columbia Press, 1994).

Cadava, Eduardo, Peter Connor and Jean-Luc Nancy, eds., *Who Comes After the Subject?* (London: Routledge, 1991).

Caird, Edward, *Kant's Critical Philosophy*, 2 vols. (Glasgow: James Maclehose, 1889).

Cassam, Quassim, 'Transcendental Arguments, Transcendental Synthesis, Transcendental Idealism', *The Philosophical Quarterly* vol. 37 no. 149 (1987) 355–378.

Caygill, Howard, *Art of Judgement* (Oxford: Blackwell, 1989).

Clark, William, Jan Golinski and Simon Shaffer, eds., *The Sciences in Enlightened Europe* (Chicago: University of Chicago Press, 1999).

Clarke, Edwin and L. S. Jacyna, *Nineteenth Century Origins of Neuroscientific Concepts* (Berkeley: University of California Press, 1987).

Coleman, William, *Biology in the Nineteenth Century* (Cambridge: Cambridge University Press, 1977).

Connor, Peter, ed., *The Community at Loose Ends* (Minneapolis: University of Minnesota Press, 1991).

Corlett, William, *Community Without Unity* (Durham, NC: Duke University Press, 1993).

Courtine, Jean-François, et al, *Of the Sublime: Presence in Question*, trans. J. S. Librett (Albany, NY: SUNY Press, 1993).

Davy, Humphrey, *On Geology* (Madison, NJ: University of Wisconsin Press, 1982).

Deleuze, Gilles, 'Second Lesson on Kant, 21st March 1978', trans. Melissa McMahon (http://www.imaginet.fr/deleuze/TXT/ENG/210378.html).

———. *Foucault*, ed. and trans. Sean Hand (London: Athlone, 1988).

———. *The Logic of Sense*, ed. Constantin Boundas, trans. Mark Lester with Charles Stivale (New York: Columbia University Press 1990).

———. *Empiricism and Subjectivity. An Essay on Hume's Theory of Human Nature*, trans. Constantin V. Boundas (New York: Columbia University Press, 1991).

———. *Bergsonism*, trans. Hugh Tomlinson and Barbara Habberjam (New York: Zone, 1991).

———. *Difference and Repetition*, trans. Paul Patton (London: Athlone, 1994).

———. *Negotiations*, trans. Michael Hardt (New York: Columbia University Press, 1995).

Deleuze, Gilles and Félix Guattari, *Anti-Oedipus*, trans. Robert Hurley, Mark Seem and Helen R. Lane (Minneapolis: University of Minnesota Press, 1983).

———. *A Thousand Plateaus*, trans. Brian Massumi (London: Athlone, 1988).

———. *What Is Philosophy?*, trans. Hugh Tomlinson (London: Verso, 1994).

Depew, D. J. and B. H. Weber, *Darwinism Evolving: Systems Dynamics and the Genealogy of Natural Selection* (Cambridge, MA: MIT Press, 1996).

Derrida, Jacques, *Of Grammatology*, trans. G. C. Spivak (Baltimore: Johns Hopkins University Press, 1976).

———. *Writing and Difference*, trans. Alan Bass (London: Routledge, 1978).

———. 'Economimesis', trans. Richard Klein, *Diacritics* 11:2 (1981) 3–25.

———. *The Truth in Painting*, trans. G. Bennington and I. McLeod (Chicago: University of Chicago Press, 1987).

———. 'Beyond the Pleasure Principle', in *The Post Card: From Socrates to Freud and Beyond*, trans. Alan Bass (Chicago: The University of Chicago Press, 1987).

———. *Archive Fever: A Freudian Impression*, trans. Eric Prenowitz (Chicago: University of Chicago Press, 1996).

———. *Resistances of Psychoanalysis* (Stanford: Stanford University Press, 1998).

di Giovanni, George, 'Kant's Metaphysics of Nature and Schelling's *Ideas for a Philosophy of Nature*', *Journal for the History of Philosophy* 17 (1979) 197–215.

Edwards, W. N., *The Early History of Palaeontology* (London: British Museum, 1976).

Escoubas, Éliane, 'Kant or the Simplicity of the Sublime', in *Of the Sublime: Presence in Question*, Courtine, et al, trans. J. S. Librett (Albany, NY: SUNY Press, 1993).

Förster, Eckart, ed., *Kant's Transcendental Deductions* (Stanford: Stanford University Press, 1989).

Foucault, Michel, *The History of Sexuality*: *Vol. One*, trans. R. Hurley (Harmundsworth: Penguin, 1981).

———. *Archaeology of Knowledge*, trans. A. M. Sheridan Smith (London: Tavistock, 1995).

Frasca-Spada, Marina, *Space and Self in Hume's* Treatise (Cambridge: Cambridge University Press, 1998).

Freud, Sigmund, 'The Economic Problem of Masochism', in *On Metapsychology: The Theory of Psychoanalysis*, trans. James Strachey (Harmondsworth: Penguin, Penguin Freud Library, vol. 11, 1991).

Friedmann, Michael, *Kant and the Exact Sciences* (Cambridge, MA: Harvard University Press, 1985).

Fulda, Hans-Friedrich und Rolf-Peter Horstmann, eds., *Hegel und die „Kritik der Urteilskraft"* (Stuttgart: Ernst Klett Verlag, 1990).

Gasché, Rodolphe, *The Tain of the Mirror: Derrida and the Philosophy of Reflection* (Cambridge, MA: Harvard University Press, 1986).

———. *Inventions of Difference: On Jacques Derrida* (Cambridge, MA: Harvard University Press, 1994).

Gillespie, Charles Coulston, *Genesis and Geology*, 2nd edn (Cambridge, MA: Harvard University Press, 1996).

Guyer, Paul, *Kant and the Claims of Knowledge* (Cambridge: Cambridge University Press, 1987).

———. 'Reason and Reflective Judgment: Kant on the Significance of Systematicity', *Noûs* vol. 24 no. 1 (March 1990) 17–43.

Hansen, LeeAnn, 'Metaphors of mind and society: the origins of German psychiatry in the revolutionary era', *Isis* 89 (1998) 387–409.

Harvey, Irene, *Derrida and the Economy of Differance* (Bloomington and Indianapolis: Indiana University Press, 1986).

———. 'Derrida, Kant and the Performance of Parergonality', in *Derrida and Deconstruction*, ed. Hugh Silverman (London: Routledge, 1989).

Hegel, G. W. F., *Aesthetics: Lectures on Fine Art*, vol. 1, trans. T. M. Knox (Oxford: Clarendon Press, 1975).

———. *Science of Logic*, trans. A. V. Miller (Atlantic Highlands, NJ: Humanities Press, 1989).

Heidegger, Martin, *Die Frage nach dem Ding* (Tübingen: Max Niemeyer Verlag, 1962).

———. *What is a Thing?*, trans. W. B. Barton jnr. and Vera Deutsch (Chicago: Henry Regnery, 1967).

———. 'The Origin of the Work of Art', in *Poetry, Language, Thought*, trans. Albert Hofstadter (New York: Harper and Row, 1975).

———. *Early Greek Thinking: The Dawn of Western Philosophy*, trans. David Farrell Krell (New York: Harper and Row, 1975).

———. *The Basic Problems of Phenomenology*, trans. Albert Hofstadter (Bloomington and Indianapolis: Indiana University Press, 1982).

———. '...dichterisch wohnt der Mensch', in *Vorträge und Aufsätze* (Pfullingen: Neske, 1985).

———. *The History of the Concept of Time*, ed. and trans. Theodore Kisiel (Bloomington and Indianapolis: Indiana University Press, 1985).

———. *Sein und Zeit*, 16th edn (Tübingen: Max Niemeycr Verlag, 1986).

———. *Vom Ereignis: Beiträge zur Philosophie, GA 65* (Frankfurt am Main: Klostermann, 1989).

———. *The Concept of Time*, ed. and trans. Will McNeill (Oxford: Blackwell, 1992).

———. 'On the Essence of Truth', in *Basic Writings*, trans. David Farrell Krell (San Francisco: Harper Collins, 1993).

———. *Being and Time*, trans. John Macquarrie and Edward Robinson (Oxford: Blackwell, 1995).

———. *Aristotle's Metaphysics Theta 1–3*, trans. Walter Brogan and Peter Warnek (Bloomington and Indianapolis: Indiana University Press, 1995).

———. *Kant and the Problem of Metaphysics*, 5th enlarged edn, trans. Richard Taft (Bloomington and Indianapolis: Indiana University Press, 1997).

Herz, Marcus, *Versuch über den Schwindel* (Berlin: Voss, 1791).

Hildyard, Nicholas, 'Ethnic Conflict and the Authoritarian Right', Briefing Document (London: The Cornerhouse, January 1999).

Hodge, Joanna, 'Sexual difference as transcendental aesthetic: Irigaray reading Kant', in *Reading Ethics of Sexual Difference*, eds. Bergoffen and Silverman (Evanston: Northwestern University Press, 2001).

———. 'Forays of a Philosophical Feminist: Sexual Difference, Genealogy, Teleology', in *Feminists Transforming the Political*, eds. Ahmed, Lury, McNeil, Kilby and Skeggs (London: Routledge, 2001).

Horstmann, Rolf-Peter and Michael J. Petry, eds., *Hegels Philosophie der Natur: Beziehungen zwischen empirischer und spekulativer Naturerkenntnis* (Stuttgart: Klett-Cotta, 1986).

Hume, David, *A Treatise of Human Nature* (1739–40), eds. L. A. Selby-Bigge and P. H. Nidditch (Oxford: Clarendon Press, 1978).

Hutchings, Kimberly, *Kant, Critique and Politics* (Edinburgh: University of Edinburgh Press, 1994).

Irigaray, Luce, *Le langage des dements* (The Hague: Mouton, 1973).

———. *Speculum of the Other Woman*, trans. Gillian C. Gill (Ithaca, NY: Cornell University Press, 1985).

———. 'The "Mechanics" of Fluids', in *This Sex Which Is Not One*, trans. Catherine Porter (Ithaca, NY: Cornell University Press, 1985).

Jantzen, Grace, *Becoming Divine* (Manchester: Manchester University Press, 1999).

Kielmeyer, Carl Friedrich, *Natur und Kraft: Carl Friedrich Kielmeyers gesammelte Schriften*, ed. F. H. Köhler (Berlin: Kieper, 1938).

Kitcher, Patricia, *Kant's Transcendental Psychology* (Oxford: Oxford University Press, 1990).

Lacan, Jacques, *Écrits, A Selection*, trans. Alan Sheridan (London: Tavistock, 1977).

———. 'Kant with Sade' trans. James Swenson, *October* 51, 1989.

Lacoue-Labarthe, Philippe, *Poetry as Experience*, trans. Andrea Tarnowski (Stanford: Stanford University Press, 1999).

de Lamarck, Jean Baptiste, *Recherches sur l'organisation des corps vivants* (Paris: published by the author, 1802).

Langton, Rae, *Kantian Humility. Our Ignorance of Things in Themselves* (Oxford: Oxford University Press, 1998).

Larson, James, *Interpreting Nature: The Science of Living Form from Linnaeus to Kant* (Baltimore: Johns Hopkins University Press, 1994).

Lecercle, Jean-Jacques, 'The Pedagogy of Philosophy', *Radical Philosophy* 75 (1996) 44–6.

Leibniz, G. W., 'Monadology', in *Philosophical Essays*, trans. R. Ariew and D. Garber (Indianapolis: Hackett, 1989).

Lenoir, Timothy, 'Kant, Blumenbach and vital materialism in German biology', *Isis* 71 (1980) 77–108.

Lippitt, J., ed., *Nietzsche's Futures* (London: Macmillan Press, 1999).

Livingston, Donald W., *Hume's Philosophy of Common Life* (Chicago: University of Chicago Press, 1984).

Longuenesse, Béatrice, *Kant and the Capacity to Judge*, trans. Charles T. Wolfe (Princeton: Princeton University Press, 1998).

Lyell, Charles, *Principles of Geology* (1830–33), ed. James A. Secord (Harmondsworth: Penguin, 1997).

Lyotard, Jean-François, *The Postmodern Condition: A Report on Knowledge*, trans. Geoff Bennington and Brian Massumi (Manchester: Manchester University Press, 1984).

———. *Just Gaming*, trans. Wlad Godzich (Manchester: Manchester University Press, 1985).

———. *The Differend: Phrases in Dispute*, trans. Georges Van Den Abbeele (Minneapolis: University of Minnesota Press, 1988).

———. 'Analysing Speculative Discourse as Language-Game' in *The Lyotard Reader*, ed. Andrew Benjamin (Oxford: Blackwell, 1989).

———. *Heidegger and 'the jews'*, trans. Andreas Michel and Mark Roberts (Minneapolis: University of Minnesota Press, 1990).

———. *The Inhuman: Reflections on Time*, trans. Geoffrey Bennington and Rachel Bowlby (Cambridge: Polity Press, 1991).

———. 'The Subject in *statu nascendi*', in *Who Comes After the Subject?*, eds. Cadava, Connor, Nancy (London: Routledge, 1991).

———. *Lessons on the Analytic of the Sublime*, trans. E. Rottenberg (Stanford: Stanford University Press, 1994).

Makkreel, Rudolf, *Imagination and Interpretation in Kant: The Hermeneutical Import of the* Critique of Judgment (Chicago: University of Chicago Press,

1990).

Mehlman, Jeffrey, ed., *The French Freud*, Special Issue of *Yale French Studies* no. 48 (1972).

Nancy, Jean-Luc, *The Inoperative Community*, trans. Peter Connor and Lisa Garbus (Minneapolis: University of Minnesota Press, 1991).

Nietzsche, Friedrich, *The Will to Power*, trans. W. Kaufmann and R. J. Hollingdale (New York: Random House, 1967).

———. *The Anti-Christ*, trans. R. J. Hollingdale (Harmondsworth: Penguin, 1968).

———. *Thus Spoke Zarathustra*, trans. R. J. Hollingdale (Harmondsworth: Penguin, 1969).

———. *Beyond Good and Evil*, trans. R. J. Hollingdale (Harmondsworth: Penguin, 1973).

———. *The Gay Science*, trans. W. Kaufmann (New York: Random House, 1974).

———. 'On Truth and Lies in a Nonmoral Sense', in *Philosophy and Truth – Selections from Nietzsche's Notebooks*, ed. D. Breazeale (Atlantic Highlands, NJ: Humanities Press, 1979).

———. *Ecce Homo*, trans. R. J. Hollingdale (Harmondsworth: Penguin, 1979).

———. *Daybreak*, trans. R. J. Hollingdale (Cambridge: Cambridge University Press, 1982).

———. *On the Genealogy of Morality* , trans. C. Diethe (Cambridge: Cambridge University Press, 1994).

Owen, Richard, *The Hunterian Lectures in Comparative Anatomy, May and June 1837*, ed. Phillip R. Sloan (London: Natural History Museum, 1992).

Rajan, Tilottama and David L. Clark, 'Speculations: Idealism and its Rem(a)inders', in *Intersections: Nineteenth-Century Philosophy and Contemporary Theory*, eds. Rajan and Clark (Albany, NY: SUNY Press, 1995).

Reil, Johann Christian, 'Von der Lebenskraft', *Archiv für die Physiologie* vol. 1 issue 1.

Roudinesco, Elisabeth, *Jacques Lacan* (Cambridge: Polity Press, 1997).

Russell, Bertrand, 'The Philosophy of Logical Atomism', in *Logic and Knowledge*, ed. Robert Charles Marsh (London: Allen and Unwin, 1956).

Sallis, John, *Spacings – of Reason and Imagination in Texts of Kant, Fichte, Hegel* (Chicago: Chicago University Press, 1987).

Schenchzer, Johann, *Homo diluvii testis* (Tiguri, 1726).

Sloan, Phillip R., 'Buffon, German biology and the historical interpretation of species', *British Journal for the History of Science* 41 (1979) 107–153.

Steffens, Henrich, *Lebenserinnerungen* (Jena: Eugen Diederichs, 1908).

Stendhal, *Love*, trans. G. and S. Sale (Harmondsworth: Penguin, 1975).

Stengers, Isabelle, 'Ambiguous Affinity: The Newtonian Dream of Chemistry in the Eighteenth Century', in *A History of Scientific Thought*, ed. Michel

Serres (Oxford: Blackwell, 1995).

Treviranns, Gottfried Reinhold, *Biulugic, oder Philsophie der lebendigen Natur*, 6 vols. (Göttingen: Rower, 1802–22).

Tuschling, Burkhard, 'Apperception and Ether: On the Idea of a Transcendental Deduction of Matter in Kant's *Opus postumum*', in *Kant's Transcendental Deductions*, ed. Eckart Förster (Stanford: Stanford University Press, 1989), pp. 193–216.

———. 'Intuitiver Verstand, absolute Identität, Idee. Thesen zu Hegels früher Rezeption der „Kritik der Urteilskraft"', in *Hegel und die „Kritik der Urteilskraft"*, eds. Hans-Friedrich Fulda und Rolf-Peter Horstmann (Stuttgart: Ernst Klett Verlag, 1990) pp. 175–88.

———. 'The System of Transcendental Idealism: Questions Raised and Left Open in the *Kritik der Urteilskraft*', *Southern Journal of Philosophy* 30 (1992, supplement) 109–127.

Westphal, Kenneth, 'Affinity, Idealism and Naturalism: The Stability of Cinnabar and the Possibility of Experience', *Kant-Studien* 88 (1997) 139–189.

Whitford, Margaret, *Luce Irigaray: Philosophy in the Feminine* (London: Routledge, 1991).

Wolff, Christian, *Rational Thoughts on God, the World and the Human Soul as well as Things in General*, in *Metafisica Tedesca*, ed. Raffaele Ciafardone (Milan: Rusconi, 1999).

Wolff, Robert Paul, *Kant's Theory of Mental Activity: A Commentary on the Transcendental Analytic of the* Critique of Pure Reason (Cambridge, MA: Harvard University Press, 1963).

Zammito, J. H., *The Genesis of Kant's* Critique of Judgment (Chicago: University of Chicago Press, 1992).

Index